Strangers in a Strange Land

*A Festschrift in Honor of Bruce C. Birch
upon his Retirement as Academic Dean of
Wesley Theological Seminary*

Lucy Lind Hogan &
D. William Faupel , editors

Emeth Press

Strangers in a Strange Land, A Festschrift in Honor of Bruce C. Birch upon his Retirement as Academic Dean of Wesley Theological Seminary

Copyright © 2009 D. William Faupel
Printed in the United States of America on acid-free paper

All rights reserved. No part of this book may be reproduced, or stored in a retrieval system or transmitted in any form or by any means, electronic, mechanical, photocopying, recording, scanning or otherwise, except as permitted by the 1976 United States Copyright Act, or with the prior written permission of Emeth Press. Requests for permission should be addressed to: Emeth Press, P. O. Box 23961, Lexington, KY 40523-3961.
http://www.emethpress.com.

Library of Congress Cataloging-in-Publication Data

Strangers in a strange land : a festschrift in honor of Bruce C. Birch upon his retirement as academic dean of Wesley Theological Seminary / Lucy Lind Hogan & D. William Faupel, editors.
    p. cm.
Includes bibliographical references and indexes.
ISBN 978-0-9797935-9-2 (alk. paper)
1. Theology. 2. Strangers--Religious aspects--Christianity. I. Birch, Bruce C. II. Hogan, Lucy Lind, 1951- III. Faupel, David W.
BR50.S768 2009
230--dc22   2009010556

(on front cover)
Titus Arch in Rome. Enlarged Relief used by permission from Beth Hatefutsoth, the Nahum Goldmann Museum of the Jewish Diaspora, Tel Aviv

Contents

Foreword
    David F. McAllister-Wilson..5

Biographical Sketch of Bruce C. Birch 7

Introduction
    Lucy Lind Hogan & D. William Faupel..................................9

1. Democrats in Exile: 2004-2008
    Shaun A. Casey..13

2. Culture Care: Theological Education and Christian Mission
    Sathianathan Clarke...19

3. Dante: From Exile to Pilgrim
    Deryl A. Davis...29

4. Unmasking: Esther, Exile, and Creativity
    Denise Dombkowski Hopkins...43

5. Memory, Identity and Hope: The Exile and Christian Formation
    Jessicah Krey Duckworth and Susan B. Willhauck...................51

6. From the Margins: God's Strategy for Renewal?
    D. William Faupel...59

7. Reflections on the Use of "Exile" as a Christian Category
    Craig C. Hill..75

8. Who is the Stranger? Preaching in the Diverse Church
    Lucy Lind Hogan...79

9. Playing in Exile
   Michael S. Koppel..89

10. The Exile Question of African Americans: "Lord, How Come We Here?"
    William B. McClain..97

11. Black Abolitionists: Faithful Voices in Exile
    Beverley Eileen Mitchell..105

12. Pastoral Reflections on Exile and Hope
    Mary Clark Moschella..113

13. "How Can We Sing the Lord's Song in a Foreign Land?" Narrative Collapse in Small Churches
    Lewis A. Parks..121

14. The Gospel for an Uprooted People: Perspectives on the Fourth Gospel
    Sharon H. Ringe...129

15. Art in Theology-Land
    Deborah Sokolove..137

16. "Hallowed Be Thy Name!" The Theological Significance of the Avoidance of God's Name in the New Testament
    R. Kendall Soulen...145

17. Some Thoughts on the Exodus and the Exile
    Josiah Ulysses Young II...151

The Publications of Bruce C. Birch
    Eleanor Marshall Gease & Howertine Farrell Duncan.............157

Index of Names..167

Index of Subjects...173

About the Authors...181

Foreword

"Sing to the Lord a new song." Recalling this piece of scripture from the Psalmist and Isaiah may be the best way to sing the praises of our Bruce Birch, teacher, scholar, colleague and friend. It is his signature line and the spiritual of his labor.

His vocation was lived out in the strange land of the late twentieth century. Perhaps, if he had been born in another time, Dr. Birch would only have been another important biblical scholar. His contribution to his academic field and his leadership in his guild stand on their own as a great legacy. But it was his destiny to work in an age when the Mainline Protestant Church was losing its confidence and his academic field of study was dominated by a deconstruction of old forms and conventions. So, he became both a Jeremiah and a Nehemiah for his time. His scholarly contribution is a reconstructive approach to the ancient text. It honors all that has come before, but makes possible a new and confident appropriation.

Bruce Birch is a scholar of the church. His ordination is central to who he is and what he does. His books are for the church and its leadership. He has been elected and appointed to top positions in his denomination while his face and his voice and his texts appear in countless church libraries. But he also sings in the choir of the congregation whose pastor is his wife, Susan Halse. Birch's scholarship lives because it is grounded in the actual life of the church.

His heart is in the classroom. A first class scholar, he nevertheless could walk into a session as Elvis singing "All Shook Up" to make a point. His students saw his righteous anger at injustice, his exuberance at discovery and his tears when the waters ran deep. And so, legions, numbering in the thousands, found their voice in his classroom. How can the impact of over 30 years of good teaching be measured? Students who thought the Old Testament was just old and others whose cherished image of it was rent asunder by historical biblical criticism all rediscovered its richness. How many since have preached the Good News from the Old Testament because of Professor Birch?

And the Gospel he preaches is infused with *tzedek* (righteousness) and *hesed* (steadfast love). Birch is a child of the 60s, and his hermeneutic is to keep before us a vision of a more just and loving church and world. In a word, the theme of Birch's work is "shalom," a mantra that generations of those of us who are his students first learned from him.

Then, Professor Birch became Dean Birch and we found that he practiced what he taught. To every conflicted situation he brought a leadership style infused with shalom. Working closely with two presidents, Dean Birch made Wesley's diversity work, demonstrating the power that can come from a collaborative, inclusive and appreciative approach. His seminary has become a truly "church-based seminary" because of his leadership.

And now, in the spring of 2009, the flowers appear on the earth and the time of singing has come. The contributors to this volume raise our voices in loving honor of Bruce Birch who made the old song new again.

David F. McAllister-Wilson
President, Wesley Theological Seminary

Bruce C. Birch:
A Biographical Sketch

A son of the prairie, Bruce C. Birch was born and raised in Wichita, Kansas, the son of Lauren and Marjory Birch. Drawn to service, Bruce was active both in his local church, but quickly became involved in a number of state church groups. Bruce was also a committed member of the Boy Scouts and attained the rank of Eagle Scout before leaving Wichita to attend Southwestern College in Winfield, Kansas.

At Southwestern, Bruce pursued majors in History/Political Science and Religion/Philosophy. During his junior year in the spring of 1961, Bruce traveled to Washington, D.C. to participate in the Washington Semester at American University not knowing that, just ten years later, he would return to begin his tenure at Wesley which is adjacent to the University.

Upon graduating *Magna cum laude* from Southwestern, Bruce began his studies at Perkins School of Theology, Southern Methodist University in Dallas, Texas. There he graduated with honors in 1965 and moved to New Haven and further graduate study at Yale.

At Yale, Bruce was a Woodrow Wilson Fellow in 1965-66, and received his M.A. in 1967. In 1967-68, he was a Woodrow Wilson Dissertation Fellow and received his M.Phil. in 1968 and his Ph.D. in 1970. Bruce's dissertation was "The Rise of the Israelite Monarchy: The Growth and Development of 1 Samuel 7-15."

With an Association of Theological Schools Research Fellowship, Bruce did post-doctoral study at Tübingen University in West Germany in 1977-78.

Before beginning his teaching at Wesley Theological Seminary in 1971, Bruce taught at Iowa Wesleyan College in Mount Pleasant, Iowa, and Erskine College in Due West, South Carolina.

National attention came early in Bruce's career. In February of 1976 a portrait of Bruce appeared on the cover of U.S. News and World Report. He, and seven others, were pictured below a headline announcing, "Young Builders of America – 8 Who Have Made Their Mark." Along with Rep. Barbara Jordan of Texas and Nobel Prize winning biologist, David Baltimore, the thirty-four year old Bruce was honored as "one of the most outstanding young theologians in

America." Noting that he is a "tousle-haired ex-Kansan," the article asked Bruce to explain his mission. "I want students to learn that the Old Testament is a great resource for their lives, and not just a history book, and I think I'm succeeding."[i] We can report that, thirty-three years later, he did, indeed, succeed.

Unfortunately, as the preacher, *Qohelet* observed, "there is nothing new under the sun" (Eccl. 1:9b). A prescient comment by Bruce in that 1976 article about the then current political climate remains true today; "We are constantly coming up against situations which make the future look gloomy . . . The church ought to point toward hopeful solutions even when there seems to be no way out."[ii]

Bruce is an ordained elder in the United Methodist Church and is a member of the Baltimore-Washington Conference. He has served as a delegate to General and Jurisdictional Conferences and on the United Methodist General Board of Church and Society.

At the 2008 meeting of the Society of Biblical Literature, Bruce was elected as Chair of the Executive Council of the Society. He has also served on the steering committee for the Chief Academic Officers Society of The Association of Theological Schools as well as several committees for Middle States Commission on Higher Education.

In 1998, Bruce began his tenure as Dean of the Seminary at Wesley Theological Seminary and in 1999 was awarded the Woodrow W. and Mildred B. Miller Chair of Professor of Biblical Theology.

Notes

1. "Young Builders of America Who Have Made Their Mark," *U. S. News and World Report,* Vol. 80:6 February 6, 1976. p. 45.
2. *Ibid.*

Introduction: Ancient Testimonies for Contemporary Challenges

I come to you in the name of the Lord of hosts.
1 Samuel 17:45

How could we sing the Lord's song in a strange land?
Psalm 137:4

In the fall of 1971, the faculty of Wesley Theological Seminary gathered for their first meeting of the new academic year. Included in that gathering was the newest member of the faculty, an Old Testament scholar, Bruce Birch who had come from teaching at Erskine College. He reports that he felt very much like a stranger in a strange land as he looked around the room at the mostly male faculty. His bell-bottomed pants and plaid sport coat, not to mention his mustache and side-burns, stood in sharp contrast to the black suits and dark ties worn by all of the other, clean shaven men seated at the table. But, as he also will report, he was welcomed warmly into that faculty that would become his home and family for the next thirty-eight years.

Over those years the size and composition of the student body and faculty of Wesley changed dramatically. Wesley moved from being a small, largely white, male, United Methodist community to one of the largest free-standing seminaries in the United States, and one that reflects the marvelous racial, gender, denominational, ethnic, and global diversity that is the Body of Christ.

Now, after nearly forty years, Bruce Birch is preparing to leave active teaching and administration at Wesley Theological Seminary in Washington, D.C. During his tenure at Wesley, Dean Birch has shaped faculty, students, staff, administration, and the broader community through his outstanding teaching and thoughtful scholarship and writing.

It is an honored tradition in the academic community to pay tribute to a retiring colleague with a *Festschrift* – celebration writing. In that sense this volume is not unusual. What is unusual, however, is the fact that, rather than being a collection of the honoree's colleagues, i.e, those in the biblical, Old Testament academy, this represents a variety of academic disciplines: Hebrew Scriptures, New Testament, theology, history, pastoral theology, homiletics. It is a celebration of Bruce by his colleagues at Wesley.

To honor their dean on the occasion of his retirement, the faculty of Wesley Theological Seminary offer this *Festschrift* devoted to the theme of exile. They wish to demonstrate how this theological theme, that has been very important in Bruce's teaching and scholarship, is expressed in their teaching and writing. And they wish to show how, under the influence of Bruce Birch, this crucial narrative found its way into and through the various academic disciplines, theological education, and in the life of the church.

Fresh Testimonies

In the introduction to his book, *Let Justice Roll Down*, Bruce Birch describes an encounter with a woman who was doing work in his home. When he told her that he was writing a book which would explore the relationship of the Old Testament in Christian ethics, he reports that he was encouraged and affirmed in his task by her observation— "I didn't think there was anything in the Old Testament that related to Christian ethics. Christians are beyond that 'eye for an eye' stuff."[1]

Bruce recognized that the Old Testament seems a strange land for many modern readers. It tells the stories of the faithful as well as the failures who turned to dust long ago. The pages are filled with the tales of marching armies, shepherd kings, sacrificing priests and prostitutes, whales and witches. Yet, as strange as it all can be, he knew that there was much more to the Old Testament than that "eye for an eye stuff." And so, he has devoted his entire career; his teaching, his world-wide lecturing, and his extensive writing, to drawing fresh testimonies from those ancient stories. He has sought to uncover, in those narratives, witnesses that will bring the living, lively word of the Lord to those seeking to live lives of faith and who are confronting the challenges of singing the Lord's song in today's world.

Bruce has also sought, through his teaching and deanship, to demonstrate the importance of interdisciplinary dialogue. His has not been a narrow vision of scholarship; rather he has endeavored to shape a community at Wesley that understands the connectedness of all their teaching. Toward that end he has stepped out of the biblical scholar's classroom and taught Old Testament with those in the arts, preaching, and many others.

Singing the Lord's Song

What happens when we are ripped from all that is familiar; when we find ourselves strangers in a strange land? Where is God in all of this? Has God, in fact, visited this upon us? Who are we? How are we to live? How are we to relate to the strangers? Can we sing the Lord's song when we feel as though we have been abandoned by our God?

Two narratives were central to the Jewish identity, the exodus and the exile. The former is the story of release from captivity by God with the subsequent wandering through the wilderness until the eventual deliverance into the promise land. And the latter is the story of being ripped from that Promised Land and into captivity once more. The experiences and insights gained in these central events shaped Jewish consciousness and, subsequently, Christian identity as well. Exploring the meaning and witness of wilderness and exile, and their contemporary application, has been a major focus of Bruce's scholarly work.

As people of the word, who make their livings speaking and writing words upon words upon words we, the Wesley Theological Seminary faculty, find that our words seem inadequate to thank Bruce for his thoughtful, dedicated, and inspired leadership over these many years; first as colleague, then as our dean. Bruce was one of those rare colleagues and deans who worked tirelessly and always put students and colleagues first. We hope that Bruce and you, the reader, will appreciate our efforts to explore this foundational theme of exile that was so important in Bruce's scholarship as our way of saying thank you and wishing God's speed to Bruce as he begins this new journey in his life.

Lucy Lind Hogan

D. William Faupel

Notes

1. Birch, Bruce. *Let Justice Roll Down, The Old Testament, Ethics, and Christian Life.* Louisville: Westminster John Knox Press, 1991.

1

Democrats in Exile, 2004-2008

By Shaun A. Casey

Introduction

While it might be tempting to draw explicit parallels between Israel's exile in Babylon and the Democratic Party's exile from the White House in the early years of the twenty first century, I am going to resist the impulse. There are a multitude of reasons for this, not the least of which is that I do not believe there are any theological warrants justifying any special covenantal relationship between God and the Democrats, despite what some might think. This, of course, is in contrast to the relationship between God and Israel. Rather, in this essay I will trace what I see to be the major efforts of Democrats at the national level to understand the party's poor performance among major religious demographics such as Roman Catholic and white Evangelical voters in the 2004 presidential election. It is my thesis that after significant introspection and debate the Democratic Party produced a robust electoral strategy toward people of faith and that this aided the Obama victory.

I will proceed in three main steps. First, I will look at the immediate aftermath of the 2004 presidential race and describe the various responses to the perceived role of religion in that election. Second, I will examine in some detail a speech that Sen. John Kerry gave at Pepperdine University in September 2006. Finally I will show how Barack Obama's campaign built on the emerging trends after 2004 among Democrats addressing religion directly.

Responses in the Wake of John Kerry's Defeat

In the wake of John Kerry's defeat in 2004 there was much weeping and gnashing of Democratic teeth. They searched for God in the exit polls and found much grief. Kerry lost the Catholic vote and carried a very low percentage of the white Evangelical vote. In the political jargon of the day the Republican Party had successfully framed the message among voters that the Democratic Party was the anti-God party. There seemed to be a consensus within the Party and the media that Democrats had a tin ear for religion in contrast to President Bush's juggernaut among Catholics and Evangelicals. If Democrats wanted to regain the White House, it would have to disrupt this frame and find a way to speak to persuadable faith oriented voters. Democratic enclaves pondered this question ceaselessly in early 2005.

In addition to the internal self-examination by party regulars several monographs began to appear creating a genre of religion themed election books. The first of these was *God's Politics: Why the Right Gets it Wrong and the Left Doesn't Get It* by Jim Wallis. Wallis was ubiquitous in his promotion of the book and by the end of 2005 people were debating just what Democrats needed to learn from 2004 and what they needed to start doing to prevent a repeat of the debacle.

Two other books are noteworthy in the ensuing wave: *The Party Faithful: How and Why Democrats are Closing the God Gap* by Amy Sullivan and *Souled Out: Reclaiming Faith and Politics after the Religious Right* by E.J. Dionne. All three argued that the Religious Right was in some decline and that Democrats needed to address faith communities directly. There was a modest sort of backlash among secular writers and others who were religiously unaffiliated, but the dominant voices among Democrats acknowledged that the lack of an effective strategy to Catholics and Evangelicals spelled continued electoral trouble.

Far more important than the literary response was the action taken by party leaders. Governor Howard Dean, chairman of the Democratic National Committee, launched a faith in action working group under the leadership of his chief of staff, Leah Daughtry. This group of interfaith advisers met periodically with the DNC staff to advise party leaders on the particular issues of various major religious communities and helped Dean land speaking engagements in venues traditionally shunned by Democrats. The DNC also assembled a faith outreach staff of unprecedented size. As part of the DNC's fifty state strategy state Democratic Party offices were encouraged to begin to map the religious terrain in their states and to do faith outreach at the state level.

At the same time Democrats in Congress began to deliberate on how they might reach out to faith communities more effectively. Speaker of the House Nancy Pelosi and Senate Majority Leader Harry Reid appointed staffers to organize faith caucuses for members to meet with religious leaders and recommend ways to communicate more effectively. In these venues Democrats discovered a long line of previously frustrated religious leaders who were more than happy to share their wisdom, complaints, and requests.

In addition to these formal rubrics a host of independent entities sprang up to give renewed energy among progressive religious constituents. Mara Vanderslice, who was the religious outreach coordinator for John Kerry's 2004 presidential campaign, co-founded Common Good Strategies with Eric Sapp and began to advise various Democratic candidates during the 2006 midterm elections. Their clients did very well in that election cycle, adding to the emerging narrative that Democrats could fight back with some success among what had come to be seen as traditionally Republican faith constituencies. By 2008 Burns Strider, who had staffed the Democratic faith outreach efforts in House Speaker Nancy Pelosi's office and was the religion staffer for Hillary Clinton's presidential campaign, founded his own consulting firm, the Eleison Group. His stable of clients also fared very well in various 2008 House and Senate races.

In addition to these consulting firms, a number of nonprofit organizations emerged to rally various progressive religious groups. Among the more successful were Faith in Public Life and Catholics in Alliance for the Common Good. Faith in Public Life sponsored a Compassion Forum at Messiah College in Grantham, PA during the presidential primary season in which Hillary Clinton and Barack Obama answered questions from a wide range of religious leaders and journalists. John McCain turned down an invitation to join them. Thus progressive religious leaders were able to shape the election discourse in such a way that the exclusive franchise of Republicans on faith issues in an election was broken.

Kerry's 2006 Pepperdine Speech

While this apparatus was emerging among Democrats, leaders were also addressing audiences, both public and private. One of the more interesting speeches was given by John Kerry in 2006 at a point where he was widely viewed as contemplating running for president again in 2008. In September 2006 he spoke in Malibu, CA, at Pepperdine University, a college affiliated with the Churches of Christ.[1] Presumably exactly the type of constituency Democrats needed to do better with if the Republican lock on Evangelical voters was to be diminished.

Kerry began his speech by acknowledging the toxic environment regarding his faith during the 2004 campaign. He noted that he would not make this mistake again. He would portray his faith on his own terms rather than allowing his opponents to spin a tale to suit their ends. No Democrat running for president in 2008 would allow this to happen to them either. Religion had become weaponized in presidential politics and Democrats who failed to tell their own faith stories soon found themselves responding to attacks about the nature of their beliefs. Kerry learned the lesson one election cycle too late.

The first large section of the speech was autobiographical. Kerry spoke about growing up with a pre-Vatican II Catholic faith. He experienced a crisis of faith during and after the Vietnam War. His faith during combat was a naïve sort of quid pro quo: "deliver me from death God and I will be good". It took him a long time to process and understand the horrors he had witnessed. He described these post-war years as wandering in the wilderness where he sought to understand the meaning and direction of his life. Then, "suddenly and movingly, I had a revelation about the connection between the work I was doing as a public servant and my formative teachings. Indeed, the scriptures provided a firmer guide about values applied to life — many of the things you are wrestling with now today."[2]

At that point Kerry pivoted to explicate one of his favorite passages in scripture, Mark 10:35-45, that underwrote the connection between his faith and his vocation as a public servant. This is the periscope in which James and Andrew approach Jesus with a special request for the seats of power next to Jesus in his glory. The other ten disciples become angry when they learn of this insiders' plea and Jesus responds with a lengthy statement on greatness in the kingdom based on service in contrast to Roman political power models based on hegemony and coercion. For Kerry this passage provided the theological warrants for his public engagement as a Christian.

From there he segued into a series of questions raised by the U.S. Catholic bishops in their statement to Catholic voters prior to the 2004 presidential election. In doing this Kerry affirmed that the bishops had indeed raised important moral questions that voters needed to ponder as they formed their choice for the voting booth. These questions dealt with topics such as how to respond to the attacks of 9/11, how to protect the weakest in society including the unborn, how to prevent the deaths of 30,000 children every day due to poverty, how to support marriage, how to provide access to affordable health care, how to combat prejudice and war, how to search for the common good, when and why to use lethal force, and how to join with other nations to seek answers to international problems.

The last major section of the speech featured an in depth analysis of four major policy areas where Kerry believed people of faith from every background could work together with other people of good will towards public policies that contribute to the common good. The four issues were poverty, the environment, abortion, and war. I will concentrate on his discussion of abortion because I believe his viewpoint represents a major turning point for Democratic presidential politics and one that influenced President Obama's position as well.

Kerry began with the observation that while there were 1.3 million abortions a year and that abortion was highly divisive there was a common ground to be found:

> Everyone can agree that that is too many and on a shared goal of reducing the need for abortion in the first place. And I believe our first step is to unite and accept the responsibility of making abortion rare by focusing on prevention and by supporting pregnant women and new parents.
>
> Even as a supporter of *Roe V. Wade*, I am compelled to acknowledge that the language both sides use on this subject can be unfortunately misleading and unconstructive. Unfortunately, this debate has been framed in an overly partisan setting with excessive language on both sides—none of which does justice to the depth of moral conviction held by all. There's been demonization rather than debate. Distrust rather than discussion. Everyone is worse off for it. Instead of making enemies, we need to make progress.

What Kerry did next was to move the discussion to specific legislation that if enacted would help to reduce the number of abortions not by criminalizing women or doctors, but by reducing the demand for abortion.

> What would progress look like? Many people are surprised to learn that the most dramatic decline in America's abortion rate took place under the last Democratic administration when poverty declined, more people graduated from

college, employment grew at record rates, and the economy grew at record levels. Unfortunately, the economic policies of these last six years increase the pressure on women with unplanned pregnancies to seek abortions.

In addition to focusing on policies that will prevent unintended pregnancies in the first place, I believe we should also embrace and expand a proven set of economic measures to again make significant progress on reducing the number of abortions in America. This would mean raising the minimum wage, expanding educational opportunity, giving tax credits for domestic adoptions, providing universal health insurance, expanding the Earned Income Tax Credit, and expanding federally funded child care.

This was the most interesting and innovative part of his speech. In essence Kerry argued that he agreed abortion was too high in our society but he disagreed with the argument that criminalizing abortion would significantly reduce abortion. At the pragmatic policy level he believed that people of goodwill across a political, theological, and philosophical spectrum could work together to pursue specific policies that would significantly reduce abortion. His quarrel with the leadership of the Catholic Church had less to do with the moral status of abortion and more to do with the proper political means to pursue and achieve reduction. This was a powerful move and one that could be defended on Catholic grounds as well.[3]

He concluded the speech with a call to address:

> these four great challenges—fighting poverty and disease, taking care of the earth, reducing abortions, and fighting only just wars—as godly tasks on which we can transcend the culture wars and reach common ground.
>
> And for all the anger and fear so often expressed about the intersection of politics and religion, I believe that a vision of public service based upon serving rather than being served is ultimately a vision of hope and not despair. The Scripture says, again and again, "be not afraid." God is not through with humanity. Shame on us if we use our faith to divide and alienate people from one another or if we draft God into partisan service.
>
> Shame on us if we sow fear for our own advantage. As God gives us the ability to see, let us take up the tasks associated with loving our neighbors as ourselves. We can take up God's work as our own. The call of Jesus, and of every great religious leader, to everyone is one of service to all and not the pursuit of power. Each of us needs to do our best to answer that call, and help each other hear it in a common spirit of obedience, humility and love.

In sum, Kerry did several things which signaled a sea change for how Democrats would approach their "religion problem" in the future. First of all, he showed up and spoke to an audience that was not from his own tradition. As a Catholic he chose to give an address at a university affiliated with an Evangelical tradition. Second, he spoke autobiographically and confessionally. He embraced his own story and told it in authentic terms that allowed an audience that did not share that story to identify with common points. Third, he grounded his own political values in both biblical terms and also in terms of Catholic social teachings. He did not seek to translate his own idiom into some fictional neutral common language. And finally, he pointed out specific public policy implications that stemmed from his theological position. In total, Kerry faced down the stereotype that all Democrats were atheists and unable to speak to people of faith. In so doing he refused to use religion as a political strategy to divide Americans. Instead he chose to call for cooperation between people of faith in pursuit of shared values and policies.

Barack Obama Follows Kerry's Example in 2008

It should be clear that the campaign of Barack Obama represented the final exodus of the Democratic Party from not only its political exile but from its fear of engaging faith communities, particularly Evangelicals and Catholics. He extended the impulses that Kerry displayed in his Pepperdine speech. Obama called for direct engagement with religious leaders and he gave several ground-breaking speeches on the role of religion in politics. He built the most extensive and robust national campaign staff for religious outreach in a Democratic presidential campaign in history. While it would be inaccurate to claim this move was responsible for his victory, it is fair to say it did him no harm.

Let me also hasten to add a word of tribute to Dean Bruce Birch. Bruce has been my only dean for the entire length of my teaching career. His legacy of public engagement has greatly shaped my own work. It was with his encouragement and support that I joined the Obama campaign's religious outreach staff during the general election. It has been a profound honor to work with him and I benefit from his counsel constantly. I offer this essay as my thanks.

Notes

1. For the full text of the speech see http://www.washingtonpost.com/wp-dyn/content/article/2006/09/18/AR2006091801046.html. Accessed February 20, 2009.

2. Ibid.

3. Time and space do not allow me to flesh this argument out in any detail. Suffice it to say that one can turn to the work of theologian John Courtney Murray for this sort of pragmatic question about the best means available to work for moral change in a liberal democracy.

2

Culture Care, Theological Education, and Christian Mission[1]

By Sathianathan Clarke

Introduction

Culture mediates between the Gospel and the world. Thus far culture, Christian Gospel and the world were thought of as relatively fixed entities. In general our worldview assumed that culture and Gospel were like gift boxes or care packages that could be loosely or tightly put together (depending upon the theological confidence or diffidence or shall I say ideological arrogance or fuzziness!) in seminaries (I will use this term to also cover divinity schools) to be delivered to churches for distribution around the world. Often the role of theological institutions was to help students differentiate between the one Gospel and the many cultures and then to work out a convincing fit between the two that could be taken into the world.

Our twenty-first century has seen a dramatic change in the conceptions of all three entities. Culture is now more pliant and dynamic. It is no longer a tool kit of stable commodities. Rather shape-shifting is almost its most enduring feature. The complexity and dynamism of culture may have made it less easy to analyze. Yet, it has not become any less influential in the life of human communities. The gospel is also resplendently diverse and creatively multiplex. In spite of the colonial drift toward abstracting and essentializing the Gospel as a singular deposit placed in the lap of the West, a careful look at the whole world makes one aware of the rich and spectacular ways in which irruptions and interruptions of the Christian gospel have already brought forth multifold fruit and flower harvests in various parts of the globe. The world though is most radically changed in our global era. It is smaller, flatter and more networked than ever. In one sense we might say that there is no world out there anymore waiting to be entered. The world has taken the offensive and pervaded every realm of life in most human societies. No longer do we prepare students to enter into the real world. Rather the world with all its cultural trappings has infiltrated our communities. It has come into our homes, our churches, our restaurants and our seminaries via e-ideas, images, text messages, communication forms, sound

19

bites, cuisines, airwaves, and even culturally different persons, often at lightening speed, mostly unannounced, and sometimes even unnoticed.

In its objective of impacting the life of our shrinking world with the good news of God's love available in Jesus Christ seminaries are entangled in various aspects of local and global culture. Some of these cultural configurations seep in through the proliferation of high speed communication gateways, some of these cultural patterns are embodied within the diversity of the gathered community of faculty, administrators, staff and students, and some of these cultural frames are transmitted through the 'deep structures' built into institutional commitments and educational curricula. In this paper, taking cognizance of this change just described I set out to do four things. First, I offer a succinct sketch of culture in relation to the U.S. seminary. Second, I outline an argument to think theologically about culture. Third, I explore institutional possibilities for honestly dealing with culture in a theological setting. Finally, I conclude with a difficult but necessary missiological opening for theological education. In a world that needs mending from the new wave of religious conflicts, I suggest that we cannot ignore the Christian vocation for reconciliation and healing among cultures and religions. This implies that we re-imagine the theological relationship of culture to religion in our new century.

Old Culture Components (Ideational, Performative and Material) in New Culture Zones (Classrooms, Chapels, and Cafeterias)

Culture is still one of the most slippery and complicated terms.[2] It has so many different meanings, histories, usages, and referents. Robin Alexander draws our attention to the complication of coming up with conceptual clarity with regard to the notion of culture:[3]

> One clue to the difficulty is the frequency with which the word carries appendages of one kind or another: **adjectives** which demarcate, claim, reject, compare and in any event tacitly evaluate kinds of culture—'high', 'popular', 'mass', 'majority', 'minority', 'youth', ethnic', 'gender'; **nouns** which indicate what people and groups do with culture and what culture does to people — cultural 'capital', 'reproduction', 'transmission', 'oppression', 'politics', 'relativism'; **prefixes** which place culture temporarily, spatially or taxonomically — 'postmodernist culture', 'subculture', 'micro-culture.' More recently, the word has acquired such pervasive usage that it can be **appended** to virtually any sphere of activity to signal its distinctiveness and otherness — 'business culture', 'institutional culture', 'professional culture', 'research culture'.

Because of the incredible intricacies surrounding the concept of culture, rather than try to define it let me identify some overall features emerging in the discourse on culture. Specifically, I will seek to capture the properties and dynamics of culture as I see them played out within the culture zones of theological communities. In what follows, I draw upon Robert Schreiter's description of three important dimensions of culture as a useful starting point.[4]

1. "Culture is Ideational." Culture provides a kind of "scaffolding" for human living. Thus it involves communal systems or frameworks of meaning. In general these frames for capturing life in all its complexity "serve both to interpret the world and to provide guidance for living in the world." Although culture in its ideational reach serves as an organizing schema with universal propensities it, nonetheless, is embodied in specific beliefs, norms, attitudes, and rules of behavior. It is important to underscore this ideational dimension of culture since such meta-systemic and meaning-ordering tendencies appear to mirror religious or theological orientations. Often theological education assumes that all ideational features of culture are sacrificed by students in an effort to hold on to a broader Christian theological framework. I think we need to rethink this easy generalization. I believe that African American or Latino or Caucasian or Asian cultural systems operate as co-constituting orientations in our seminary campuses and classes. Often they operate as implicit, even hidden, cultural templates into which theological frameworks are made to fit.

2. "**Culture is also Performance.**" Culture is not only in the minds of the gathered theological community but it is also acted out through their bodies even as it is lived out in the social body of society. Thus, it encompasses rituals, which connect certain members of a given community together. What is assumed to be a shared meaning system is lived out through different ritualized social practices in everyday community.

In these terms culture is an arena, which provides communities "with a participatory way of embodying and enacting their histories and values." While this aspect of culture is played out in subtle ways in the dynamics in classrooms there is much more reason to believe that culture as performance is enacted by members of seminaries with passion and freedom in the arenas of **corporate worship** and **communal dining**. As theological faculty we have consistently emphasized the profound and intimate theological connection between the breaking of the sacrificed body of Christ in the sanctuary and the breaking of the gift of daily bread in the refectory. Within the realm of cultural performance this connection required no instruction or permission. The songs, prayers, dances, rituals, words, preaching styles, and bodily movements let loose in the sanctuary become a repertoire of performative culture that expresses community identity. So also, the interaction, choice of food, volume of discourse, and purpose of meal (nourishment or celebrative experience) are played out freely in the refectory. These ritualize a variety of cultural social texts that are acted out in theological institutions.

3. "**Culture is Material.**" For a long time the material aspect of culture was only identified with the art and architecture of the elite. Thus, whether it was the cathedrals, monuments and castles of Europe or the temples, stupas and palaces in Asia, the materiality of cultural artifacts were associated with the 'high culture' of the aristocratic and the ruling classes. This has nevertheless changed with anthropologists and sociologists turning their attention toward the local and the popular. Now we are discerning that material culture is a component of all communities. Material representations are an extension of the creativity

and originality of respective communities, which symbolize their very being. Thus, language, food, clothing, agricultural implements, architecture, musical instruments, artifacts, organization of space, and indigenous medicines all symbolize material dimensions of culture.

Theological education has for a long time been unapologetic in its **bias** concerning material culture: It rewarded linguistic symbolization and did not know how to assemble and interpret other symbolic representations in the academic life of the community. While this seems natural to educational institutions that flourish on a culture of wordiness based on the wisdom contained in the Book there is also a certain western, logo-centric, elitist and iconoclastic ethos that this mono-modality advocates. We must not ignore the fact that literary cultures have a long history of being divorced from the culture of craftsmanship. While elitists may think of manual labor as messy, blue collar business and more brawn than brain, from the perspective of the working peoples it is skeptically held that one needs the craftiness of writing profusely to escape the obligations of pursuing a culturally and economically productive craft.

Becoming Theologically Educated about Culture

What is theological education's business with culture? The first reason that theological education ought to work with culture stems from a foundational theological affirmation: God is the creator of the world in its entirety and integrity. The dualistic split between matter and spirit is no longer a serviceable metaphysical option. Thus, an easy explication that culture as matter must be relegated to the corrupt and temporal material pole even as human spirit must be enveloped into the pure and eternal spiritual pole is not tenable today. The interrelated and integrated theological vision of holistic notions of the world and human beings find legitimization both in the traditional Hebraic worldview that Jesus espoused and in the emerging world picture agreed upon by modern science. God, thus, cannot but be conceptualised apart from the totality and organicity of reality as a whole. It is our central affirmation, is it not, that all that has been and is and will be created owes its existence to God's creative grace and goodness! Culture then like all other stuff of reality cannot be unrelated and thus independent from the God as Creator.

But culture, one will object, is the work of human beings and not of God. The classical distinction between culture and nature is invoked in this objection. A wedge is driven between nature as God's work, which has to do with all that has been originally created from the beginning (inclusive of both living and non-living things), and culture as human work, which has to do with a secondary kind of creative activity. The latter is dependent on the former since culture is a phenomenon that creatively puts together what already exists in different and novel configurations. Such a conceptual differentiation between nature and culture suggests that nature because of its direct origination from God can be included into the purview of theology whereas culture represents more the 'fallen' creativity of human beings which is best discarded in any reflection on God. According to such a view, taking culture as a building block of theology only manifests the hubris of human beings: they want to reflect on their own works rather than the work of God.

There are several problems with buying into the nature-culture binary as a justification for precluding culture from theological education. Let me mention just one. I object to the characterization that all human work is fallen. Human beings complete their own existence by creating culture and like all creative acts and artefacts can either serve constructive or destructive purposes. Any judgment however can only be made after the fact by assessing their functioning in the world. Indeed, this is one of the tasks of theology, which uses the symbol of God to relativize and evaluate various representations of culture. Invoking Tillich's contribution to a theology of culture we can utilize theological bases to distinguish between autonomous and heteronomous cultures on the one hand and theonomous cultures on the other.

A second reason for theological education to work with culture is rooted in our Christological affirmation. The incarnation of Christ into human flesh embodied within a specific cultural worldview reconciles rather than further divides all aspects of the divine with all dimensions of the human being. Embracing human nature and culture after Jesus' incarnation reaffirms one key commitment of the Christian Gospel: Christians affirm and celebrate that the God-with-us is no other than the God-of-all-creation and the God-for-all-of-us. After all, if there is an overall uniqueness attributed to the Christian gospel it points to the Good News of God's incarnation into the world of humanity. God in becoming human flesh transmits historical and concrete divine grace among all of God's own. Couching this in the terminology popularized by Marcus Borg, we might say that encountering the gospel always means meeting the enfleshed and inculturated Jesus again and again for the first time.

A third reason for enlisting culture as a resource for theological education has to do with an anthropological affirmation that has theological implications. Human beings need to know themselves if they want to refrain from living as objects and embrace their responsibility as subjects. Cultures are the symbolic arrangements that manifest what human communities experience themselves to be in the world. At a most basic level, culture represents the symbolic self-reflexivity of human beings. Thus, culture represents the communities' experience of being in the world and the particular manner by which they read meaning into this reflected upon experience.

As a Christian theologian I believe that God is at the foundation of such a profound self-reflectivity. It is because human beings participate in God's image that they are able to be self-reflexive. After all, only human beings have the capacity to become objects to themselves and reflect on themselves in relation to God and other realities around them. Furthermore, just as this image of God is relational, through the interconnectedness of the Trinity, human beings communicate this symbolic self-reflexivity socially. Theological symbols also emanate from and are interpreted through this connected and cumulative cultural pattern of self-reflexivity. This anthropological affirmation thus has obvious theological consequences. In as much as theology is a communal activity it can only be done with the means of symbols, which are themselves the creation of human beings in the form of language, cult, music, ritual and art. Any reference to God cannot be expressed apart from symbols, which are cultural creations. Theology would need to go into a mode of silence if it turns its back on culture. All efforts to empty theology of the rudiments of culture thus are not in the realm of possibility.

At the Intersection of Culture and Theological Education: Harnessing Culture; Enhancing Community; and Augmenting Gospel

The challenge for theological education regarding dealing with cultures in our community settings ought to be somewhat clearer. To start with new frontiers of cultural interplay are recognized. This involves a cultural shift in viewing our vocation as faculty, staff and administrators. Western bureaucracy has made our office space or the class room the primary sphere within which we do all our work that matters institutionally. We do not think of the chapel and the cafeteria as zones that we ought to claim, study, and utilize for the purposes of learning from students and teaching them about exchanging cultural gifts in an effort to build multicultural community. As a person from India, I make use of any form of eating in my class at Wesley Theological Seminary as a way to introduce my students to another cultural set of rules for food exchange, which come from my own communitarian, developing-world, Christian culture. In a context of economic inequality like Indian, since it cannot be assumed that everyone gathered in class has eaten sufficiently, any move to eat in public implicitly brings with it an open invitation for anyone to share in the food on display. Much to the amazement, why even irritation, of some of my American students I would thus, without batting an eyelid, help myself to a couple of M&Ms or nuts or chips or even a piece of a cookie, when a student decides to eat in my class. The cultural knowledge that is communicated is an important one for individualistic-minded western students. Hospitality is first of all about sharing food in a world of unequal resources; only secondarily is it about accepting each other. I have a feeling that my message is bearing fruit. Recently I have been noticing a cup cake or a cookie left for me on my desk during class break!

But recognizing and exchanging cultural frameworks, patterns of social expression and material symbols may lead us to wrongly conclude that theological institutions merely fulfil a role of being repositories of multiculturalism. Surely seminaries do not purport to be living museums of cultural diversity in glorious witness to the creatively that God has bestowed upon human beings. Like Seyla Benhabib, I too do not believe in "pure multiculturalism," which has the objective of keeping pristine forms of culture alive. While there is a legitimate argument that can be made for preservation of endangered cultural practices and forms, I believe that theological communities continuously grow, discard, transmit, transform and reconfigure cultural conceptions, patterns and expressions. Rather what is more important to my argument is that theological institutions bear the responsibility to provide a just system within the community whereby cultural orientations of various groups have a reasonable chance to be represented and respected. Enhancing Christian community involves enriching each other culturally through the process of mutual respect and reciprocal interchange for the sake of sharing in the fullness of the gospel.[5]

There is a power element involved in theological education's ability to harness multiple cultures and enhance plurality of communities for augmenting the gospel. Theological education in the United States must acknowledge and confront its long and intricate history of privileging western, Eurocentric philosophical roots and ministerial objectives. More serious than reflecting and living in a fragmented and disjointed cultural universe is, I believe, the burden and distress of living under someone else's cultural orientation. This is what reduces communities to objects. When a community starts living under the imposed cultural universe of another dominant community then it is being forced into pursuing its own selfhood according to the reflexivity of another's subjectivity. Clearly this is manipulative and destructive. But it is also enslaving. The plurality of configurations of God, human being, and world and their interrelationships, which are the cultural products of a long and rich process of various communitarian self-expressions, must be given fair prospect for circulation in theological education. Not only do they symbolize the gift offering of a community's valuable memories of God's faithful encounters with them in their own modes and moods. But these cultural frames and symbols also generate an authentic and organic resource pool to ward off the overreaching dominant cultural patterns that endeavour to homogenize theological representation. This no doubt has serious implications for financial aid, 'preferential option' commitments for underrepresented minority communities, faculty and staff hires and training concerning how to walk the tight rope of multicultural expressions and expectations in theological institutions.

What constitutes justice in identifying and circulating all segments of the community's cultural conceptual, performative and material components becomes an important question for theological educators. Along with this question is the matter of how classrooms, chapels and cafeterias can be arenas that promote mutually respectful and reciprocally interactive cultural interchange within the contours of a multiple informal and mutually forming community. The art and practice of negotiating and nurturing respect, equality, and reciprocity in exchanging cultural models enhances community living but also helps builds resourceful Christian leaders for transforming the life of the world. I suggest a few important thoughts to be kept in mind as seminaries harness cultures for the purpose of enhancing communities and growing Christian leaders for the sake of furthering the fullness of the Christian gospel.

1. Institutional planning to consciously and critically understand student and staff cultures communicates commitment of theological schools to affirm themselves as diversely gifted communities that manifest the creative providence of God.

2. Institutional affirmations of the commonality of Christian Gospel must not conceal the competing feature of cultures.

3. There is a ministerial rationale for theological institutions to work more deliberately and creatively with cultures. Theological education's sourcing of cultures in its institutional life becomes a skill that is transferred to students as they enter churches and communities that are saturated with such difference.

4. Cultural plasticity and theological elasticity do not lead to watering down the Christian Gospel. Rather it means stretching divine matters to bring life that matters to specific peoples and particular contexts.

Mission-shaped Seminaries: It's for the Life of the World, Stupid!

It must be explicitly attested that all this talk about sourcing the culture zones of the classroom, chapel and the cafeteria to forge authentic and organic Christian community is aimed toward affecting life among the whole multicultural world of God's children. In a round about manner the multiple cultural orientations of the world, which seeps into the theological communities, after a process of circulation, contestation, exchange, and transformation become resource for students as they go back to serve the purposes of the Gospel in our contemporary culturally plural world.

One interesting trait about the western theological tradition has to do with a long and strong conviction that culture can be separated from religion. While many theological seminaries are quite comfortable to delve deeply into various aspects of culture there is still some apprehension when religion is suggested to be a compelling and well-organized cultural system. Tillich's initial proposal provides a middle ground. He suggests that "religion is the substance of culture, [while] culture is the form of religion."[6] This view may not be good enough. It indicates that culture itself, devoid of religion, is substance-less and vacuous, which certainly is false. But more importantly, it is based on the questionable presupposition that substance and form are separable and distinct from each other. Such an uncoupled understanding is far removed from most non-Western interpretations concerning the relationship between culture and religion. In fact, in India there is no word for religion. The term *Dharma* is intimately tied up with various dimensions of social and cultural life. In western academic discourse, if there is one positive outcome from Samuel Huntington's 'clash of civilization thesis' it may have to do with his conflation of culture blocks with the larger framework of religiously grounded civilizations. In Huntington, culture and religion are reunited even if they are set up as global mine fields of violent conflict.

This brings us to the missiological concern which lies at the intersection between theological education and culture. What is the role of mission-shaped seminaries to foster new life in our world where we are witnessing the growing destructive and dangerous phenomenon of colliding religions on a global scale? One way forward, I suggest, is that we mend the breach that we have created between culture and religion. The gospel cannot only be entwined only with cultures; it also needs to be engaging religions. Indeed this is where the fault lines appear in our contemporary world. To be a mission-shaped seminary in the world has always involved the challenge of witnessing and working in the context of real cultural diversity. To prepare to be such a seminary in the world into the twenty-first century will require that we realize that this religiously plural world, which is also likely to be our local U.S. context, is sorely in need of reconciliation and healing.

It is important to register that the historical context within which we reflect upon our calling to be seminaries is quite different from a few decades ago. We agreed then that the main problem in the western world was one of moral relativism and religious apathy. The challenge thus that confronted seminaries in the twentieth century was a secularized generation that was steeped in relativism, which made it a gullible target for mammon, meaninglessness and market-driven self-indulgence. Today in the twenty-first century the challenge of being a mission-shaped seminary also comes from a shift in the opposite direction. We are witnessing the rise of a moral and religious absolutism that leads, feeds, and funds religious fundamentalism and global violence. The problem is not only relativism which is intimately tied up with the collapse of a universal moral framework. The problem in our century also stems from absolutism. The emergence of "strong religion" (Muslim, Hindu and Christian faces of religious fundamentalism) has become a major cause of violence in our world. It is within this complex of contexts, where religions are drawing physically closer together but also more hostile to each other, that I wish to place before us the question as to what it means to be a mission-shaped seminary in the context of world cultures and religions.

Notes

1. This is an expanded and revised version of a paper that was originally presented at the Closing Plenary of ATS's Student Personnel Administration Network (SPAN) Conference at Lake Buena Vista, Florida on March 29, 2008.

2. See for example, Raymond Williams, *Keywords: A Vocabulary of Culture and Society* (London, ENG: Fontana, 1976).

3. Robin Alexander, *Culture and Pedagogy: International Comparisons in Primary Education* (Oxford, England: Blackwell, 2000): 163-164. Emphasis mine.

4. Robert J. Schreiter, *The New Catholicity: Theology between the Global and the Local* (Maryknoll, NY: Orbis, 1999): 29ff.

5. See Seyla Benhabib, *The Claims of Culture: Equality and Diversity in the Global Era* (Princeton, NJ: Princeton University, 2002): 1-23. The ideas about justice, respect and

mutual reciprocity in relation to multicultural exchange is from Benhabib.

6. Paul Tillich, *Theology of Culture* (London, England: Oxford University, 1959): 42.

Works Cited

Alexander, Robin. *Culture and Pedagogy: International Comparisons in Primary Education.* Oxford, ENG: Blackwell, 2000. Benhabid, Seyla. *The Claims of Culture: Equality and Diversity in the Global Era.* Princeton: Princeton University, 2002.

Schreiter, Robert J. *The New Catholicity: Theology between the Global and the Local.* Maryknoll, NY: Orbis, 1999.

Tillich, Paul. *Theology of Culture.* London, ENG: Oxford University, 1959.

Williams, Raymond. *Keywords: A Vocabulary of Culture and Society.* London, England: Fontana, 1976.

3

Dante: From Exile to Pilgrim[1]

By Deryl A. Davis

The "Despicable, Senseless Company" of Politics

Thirteen hundred should have been a good year for Dante Alighieri. The turn of a new century found the thirty-five-year-old Florentine at the apex of his career: a celebrated poet, he had popularized an innovative style of love poetry (the *dolce stil nuovo* or "sweet, new style") which had drawn scores of artful imitators and attracted the attention of musicians, who set many of Dante's poems to song; he had married into one of Florence's leading mercantile families, likely offering prospects of considerable economic advancement; and perhaps most importantly in a notoriously politics-driven city such as Florence, he was a public bureaucrat on the rise. Things were going Dante's way.

Imagine the poet in June of that year: dressed in the rich crimson robe portraitists would later picture him in, Dante stands on an upper floor council chamber of the bargello, Florence's fortress-like "Palace of the People," holding forth on some policy matter or another while his compatriots, all scions of Florence's great families, sit in respectful silence. Or perhaps not. As eloquent a writer as Dante was, he also must have been a forceful speaker, capable of thoughtfully defending or rebutting policy points he agreed with or rejected. Early biographers note that the poet sometimes spoke out so forcefully against the papacy, in particular, that contemporary stenographers were too frightened to write down his remarks. Dante did it for them a few years later in his vitriolic outbursts against papal and Italian political machinations in the *Comedy*.

But in June 1300, the poet was among Florence's political elite: one of six priors, or councilmen, governing the city from their sequestered quarters in the bargello, looking out over the towers of the bustling mercantile city, across the swift-running Arno River, to the vast expanses of fertile vineyards and rich agricultural estates beyond. It must have been a heady experience for an ambitious person from the lower nobility, whose ancestors had inhabited the city for nigh on four centuries, but not one of whom had ever risen to such political heights. Having lately turned his prodigious talents to matters philosophical and moral, such as the true nature of nobility, it must have seemed to Dante a perfect opportunity to match intellectual and practical concerns. Unfortunately, that relationship would be short-lived.

True to form, political alliances in Florence were shifting even before Dante took office that spring. His own party, the Guelphs, had split into rival factions, White and Black. Then, less than a week after he and his fellow priors assumed office, a public disturbance broke out between the two factions that demanded immediate and vigorous response. Imagine again the poet standing before his peers in the bargello, only this time he's not holding forth on policy matters or the intricacies of foreign alliances, but offering a radical suggestion at peacemaking: rather than take the traditional approach of punishing one faction or the other, both of which had their adherents on the council, the priors should banish leaders of both parties together, allowing for an undetermined cooling off period and offering the city a chance to regain a measure of stability.

Whether or not Dante made the unusual suggestion himself, he must have known, and perhaps feared, the real effects on himself and his family: the banished would include his best friend and fellow poet Guido Cavalcanti (a leader of the Whites) and his brother-in-law, Corso Donati, leader of the Blacks. As the council voted on the measure, setting their marks to velum or perhaps dropping a symbolic marble into a plate, did Dante imagine what lay ahead for the exiles – the city gates clanging behind them, the forest with its dangers all around them, friends, family, and livelihood all out of reach? Did he dare to imagine the possibility of his own exile, adrift on a sea of violence and political chaos, some distant day in the future? For someone with Dante's imaginative gifts, it is a very real possibility, indeed.

Looking back later, the poet saw his brief time in political power as the beginning of his undoing. No wonder, perhaps, that his *Inferno* and the antechambers of his Purgatory are filled with politicians. Or that the poet has his illustrious ancestor in Paradise, Cacciaguida, castigate Dante's fellow politicians as "the despicable, senseless company" that "shall turn on you." Had not Dante done the same, albeit out of political necessity, to his own friend (who died in exile) and his brother-in-law? Politics is hell indeed. One need not look far to understand why, when the poet came to write his fictional pilgrimage through the afterlife, he would set it in the remarkable, ominous year of 1300 – the year of his priorate, of his greatest success, and the beginning of his downfall. (Thirteen hundred also was the Roman Catholic Church's first "Jubilee Year," proclaimed by Boniface, when pilgrims were encouraged to make a penitential journey to Rome—and help fill Boniface's coffers. Dante is no doubt juxtaposing his heavenly pilgrimage with this earthly one.)

Did pride, as in a Greek tragedy, play a role in the reversal of the poet's fortunes? There's no way of knowing for sure, but Dante does admit to that most grievous of the "deadly" sins in *Purgatorio*, when he confesses to the penitent Sapia, "I feel on me the weight those souls [the proud] must bear." The picture being evoked is of the souls of the proud, on the first terrace of Purgatory, bent to disfigurement by the huge stones they carry in penance for their sin. Writing several decades after Dante's death, the Florentine chronicler Giovanni Villani rather glibly asserts that the poet was "somewhat haughty and reserved and disdainful," but it is impossible to know how accurate this depiction is. Whatever the case, Dante came to view politics, short of universal monarchy, as an inherently corrupt and blindingly prideful business (witness Farinata in *Inferno* X or Omberto Aldobrandesco in *Purgatorio* XI), and he often may have deplored his own involvement in it.

That was likely the case in November 1301, when the poet, on an embassy to Rome, found himself on the receiving end of a political coup d'etat back home in Florence. Engineered by Pope Boniface VIII, the man Dante had come to see, and carried out by Boniface's ally Charles of Valois, the coup saw Florence overrun by Black Guelfs under the leadership of none other than Dante's brother-in-law, Corso Donati – a person, one imagines, not much disposed to treat the poet kindly. He wasn't, nor were his allies. Dante was sentenced to an initial banishment of two years, based upon false charges of graft. However, when the poet refused or was unable to return to Florence to face these trumped-up charges, a more terrible sentence was imposed: should Dante ever seek to return to the "city of blossoms" (*Firenze*), he would be burned at the stake. It was a punishment as gruesome as some of the more vivid torments the poet would evoke in his *Inferno*, although not so lengthy. (Apparently, it also was a punishment the poet had witnessed himself, as he suggests in *Purgatorio XXVIII*. "I recalled what human bodies look like burned to death" the poet tells us, when seeing the shades of the lustful in the purifying fires of Purgatory.)

If, while setting his mark to the banishment of Guido Cavalcanti and Corso Donati in 1300, Dante had dared to imagine what exile might be like, he experienced its shocking force firsthand in the spring of 1302. In March of that year, the 37-year-old poet found himself instantly bereft of home, family, friends, possessions, and livelihood. In contrast to the banishments of Cavalcanti, Donati, and their fellows, there would be no opportunity for Dante to return home, say his farewells, gather his belongings, or – essential for a poet - collect his manuscripts. He had lost country and legal status, too, since fourteenth century Italy was no more than a patchwork of rival, warring city-states and principalities with laws and customs particular to themselves. Outside of its urban centers, Italy could be a wild and uncivilized place, especially for cosmopolitans like Dante.

Imagine the poet again: the crimson robe has been replaced by a worn, muddied cloak which he holds tightly to his chest in an effort to defend against the cold. Shoulders hunched forward, he leans toward a pitiful fire which is too small to provide real comfort. Hearing footsteps behind him, the poet turns quickly to identify an intruder, finding only another wayfarer seeking shelter. Looking up through barren branches toward a waning moon, he thinks of home, or simply the possibility of it. And he imagines characters – perhaps many of them– predicting the arrival of this fateful day. Their voices grow louder in his mind, as he listens intently, straining for some word of hope, some promise amid the prophecies of woe. The wind rises, shakes the empty boughs, and the voices disappear one by one. As the poet bends to stir the fire, there is only silence.

This may be a romantic reading of the poet's exile, but not, I think, too far from the mark. It's entirely possible that Dante literally, as well as metaphorically, woke one morning to find himself "alone in a dark wood," as he famously puts it in the beginning of *Inferno*. Indeed, he may have seen the gates of his own city closed behind him, as he certainly saw the wilderness (its antithesis) stretching before him. The powerful image of the "dark wood," recurring throughout the *Comedy* and at times associated with Florence, is always representative of the chaos, confusion, and terror of losing one's way, of getting off "the straight path" and finding oneself alone and in need of help. This is the literal and figurative condition of exile in which the poet found himself. For Dante the man – soon to be the pilgrim - it was a condition of spiritual dislocation, as well.

Modern readers will be tempted to think of exile as a state of happy abandon or a license to escape authority with impunity, seduced as we are by images of Romantic poets like Byron or Shelley cavorting under Italian skies, Ernest Hemingway passing the wineskin at bull fights in Spain, or French existentialists proclaiming political, moral, and religious free agency from the comforts of a West Bank cafe. Then there is the host of self-exiled or politically exiled artists such as Joyce, Picasso, Beckett, Pound, Stein, Ionesco, Nabokov, Neruda, Kundera, and many others whose best work was forged in the often happy, or at least liberating, crucible of exile. Can one imagine *Ulysses* composed under lamplight in a Dublin rooming house? Or *The Waste Land*'s extensive, perhaps giddy, revisions undertaken in an Edwardian parlor on Beacon Hill? Modern films have reinforced the idea that exile, including self-exile, is a state of ultimate freedom and creativity which we would all wish to inhabit. We see handsome characters played by the young Marlon Brando, James Dean, or more recently, Brad Pitt. We may think of Gauguin's South Sea island or the pleasantly sunburnt landscapes inhabited by Georgia O'Keefe and D. H. Lawrence. Few of us, however, think of Dostoevsky's Siberia or Solzhenitsyn's gulag.

Exile is "curiously compelling to think about, but terrible to experience" wrote the late cultural critic Edward Said, who as a Palestinian-American whose family lands were taken by Israelis in the 1948 Arab-Israeli War, knew whereof he spoke. Exile often has been good for literature – indeed, we can thank Dante's banishment for the *Comedy*—but the toll in human suffering, at least for those who do not choose their exile, cannot be discounted. For a civic man like Dante—a politician in need of constituents, a poet in need of an audience – exile was a kind of death, requiring him to "leave behind those things/you love most dearly," as Cacciaguida tells the pilgrim in *Paradiso*. That not only meant family, friends, social and political positions, and livelihood, but also his artistic peers, the group of young poets for whom he had written the verse commentary *Vita Nuova* a decade earlier, and the musicians who had set his poems to popular song. His exile would be cultural, as well, perhaps involving loss of fame and reputation.

Readers should not forget that Dante's imaginative journey through the afterlife is, in the act of composition, simultaneous with his exilic wanderings, and that Dante-pilgrim moves between circles of Hell, terraces of Purgatory, and spheres of Heaven at the same physical time as Dante-exile moves from patron to patron and court to court, in search of a permanent home. While the circles of Hell go downward, Purgatory's terraces rise upward, and Heaven's spheres expand beyond earthly bounds, the exile's itinerary is largely circular: beginning in Verona in northeast Italy, he moves to Liguria in the northwest, possibly retreats to Bologna in the north-central part of the country, moves back to Verona under the patronage of Cangrande della Scala (the "Greyhound" of *Inferno* I), and finally seeks refuge in coastal Ravenna under the protection of Guido Novello da Polenta, nephew of Francesca da Rimini (*Inferno* V). Twenty years of itinerant exile must have seemed like a posthumous existence to a man who had lived his entire life in his native city, whose art and identity were inseparably bound to it, and who was never able to relinquish the hope that he might one day return. ("If ever it happen that this sacred poem/. . . wins over those cruel hearts that exile me/...shall return, a poet...," he writes in *Paradiso*, the canticle completed only shortly before his death.) When it came time to put a title to his greatest work, Dante felt compelled to remind future readers from whence he had sprung, regardless of the roads traveled since. It was *The Comedy of Dante Alighieri, Florentine by Birth* - and then he added a jab at those who had driven him from home – *But Not By Custom*.

Imagine again the poet in exile: this time, not in a dark wood, but in the regal confines of a feudal court. Rich tapestries, rather than barren trees, tower above him; he is no longer alone, but surrounded by people, all dressed in fine silks and brocaded robes. They are busy with social employment - important greetings, significant conversation, and careful observance of events at hand. The mood, while formal, is festive and inviting. These are people who know and enjoy their status in the world. Only Dante seems out of place. The poet stands center stage, hands clasped at the waist, jaw resolutely set, eyes fixed forward, oblivious to everyone and everything around him. His piercing gaze moves out from the scene itself into something beyond, as if he were looking through a transparent glass toward something no one else could see. The past? The future? Whatever the case, the effect, should any bystander catch his gaze, is chilling.

Fortunately, we don't have to imagine this scene on our own. The English Victorian artist Frederick Leighton captured it in his painting *Dante in Exile* (completed in 1864, about the time that Dante's ashes were removed from his tomb in Ravenna, and promptly lost). In the painting, Leighton depicts a man supremely alone, despite the bustle of activity around him. He seems driven by inward necessity, not by any external condition or circumstance. Standing ramrod straight, in magnificent isolation, he commands our complete attention. None of the painting's other figures have any consequence. Reaching out to no one and no thing, he appears utterly self-contained, a fortress within himself.

Little question, then, as to who or what the poet is staring at from inside Leighton's painting. It's us, of course. Out of the rich hues of the artist's palette, the poet looks down the decades at modern men and women whose lives, in their interiority and disparateness, reflect his own, or so we may imagine. Whether the artist was conscious of it or not, he has captured the very modern state of alienation. He has given us a man without community or connection, at odds with everything around him including, perhaps, himself.

Every age finds a reflection of itself in Dante: For Europeans of the late Middle Ages and Renaissance, he was the stately Father of Italian Literature, forging a national language out of the rough-hewn Florentine dialect and challenging the intellectual supremacy of Latin. For Enlightenment sages, he was a philosopher in pursuit of truth, struggling to liberate himself and others from the tyranny of bad ideas. For the Romantics, he was a rebel, challenging political and ecclesiastical authority and asserting brotherhood, freedom, and Italian nationalism. And for our uncertain, postmodern age, he is the ultimate spiritual guide, a man who has looked deeply into "the lake" of his heart (*Inferno* I) and described the emptiness he saw there; who has descended to the pit of Hell, witnessed its torments – personal, social, political – and returned to show us a better way. He is the exile who finally made his way home.

A Politician Turned Penitent

Dante's banishment from Florence was the great turning point of his physical life. It may have been the turning point of his spiritual life, too. By 1304, two years into his exile, the poet had turned his back on the "despicable, senseless company" of partisan politics and become "a party of one," as Cacciaguida predicts in *Paradiso* VII. Sometime thereafter, he began conceiving the great spiritual journey of the *Comedy*, which was probably begun between 1307 and 1309. Did the pain and dislocation of exile prompt Dante to reexamine his soul's wellbeing, along with that of his body? It's hard to imagine otherwise, given the *Comedy*'s focus on sin and redemption, and the fact that the poet steps into the story himself as the fictional traveler to eternity.

"Midway through our life's journey/I woke to find myself in a dark wood,/Having lost the straight path," Dante writes in the poem's opening lines. And in case the reader hasn't grasped that this is a moral, perhaps a spiritual, lapse, the poet adds a few lines later: "How I entered there I cannot truly say,/I had become so sleepy at the moment/When I first strayed, leaving the path of truth." What error caused the poet to wander from "the path of truth," has been hotly debated among critics for 700 years. The poet himself seems deliberately obscure on the point, as if to suggest that sinful error and moral transience occur incrementally and without warning, the insidious effects of small, seemingly innocuous, actions. What is clear is that, whether Dante is conscious of it or not, he has chosen a way that is not right or true, the ultimate result of which is beyond his complete understanding. Although he "cannot truly say" when he entered the wood, he clearly accepts responsibility for being there: "La verace via abandonnai," he says. "I left the path of truth."

If Dante's exile represents a spiritual, as well as physical, turning point in his life, when the poet re-examines the state of his soul along with his body, it's likely that this turning point followed a lengthy period of spiritual estrangement. An important clue comes two-thirds of the way through the *Comedy*, when the wanderer is reunited with his beloved Beatrice, the Florentine woman (now in spirit form) who is Dante's divinely appointed guide to Paradise. Their dramatic meeting – set 10 years after her death - is all the more striking because of Beatrice's surprising behavior toward her longtime devotee. Instead of welcoming the long-suffering traveler, who has after all just made his way through the depths of Hell and up the steep slopes of Purgatory in anticipation of seeing her, Beatrice greets him with the charge of infidelity:

> *There was a time my countenance sufficed,*
> *As I let him look into my young eyes*
> *For guidance on the straight path to his goal;*
> *But when I passed into my life of Life, that man you see*
> *Strayed after others and abandoned me.*
> *When I had risen from the flesh to spirit,*
> *Become more beautiful, more virtuous,*
> *He found less pleasure in me, loved me less,*
> *And wandered from the path that leads to truth,*
> *Pursuing simulacra of the good,*
> *Which promise more than they can ever give.*
> (Purgatory, XXX,112-132)

The suggestion, of course, is that Dante has been a faithless lover, and more explicitly, that he has turned his back on the guidance Beatrice offered toward "the straight path to his goal." Was it a betrayal of Beatrice that caused the pilgrim to stumble into the dark wood, straying "after others" and only pursuing "simulacra of the good"? As critics have noted over the centuries, Beatrice is a multi-faceted character: at once an allegory of divine love and redemption, she also is the very real embodiment of Dante's romantic passions, a Florentine woman who became, even in her brief lifetime, an imaginative lens through which the poet pictured God. As early as the *Vita Nuova*, written more than a decade before the *Comedy* was begun, Beatrice takes on Christological associations: she is a "miracle" worthy of the sort of contemplation given to the Trinity; her appearance causes the poet to glow with a "flame of charity" and to forgive anyone who has injured him; she is called to heaven by God himself, who experiences "sweet longing" for her and who enthrones her in glory "by virtue of her perfect goodness"; and finally, "the marvel of her loveliness" is "transformed to spiritual beauty" in paradise, "Diffusing everywhere/A light of love which greets the angel-host/Moving their intellect…/To wonderment."

It is tempting to ask how much of this Dante literally believes, and how much is a daring, innovative play on the medieval Cult of the Virgin and the influential courtly love tradition. Certainly, Dante knew that this poetic commentary devoted to Beatrice's memory, but written for his artistic peers (Guido Cavalcanti in specific), would be read with these tropes in mind. Nevertheless, Beatrice's symbolic importance cannot be doubted. She is Dante's personal addition to the pantheon of saints, mediating between the poet and the divine. In her "sacred eyes," the pilgrim of the *Commedia* will see Christ himself (*Purgatorio* XXXI).

Which adds a level of complexity to charges of betrayal. In the *Vita Nuova*, the poet admits that, after Beatrice's death in 1290, he turned to another "gracious lady" for solace, a woman who took pity on his suffering, and in whose features he perceived "the self-same Love" he once observed in Beatrice. His heart is "stirred to tumult" by the sight of this lady, so that feelings of loss and joy are now commingled, confusing the poet's physical senses:

> *My wasted eyes I find I cannot keep*
> *From gazing at you ever and again,*
> *For by a tearful longing they are led.*
> *Beholding you then so augments their pain*
> *They are consumed by their desire to weep,*
> *Yet in your presence tears they cannot shed.*

However, it doesn't take long for the poet to recognize, and deeply regret, his apparent inconstancy. "The sight of this [new] lady had such an effect on me that my eyes began to delight too much in seeing her," he writes, reminding himself in a poem following, "While life endures you should not ever be/Inconstant to your lady who is dead."

Readers may feel the poet protests too much. After all, Beatrice is dead; why shouldn't he be free to love someone else, especially a young, beautiful woman who appears to share some of Beatrice's attributes? The question is indeed difficult to answer if both Beatrice and the "gracious lady" are no more than beautiful, if remarkably inspiring, Florentine women of the late thirteenth century. But as we have seen, Dante was already beginning to cloak Beatrice in layers of religious symbolism. Might the "gracious lady" point to something beyond herself, as well? The poet says so in his *Convivio*, or "Banquet," an uncompleted treatise on medieval thought begun in the first years of exile. There, Dante tells us that the "gracious lady" is none other than the medieval Lady Philosophy, the conceptualization of earthly wisdom that can lead toward an understanding of God. But here a problem arises: the "gracious lady" of the *Vita Nuova*, for all her gentle attributes, is clearly a distraction from Beatrice's beatified countenance guiding the poet "on the straight path." Are the lovely ladies in competition for Dante's soul, or is something else going on here?

The likely answer is that, in hindsight, Dante is giving a more specific reading of the "gracious lady" than the *Vita Nuova* supports. By the time that work was in circulation, about 1295, the poet had entered politics and turned his attention to the study of philosophy, determining to abandon the "sweet love poetry" of the *dolce stil nuovo* in order to focus on "harsher" rhymes dealing with the concrete realities of politics and social ethics. This new phase of philosophical study, clearly visible in the *Comedy*, was no doubt sparked by the personal crisis of Beatrice's death, as well as the poet's growing role in Florentine politics. For a writer of Dante's sensibilities, tensions artistic and personal would be inevitable. The "gracious lady" may indeed represent philosophy, but she almost certainly represents politics, as well, and any of the mundane realities that could – and did - steal the poet's attention from Beatrice's beatified countenance. The remarkable fact is that Dante seemed to understand this even as it was happening to him.

If an apprenticeship to politics and philosophy marked an interregnum between Dante's literary and spiritual encounters with Beatrice, it was not without its uses. Also in between was the shocking encounter with exile, a time of taking stock of everything. Reflecting on his reading of St. Augustine's *Confessions* and Boethius' *Consolation of Philosophy*, both of which appear in *Convivio*, Dante saw a pattern beginning to emerge, in which the pursuits of human love and human knowledge, ultimately unsatisfying though they may be, are the first steps in an approach to God. The poet's earthly passion for Beatrice - whom he had loved since childhood - had grown into something more, yet it remained corruptible, subject to changes of the will. After Beatrice's death, he had turned to philosophy for answers, a tendency that increased with exile, as did the questions: Why is the world so filled with chaos and violence? Why don't the evil get their just reward? Is there really any purpose behind human events? The poet eventually discovered that human wisdom, even the accumulation of it such as he had sought in *Convivio*, could not supply the necessary answers. One did not arrive at divine love by way of philosophy, as he had boldly declared in that work. There had to be something more. The philosophers could point toward the truth, but only grace could get you there, as Augustine had recounted in his *Confessions*, and as Beatrice demonstrates in the Garden of Eden atop Mount Purgatory, reminding the pilgrim of the limitations of "that school which you have followed" (XXXIII). Little surprise, then, that Dante never completed *Convivio*, his compendium of human knowledge. In the end, it simply wasn't necessary. Sometime around 1308, Dante the exile realized he had another journey to take.

A Divine Calling

In hindsight, events or transformations years in the making can seem like the work of days or even hours. So it is with Dante's transformation, if we see in the opening of the *Comedy* a reflection of its author's spiritual journey. In the space of no more than two cantos (in the context of the story, a matter of hours), we find the fictional Dante changed from exile – a man driven from home and community, fleeing what he fears - to pilgrim, a soul purposefully journeying toward a destination he longs to experience. For the spiritual man, that destination is the heavenly Jerusalem, a glimpse of God on his celestial throne; for the social man – the poet and former politician - it is a state of happiness, not just for himself, but for all humankind. In a famous and oft-quoted letter to Cangrande della Scala of Verona, probably written between 1315 and 1317, Dante explains the rationale behind the *Comedy* itself. "The whole work was undertaken not for a speculative, but a practical reason," the poet says, its purpose being "to remove those who are living in this life from a state of wretchedness, and to lead them to a state of blessedness."

It seems clear that, as Dante sat down to write the first cantos of the *Comedy*, he thought of himself in this new light. For nearly six years of exile, he had defined himself by what he lacked, by the fact of his dispossession - of home, family, property, companionship. Now, he assumed a new identity, in which exile was to be an instrument of redemption for himself and for others; wherein his aimless wandering was transformed into a purposeful journey; whereby he, the dispossessed, came into possession of something few men or women in history ever received. He had a divine calling.

Dante first makes this audacious claim in the second canto of the *Comedy*. Although religious visions and reports of angelic visitations were not uncommon in the late Middle Ages, it was still a bold thing to declare one's work directly inspired by God. Aware of the reaction such a claim might elicit, Dante expresses the idea in a subtle, almost backhanded fashion in the initial encounter between his fictional self and the Roman poet Virgil. There, Dante, as pilgrim, questions his ability to undertake the kind of cosmic journey, beginning with a descent into Hell, that Virgil says is necessary for his redemption.

"But why am I to go?" the pilgrim complains. "I am not Aeneas, I am not Paul,/ neither I nor any man would think me worthy," he declares, contrasting himself with the fictional founder of Rome, who undertook a journey to the classical underworld, and the great missionary of the early church, who claimed a mystical experience of "the third heaven." Both journeys were divinely ordained, to Dante's mind—one by a pagan diety, the other by the Christian God. Is it remotely possible that other, ordinary humans might be recipients of a similar calling?

That question is answered by Virgil, in whose mouth Dante the poet places his claim. Rebuking the pilgrim's faintheartedness, Virgil informs him of the existence of a divine rescue operation designed to return the pilgrim to the straight path and organized by none other than the Virgin Mary with help from St. Lucia and Dante's own Beatrice. "Why are you such a coward in your heart," Virgil scolds, "when three such ladies, who are blessed,/watch out for you up there in Heaven's court…?" Why, indeed, the reader may enjoin. The question is ultimately a rhetorical one. While the fictional pilgrim may doubt his ability to undertake this journey, Dante the poet is secure in his own, inviting us to "join our wills," as do the pilgrim and Virgil, and travel along for the poem's remaining 13,700-odd lines. Readers familiar with the biblical callings of Moses, Isaiah, Ezekiel and others will recognize the trope of the divine messenger who, while ultimately successful, initially doubts his ability to fulfill his mission.

The poet reasserts the claim to sacred calling throughout the *Comedy*, particularly in *Purgatorio* and *Paradiso*, where it is stated more boldly and directly. Multiple times, characters including St. Peter, Beatrice, and Dante's own ancestor Cacciaguida charge the pilgrim to relate what he has seen in the afterlife when he returns to earth, much like an interstellar John the Baptist calling medieval Italy to repent. "You, my son, whose mortal weight must bring/You back to earth again, open your mouth down there/And do not hide what I hide not from you!" St. Peter commands after delivering a lengthy tirade against papal corruption. Similarly, Cacciaguida instructs the pilgrim,

> *Let what you write reveal all you have seen,*
> *And let those men who itch scratch where it hurts.*
> *Though when your words are taken in at first*
> *They may taste bitter, but once well-digested*
> *They will become a vital nutriment.*

Dante alludes to the salutary effect his words may have in the first lines of the *Inferno* when, describing the unpleasantness involved in recounting the pilgrim's journey through Hell, he acknowledges that "if I would show the good that came of it/I must talk about things other than the good." Beatrice reinforces this idea shortly after her reunion with the poet in Purgatory, when she exhorts him to put his otherworldly experiences into writing "for the good of sinners in your world" (*Purgatory* XXXII,103-105). Thus, the stage is set for the authorial intrusion of *Paradiso* XXV, where the poet speaks directly of "this sacred poem/To which both Heaven and Earth have set their hand," and expresses hope that the divinely inspired work "Wins over those cruel hearts that exile me."

So, the poet's ultimate goal in writing the *Comedy* appears two-fold: to win the heavenly Jerusalem for himself and for others and to pry open the gates of earthly Florence—where, according to the *Convivio*, the author desires "with all my heart to rest my weary soul and end the time granted me"—along the way. Twenty years into his exile, writing the final cantos of the *Comedy*, Dante still believed the latter was possible. Despite the tragedy he had experienced, he never surrendered hope that the world, as well as he, could be redeemed, and that one day he would see his beloved Florence again. "There is no son of the Church Militant,/With greater hope than his," Beatrice declares to St. James in *Paradiso* XXV, as the pilgrim undergoes a theological examination on the Christian virtue of hope,"…and this is why he is allowed to come/From Egypt to behold Jerusalem/Before his fighting days on earth are done." How different these words, uttered on the threshold of the highest heaven, from those above the gates of Hell directing sinners to "abandon every hope"!

Beatrice's allusion to the Hebrew Exodus is of particular importance, for it is Dante's main allegorical model for the entire pilgrimage through the afterlife. Both are sacred journeys, sanctioned and guided by the divine; both entail a release from bondage into the freedom of full relationship with God – whether on Jerusalem's holy mount or in the stillness of the newly cleansed soul. Variously interpreted as Florence under the Black Guelfs; Italy enveloped in anarchy and violence; or the Church under sway of a corrupt papacy, Egypt is everything Dante has been forced to flee, while the Promised Land is the original home he, like the Hebrews of old, longs to return to – the spiritual Jerusalem in one sense; Florence in the time of Cacciaguida in another, where the native population is "pure down to the humblest artisan." Just as the Israelites cross the Desert of Sinai to enter the Promised Land, so Dante the pilgrim endures the burning sands of Hell (*Inferno* XIV) and the steep slopes of Purgatory to reach Paradise. In both cases, it is a resurrection journey by which a subject people are given new life. This point is made particularly clear in one of the most beautiful scenes in the entire *Comedy*, *Purgatorio* II, where on Easter morning Dante witnesses the souls of the dead arriving on the shores of Purgatory. Borne by an angelic boatman at the speed of light, the souls disembark singing Psalm 113, "When Israel Came Out of Egypt," a hymn of praise recalling God's delivery of the Hebrews from Egyptian bondage. Dante could be sure that contemporary readers would instantly recognize the familiar allegory of Christ's death and resurrection, which liberated the individual from bondage to sin and freed him or her to experience the grace of eternal life. Dante addresses the subject explicitly in the letter to Can Grande, where in speaking about the *Comedy*, he identifies the various meanings of the Exodus itself:

If we look only at the letter, this signifies that the children of Israel went out of Egypt in the time of Moses; if we look at the allegory, it signifies our redemption through Christ; if we look at the moral sense, it signifies the turning of the souls from the sorrow and misery of sin to a state of grace. . . .

On the literary level, the biblical Exodus is the ultimate pilgrimage narrative in a sacred scripture brimming with such journeys. The ancient Israelites were pilgrims following divine signs toward their promised home. Dante was no doubt looking for the same in the period following his final separation from partisan politics in 1303-4. He may have found them, not in the stars as does his pilgrim, but in the concrete events of the world around him. In October 1303, the poet's great nemesis, Pope Boniface VIII, died after being imprisoned by his former allies, the French—the same who had helped him wrest control of Florence two years before, driving the poet into exile. Now, that exile had an antidote to the religious corruption of Boniface and his like, "harlots" in the pageant of church history (*Purgatorio* XXXII), who claimed to speak on God's behalf.[2] Taking up his pen in righteous indignation, Dante the poet would do that himself.

There was precedent for the task the poet was undertaking, if not in medieval Europe, then in the words and actions of the ancient Hebrew prophets and of Jesus' cousin John the Baptist, the "voice crying in the wilderness." Dante probably has the latter in mind when he describes the pilgrim lost in the wilderness at the beginning of the *Comedy*, and almost certainly in

Paradiso XXV, when he envisions returning to Florence "with a changed voice and with another fleece," suggesting John's prophetic vocation as well as his famous camel hair coat. Once returned home in this new role, the poet will assume the laurel wreath—sign of literary glory—"at my own baptismal font," the very place he entered the faith. Significantly, that baptistery, "my lovely San Giovanni" (*Inferno* XIX, 17), is named after John, who also is the patron saint of Florence. The poet's intention becomes clear: if he can win over his Florentine enemies with this sacred poem, he will return home and be publicly "reborn" (the exact image is re-christened) as a prophet, like John. Dante's ancestor Cacciaguida alludes to the baptizer a few cantos earlier, when he tells the poet that "Your cry of words will do as does the wind/Striking the hardest at the highest peaks" (*Paradiso* XVII, 133-134), an obvious reference to the prophet's voice "crying" in the wilderness.

But Dante does not stop with comparisons to John the Baptist. The exhortations from Beatrice, Cacciaguida, and St. Peter to the pilgrim to write down all he sees, hide nothing, and report back to his fellow men evoke the calling narratives of Isaiah ("Go and tell this people," Isaiah 6:9), Ezekiel ("Go and speak to the house of Israel," Ezekiel 3:1), and Jeremiah ("Gird up your loins; stand and tell them everything I command you," Jeremiah 1:17). In each case, the prophets experience a vision as part of this calling: Ezekiel, exiled in Babylon, sees God on a chariot drawn by four living creatures and circumscribed by wheels of fire; Isaiah has a vision of God on a throne surrounded by seraphim; Jeremiah sees an almond tree and a boiling pot, portents of disaster for the Kingdom of Judah. Dante could and did lay claim to visions, as well, none more powerful or mysterious than that which may have given rise to the *Comedy* itself.

Near the end of the *Vita Nuova*, Dante's tribute to Beatrice written some 12 or 14 years before the *Comedy*, he includes a sonnet composed at the bequest of "two gracious ladies," perhaps friends of the late beloved and her brother Forese, Dante's close companion. The sonnet is striking both for its imagery and its inclusion of elements that would be central to the *Comedy* many years—and one long exile—later. In the poem, Dante imagines his "sigh," which we may translate as his thought, rising to heaven for "a vision of /A soul in glory, whom the host reveres." Approaching its destination, the sigh, now depicted as a "pilgrim spirit," gazes on the beatified soul and "speaks of what it sees/In subtle words I [Dante] do not comprehend.... " Several lines later, the poet reveals what he does "know well": the soul is Beatrice, whose name he hears repeatedly.

The similarities with the *Comedy* are obvious: the pilgrim spirit, the vision of Beatrice in paradise, the limitations of language and intellect when confronting the metaphysical (a recurrent theme in *Paradiso*). Strikingly different, of course, are the form and purpose of this journey: here a sigh, rather than a living man, journeys to heaven to see the beloved, rather than God, whose heavenly being dominates the entirety of the poet's thought, as he recounts in his commentary.

This is a pilgrimage of sighs—of lover's longings and desires – not of soul, a personal journey no one but the poet can take, ending in a vision of the beloved that is ultimately unrelatable and incomplete. Dante's heart remains "forlorn," longing for more.

Did Dante, as early as 1294, have an intimation of the *Comedy*? Did he imagine one day writing an epic poem about spiritual, rather than purely romantic, themes in which he, rather than Beatrice, would be the main character? The poet tantalizes us with this suggestion in the paragraph which follows the sonnet above, the final sentences of the *Vita Nuova*. There, he mentions a mysterious and "marvelous vision" that persuades him to write no more of Beatrice ("this blessed one") until he can "do so more worthily." To that end, he pledges to "apply myself as much as I can," as Beatrice well knows. The poet closes the slim volume with a kind of prayer to God:

If it shall please Him by whom all things live that my life continue for a few years, I hope to compose concerning her what has never been written in rhyme of any woman. And then may it please Him who is the lord of courtesy that my soul may go to see the glory of my lady, that is of the blessed Beatrice, who now in glory beholds the face of Him who is blessed forever.

Mourning the recent death of his beloved, the 29-year-old poet already sees her as a conduit to God, although reunion with her is still his ultimate goal. By the time he sits down to begin the *Comedy*, years later, many things will have changed: the now homeless poet will see God, not Beatrice, as his ultimate goal, and she will be transformed into his personal guide on the celestial journey. An earthly love would literally lead him toward a divine one. And although the greatest classical poet, Virgil, and the most famous medieval mystic, St. Bernard, would assist in that journey, it would be Beatrice who captured the imagination of the ages. God granted Dante's prayer, as we readers of the *Comedy* know. Weeks, perhaps days, after completing the final cantos of *Paradiso* from a temporary abode in Ravenna, Dante went to see the glory of his lady.

Notes

1. This article is reprinted by permission from the author's forthcoming book entitled: *From Darkness to Light: A Spiritual Journey Through the 'Divine Comedy'* which will be published by SPCK in the autumn of 2009.

2. In 1302, the year of Dante's exile, Boniface issued the papal bull *Unam Sanctum*, which declared that "in this Church and in its power are two swords...the spiritual and the temporal," and that "it is absolutely necessary for salvation that every human creature be subject to the Roman Pontiff."

4

Unmasking: Esther, Exile, and Creativity

By Denise Dombkowski Hopkins

If we cannot see ourselves in the stories we encounter, they have little power to shape or transform us. Great stories are those that address us, draw us in as part of larger stories that seek to claim us, and give new meaning to our own stories.
           Bruce C. Birch[1]

Bruce Birch has spent a lifetime helping students and pastors to see themselves in the stories of Hebrew Bible. Two of his courses, "The Hebrew Bible Goes to the Movies" and "The Old Testament and the Fine Arts," have pioneered the extensive use of the arts in forging connections between biblical text and interpreter.[2] As a teacher of connections, he is unsurpassed; his courses are consistently over-enrolled. As a colleague, he has modeled the vulnerability that such connections evoke in the classroom, even assuming an Elvis persona when the situation called for it! Consequently, I was recently moved to connect with the story of Esther in a surprisingly new way (for me), through biblical storytelling.

    The book of Esther is a "great" story, saturated with action, irony, suspense, drama, satire, comedy, identity crises, reversals, and conflict; it offers many hooks to pull us readers into its world. It is such a good story that it has been retold as a graphic novel, that is, an extended black-and-white comic book, published by the Jewish Publication Society.[3] I teach Esther every few years as part of a course on the Megillot, that is, the five scrolls - Ruth, Esther, Qoheleth, Lamentations, Song of Songs - read publicly in the synagogue on designated liturgical days in the Jewish tradition. Esther is read twice for the festival of Purim in the spring each year; it commemorates the deliverance from genocide of exiled Jews in the Persian Empire. When teaching Esther, I ask students to survey the book, noting structure, themes, and motifs, and then to pretend that they are publishing the book with a new, marketable title that expresses their understanding of it. The titles have illustrated in delightfully surprising ways the connections that students have made out of their own contexts with the story of Esther.

    A former corporate CEO,[4] for example, suggested the title: "What Corporate America Can Learn from Esther"; given the current global financial crisis, he was eerily prescient. He saw Esther as the Executive Vice-President who runs the company even though she doesn't own it; she knows all the employees and plays her cards right with the President and Owner of the corporation, King Ahasuerus. The President throws lavish parties at company expense to keep the staff and customers happy, goes on the road for extended periods to bring in new customers, travels with his vice-presidents (generals), and takes credit for their decisions. Haman, the Vice-President for Marketing and Sales, is given authority for new product and sales campaigns and pushes the envelope of corporate ethics; his thirst for success will ultimately prove fatal to his career (and to his life!). The eunuchs are the secretaries and assistants; overall, they are dependable, but sometimes they can be overheard sabotaging a project or a co-worker. In rare cases in the corporate world, the smaller company (the Jews), maintain their identity within the larger corporate entity (Persia) that has bought them out.

Other titles generated by my students run the gamut from, "Nowhere to Run, Nowhere to Hide," "The Sting," "Sleepless in Susa," "Pretty Woman," "Who's the Boss?," "A Comedy of Edicts," "Trading Places," "Queen for a Day," "Extreme Makeover," and "As the Kingdom Turns." In addition to titles, the course also requires a final communication event that presents the student's understanding of a text in Esther through the medium of music, visual art, drama, dance or other imaginative avenue. Deep connections with the Esther story are forged in this way. Over the years, my students have created three-act operas as well as clever songs with original lyrics to the tune of "I feel pretty, oh so pretty" (from West Side Story) or the "Triumphal March" (from "Aida"), interviewed Esther on Oprah, woven tapestries, and created chancel dramas. Bruce Birch has encouraged and modeled this kind of imagination and creativity in the classroom throughout his career.

The diversity of responses from my students to the book of Esther echoes, in part, the scholarly debate raging over the book. Scholars have disagreed in their assessments of the genre of Esther, suggesting that it is: novelistic, with elements similar to those in Greek literature; a comedy enjoyed by Jews in the Diaspora that avoids attacking existing power structures; a satire meant to remind readers of key political and theological issues; a farce full of exaggeration and caricature of the Persian court; a wisdom court legend navigating court intrigues and conflict in the Diaspora; a didactic wisdom tale meant to educate the elite; or a folk tale that makes suffering bearable.[5] Scholars have also clashed over their evaluations of Esther's actions, and even over whether it is Mordecai, rather than Esther, who is the central hero of the story. This is no surprise, since commentaries on Esther were not written until the 9th century CE[6] when questions about the book's canonicity were finally put to rest. Problematic is the fact that the book never mentions God, that Esther keeps her Jewish identity a secret and participates in the king's beauty contest, and that the story ends in bloody violence. The later additions to Esther, found in the Apocrypha, address some of these problems; they mention God more than 50 times and put prayers to God in the mouths of Esther and Mordecai.

These debates sharpen instead of dilute the focus of the book of Esther on the situation of Israel in Exile; they illustrate the creative possibilities of response to Exile. Rather than initiating a period of steady decline into legalism as many have argued, Birch considers the period of exile and return to be "a time of unusual creativity called forth in the face of severe threats to the integrity and survival of the Israelite community and its religious traditions."[7] For Birch, Esther serves as a role model for the community of Jews in Exile because she "rises from lowly status to success through perseverance, cleverness, and piety."[8] The disenfranchised become the empowered, offering hope to the powerless in every generation.

Exile as central theme in Esther emerges clearly in the intentional repetition of 2.6: "[Kish - ancestor of Mordecai] had been exiled from Jerusalem with the exiles who had been exiled with King Jeconiah of Judah, whom King Nebuchadnezzar of Babylon had exiled." Mordecai's genealogy uses words from the verbal root 'to exile' four times in one verse. To be Jewish means to know Exile and to develop structures for survival within Exile. There can be no false optimism for a quick return to Jerusalem, as Jeremiah warned after the first deportation to Babylon in 597 B.C.E.: "But seek the welfare of the city where I have sent you into exile, and pray to the LORD on its behalf, for in its welfare you will find your welfare" (Jer. 29.7). Birch argues that Jeremiah "suggests a vocation of creative minority in the larger social realities of the world,"[9] a vocation that ought to resonate with today's church. It is clear that Mordecai and Esther modeled this vocation for the exilic community. Formerly colonized peoples in contemporary culture resonate with this vocation.[10] They have hailed Esther as a model for postcolonial reading because she succeeds in an alien world by concealing her Jewishness, and once established, recovers her identity and overturns a decree against her people.[11] Esther's message is not just for Jews in the Diaspora, but also for Gentiles: Jews will survive even when the odds are against them.[12]

Esther has also become a poster child for feminist scholars in both negative and positive ways.[13] On the negative side, Esther is attacked for being a typical woman in a man's world — winning favor by using her physical beauty,[14] while Vashti is hailed as a strong woman who refuses to appear before the drunken king and his cronies and is banished (Esther 1). On the positive side, Esther is applauded for exploiting the male power structures that hemmed her in - being active and not passive;[15] Esther succeeds where Vashti fails. Sakenfeld[16] suggests rightly that Vashti and Esther present two different models of resistance to the misuse of power and authority, each valuable depending on the circumstances. Esther works within the system to save herself and others. Sakenfeld urges us not to fight over the best way to challenge power.

In questions for reflection at the end of her chapter on Esther and Vashti, Sakenfeld asks: "Do you think of yourself as more like Esther (working within the system) or more like Vashti (standing against systems you disapprove of)?"[17] This question helped to shape my interpretation of Esther when asked to present her story during the worship service at the retirement of our Wesley colleague, Diedra Kriewald..[18] My storytelling would replace the usual Scripture reading. I had invited biblical storytellers into my classroom many times and had presented Talmudic midrash (a rabbinic method of searching the Scriptures for contemporary meaning by reading in between the lines) on texts we studied, but I had never attempted biblical storytelling myself. I accepted this daunting challenge, partly to honor my colleague, Diedra, and her consistent creativity in worship, and partly to venture farther down the path that Bruce had blazed in the arts and Bible.[19]

I turned to the website of the Network of Biblical Storytellers (NOBS), founded by Tom Boomershine, to prepare myself. NOBS dedicates itself to "telling the sacred stories of the biblical tradition in post-literate, digital culture."[20] The network encourages a variety of expressions and presentations of sacred stories in oral and written form, and reminds us that there are many kinds of biblical storytelling— from midrash, to contemporization, to first person monologues. I chose the first person monologue for the worship service, feeling that I could more directly link myself with Esther's story in this way. NOBS calls biblical storytelling "a spiritual discipline that involves first committing a narrative text of scripture to deep memory (not memorizing but "internalizing" the story as images and feelings) and then engaging with the text in a lively "telling," a sacred act that binds teller and listeners in community."[21] I lived with the book of Esther for an entire week, reading and re-reading it, noting where it intersected with my story. Searching for a vehicle for this "lively telling," I decided to dress as Queen Esther at a Purim party, complete with feather boa, crown, and mask (a Mardi Gras mask of feathers and sequins that I had borrowed).[22]

On Purim, a minor Jewish holiday, the Esther scroll or *megillah* is read twice, charity is distributed, gifts of food are exchanged, and a festive meal is eaten, often accompanied by a Purimshpiel. Purimshpiels are farcical plays which parody the accepted authority of teachers, texts, and public readings of the scroll. People often dress up as the major characters in the book, wear masks, and even cross dress. Participants boo and hiss whenever Haman's name is read or mentioned. The Talmud *Megilla 7b* urges the drinking of so much wine on Purim that people can no longer tell the difference between 'blessed be Mordecai' and 'cursed be Haman.' Timothy Beal has suggested that the book of Esther is a farce and that "Purim invites us to recognize, and even to celebrate, the otherness within us that we so often try to repress or hide. Purim is, in this sense, a coming-out party. Purim crosses boundaries, and invites others to do the same."[23]

As I prepared for my storytelling of Esther, I meditated on feminist interpretations of Esther and Vashti, and on the notion of hiding that Beal sees as the key to the book. The name 'Esther' comes from the Hebrew root *satar*, 'to hide' (Hiphil). The book is preoccupied with hiding, masking, and misrepresenting otherness. Beal argues that Vashti is erased, banished from the king's presence, but her exscription "serves to mark territory by naming that which belongs outside it; yet precisely in this process of marking off for oblivion, Vashti and her refusal are also indelibly *written into* the story in a way that will be difficult to forget."[24] Beal thinks of the book of Esther as a kind of palimpsest, that is, a story written, erased, and then written over with a new story, leaving behind traces of the old.[25] This applies not only to Esther but to Mordecai as well. Like Vashti, Mordecai refused the powers by not bowing to Haman (3.2-15), who is also an outsider in the Persian court. For Beal, the book of Esther is not about models of Diaspora living but about the identity crisis brought about by Exile and dispersion. Esther's story forced me to recognize and wrestle with the 'other' in me in both my personal life and my professional career.

Keeping these approaches to Esther in mind, I positioned myself in the chancel area of Oxnam Chapel and began my monologue, clutching copies of the *National Enquirer* and *The Star* in my hands, pacing as I spoke:

"Welcome, welcome to this Purim party today as we celebrate the deliverance of the Jews from annihilation by the Persian king Ahasuerus. Let's have a terrific time. I see some great masks out there. I don't recognize many of you.

Now remember, every time I say Haman, you need to boo and hiss. I'll raise my hands to remind you.... Haman. I can't hear you...... Haman.....
I don't have time to tell the whole megillah (that's the Hebrew word for scroll) to you this morning, but here are some things you should know...

It's not easy being a woman in a man's world, let alone being a queen in it. And it's even harder being a closet Jewess in the middle of the Persian Empire, far from Judah, still grieving the Exile. I understand "double-consciousness" real well.

Now, I know what they're saying about me - I read the tabloids - *The Star*, *The National Enquirer* (holding them up and waving them around) — beauty and no brains, sex object, a puppet who follows orders, a pawn played by the men in her life - King Ahasuerus, the eunuchs, my cousin Mordecai. Just yesterday the headlines screamed, 'She's no Vashti!' - Mothers, don't let your daughters grow up to be an Esther'. They don't think I have Vashti's guts.

Well, I guess they haven't read my novel, Esther, very carefully. Did you know that it's #150 on the Amazon charts and that Oprah wants to interview me next month?

Now, I want you to know that I didn't go of my own free will into the king's harem after Queen Vashti was banished; I was "taken," (*laqach*) just as Bathsheba was 'taken' by King David. Once there, I had a choice. Give up or listen and learn to survive. They want beauty? I cleaned up real good. And partying? I showed them how to throw a banquet. I soon found favor. I stored up that favor and used it when my people needed it.

How can you not notice the delicious ironies in my story?

My favorite one is the struggle between my cousin Mordecai and Haman (HISS). My cousin told me about 2 eunuchs who were plotting to overthrow King Ahasuerus, and I warned the king and they were hanged. But the very next minute, that nasty Haman (BOO) gets promoted. No reward for my cousin, but everyone is bowing down to Haman (HISS). Except my cousin, and wow, does that ever make Haman (BOO) mad. He was infuriated.

So, to get back at my cousin, Haman (BOO) gets the king to issue a decree for the destruction of the Jews, arguing that we did not keep the king's laws and that our laws were too different. Haman (BOO) wanted a good old fashioned pogrom. The nerve of Haman (BOO) - he knows what it means to be an outsider like us - he's an Amalekite, not a Persian.

Well, my cousin Mordecai reacts to the decree by putting on sackcloth and ashes; everywhere in the Persian empire Jews are fasting, weeping, and lamenting. My cousin wants me to do something about the decree, to go to the king and intercede for our people. But Mordecai had for so long warned me to keep my Jewishness a secret, to hide it. Did you know that my name, Esther, comes from a Hebrew root meaning 'to hide'? But I wasn't the only one hiding; God was hiding, too.

Cousin Mordecai urged me to take action: "perhaps you have come to royal dignity for just such a time as this" he said. I think I always knew that. So I took charge. Everyone knew that I or anyone else couldn't approach King Ahasuerus unless called, but I told cousin Mordecai to arrange a fast for three days. Pretty gutsy and faithful, don't you think, what with all the feasting going on at court? Then I'd approach the king. "If I perish, I perish" I said.

I had been studying King Ahasuerus for a long time, and I knew that the way to his heart was through his stomach and his booze, and I knew he wouldn't want to lose another queen so publicly, so I put on my royal robes, claiming my authority, holding my breath, not quite sure what he would do. But he held out his golden scepter - I got the green light. I asked for two banquets for Haman (BOO) and the King to attend.

But nasty old Haman (BOO) couldn't bear that my cousin Mordecai was still not bowing down to him, so his wife and friends urged him to build a gallows and tell the king to have my cousin hanged on it. But here's the ironic twist - it's Haman (HISS) who winds up hanging from the gallows!!!

Why? It was because King Ahasuerus was having one of his insomniac nights, and wound up reading the court records. He realized that my cousin Mordecai was never rewarded for uncovering the plot to overthrow him. And here's the delicious part - it's Haman (HISS) who must crown and robe my cousin, and lead him through the open square of the city on a horse.!! Lovely poetic justice, don't you think?

It gets even better. At the second banquet, the king asks me again, "what is your request? Even to the half of my kingdom, it shall be fulfilled." I hadn't requested anything from him at the first banquet - wait for it, I thought. "Give me my life, and the life of my people," I said.

The king was angry and wanted to know "who is he, and where is he, who presumed to do this?" And that's how Haman ((BOO) was hanged on the gallows intended for Mordecai, and how my people escaped annihilation. That's why we're celebrating today.

So now, dear friends, it's time to take off our masks. It was time to cross over the boundaries that separate us from them, male from female, self from other. Party on!"

Those in the chancel area reported afterwards that as I removed my mask, my face hid nothing. I appeared to them to be totally vulnerable. I had become Esther; her struggles were etched in the contours of my face. I felt it, too. Thank you, Bruce.

Notes

1. Bruce C. Birch, "Old Testament Canon and Moral Address," *Canon, Theology, and Old Testament Interpretation: Essays in Honor of Brevard Childs*, G. Tucker, D. Petersen & R. Wilson, eds. (Minneapolis, MN: Fortress, 1988): 78.

2. Bruce C. Birch, "The Arts, Midrash, and Biblical Teaching," *Arts, Theology, and the Church: New Intersections*, Kimberly Vrundy & Wilson Yates, eds. (Cleveland, OH: Pilgrim, 2005).

3. J. T. Waldman, *Megillat Esther: The Graphic Novel* (Philadelphia: The Jewish Publication Society, 2005). Waldman studied at Hebrew Union College in Jerusalem. Christian graphic novelists have been at work since the 1960s. The book of Esther has also been retold for children in the video series Veggie Tales: "One Night with the King."

4. Tom Barnard is now an ordained United Methodist pastor in Virginia.

5. See a thorough review of these various approaches in Kevin McGeough, "Esther the Hero: Going Beyond "Wisdom" in Heroic Narratives," *Catholic Biblical Quarterly*, 70:1 (January, 2008): 44-65.

6. See Kimberly Vrudny, "Medieval Fascination with the Queen: Esther as the Queen of Heaven and Host of the Messianic Banquet," *Arts*, 11:2 (1999): 36-43. Vrudny discusses two medieval approaches to Esther. One, by Rhabanus Maurus in 836 CE, views Esther allegorically as the type or prefigure of the Church, King Ahasuerus as Christ, and Haman as representative of those who opposed the Church, e.g. the Jews. The "old people" of the synagogue are expressed by Queen Vashti. The second, *The Mirror of Salvation*, was a popular devotional book that illustrated these typologies.

7. Bruce C. Birch, *Let Justice Roll Down: The Old Testament, Ethics, and Christian Life* (Louisville, KY: John Knox, 1991): 280.

8. *Ibid.*, p. 311.

9. *Ibid.*, p. 304.

10. Daniel Smith, *The Religion of the Landless: The Social Context of the Babylonian Exile* (Bloomington, IN: Meyer-Stone, 1989): 8-10. Smith urges us to adopt a "Fourth World Perspective" of migrants, indigenous peoples, and refugees who live as permanent minorities in empires they cannot escape. Smith has been an important dialogue partner for Birch.

11. R.S. Sugirtharajah, ed., *The Post-Colonial Bible* (Sheffield: Sheffield Academic Press, 1998): 16.

12. See Jon D. Levenson, *Esther*, Old Testament Library (Louisville, KY: Westminster/John Knox, 1997).

13. See the review in McGeough, "Esther the Hero," 54-57.

14. Alice Laffey, *Introduction to the Old Testament: A Feminist Perspective* (Philadelphia, PA: Fortress, 1988): 216.

15. Sidnie White Crawford, "The Book of Esther and the Additions to Esther" *New Interpreters Bible, vol.* 3 (Nashville, TN: Abingdon, 1999): 872-73.

16. Katherine Doob Sakenfeld, *Just Wives? Stories of Power and Survival in the Old Testament and Today* (Louisville, KY: Westminster/John Knox, 2003): 64-65.

17. *Ibid.*, p. 66.

18. Diedra Kriewald retired in 2007 as Professor of Christian Education at Wesley

Theological Seminary.

19. This next step seemed like a natural progression, given that Bruce and I had portrayed Mr. And Mrs. Claus in Diedra's famous St. Nicholas chapel during Advent of that year.

20. See nobs.org for more information, especially "Biblical Storytelling 101."

21. *Ibid.*

22. My imagination was also sparked by a project submitted to me by Rev. David Bahr, a Doctor of Ministry student at Wesley Seminary in a class I taught on Biblical Women, Leadership, and Power in 2004. He planned a Purim Party event that included mask making, the reading of Esther, and a celebration with food, fellowship, and dancing in his local church. As part of this event, he invited people to share testimony about the ways in which they keep their identity hidden in different areas of their life, reminding them that masks are not necessary within the community of faith.

23. Timothy K. Beal, *The Book of Hiding: Gender, Ethnicity, Annihilation, and Esther* (New York, NY: Routledge, 1997): 124.

24. *Ibid.*, p. 25.

25. *Ibid.*, p. 29.

Works Cited

Beal, Timothy K. *The Book of Hiding: Gender, Ethnicity, Annihilation, and Esther.* New York, NY: Routledge, 1997.

Birch, Bruce C. "The Arts, Midrash, and Biblical Teaching," *Arts, Theology, and the Church: New Intersections,* Kimberly Vrundy & Wilson Yates, eds. Cleveland, OH: Pilgrim, 2005. pp. 105-124.

_____ *Let Justice Roll Down: The Old Testament, Ethics, and Christian Life.* Louisville, KY: John Knox, 1991.

_____. "Old Testament Canon and Moral Address," *Canon, Theology, and Old Testament Interpretation: Essays in Honor of Brevard Childs,* G. Tucker, D. Petersen, & R. Wilson, eds. Minneapolis, MN: Fortress, 1988.

Crawford, Sidnie White. "The Book of Esther and the Additions to Esther" *New Interpreters Bible,* vol. 3. Nashville, TN: Abingdon, 1999. pp. 872-73.

Laffey, Alice. *Introduction to the Old Testament: A Feminist Perspective.* Philadelphia, PA: Fortress, 1988.

Levenson, Jon D. *Esther,* Old Testament Library. Louisville, KY: Westminster/John Knox, 1997.

McGeough, Kevin. "Esther the Hero: Going Beyond "Wisdom" in Heroic Narratives," *Catholic Biblical Quarterly,* 70:1 (January, 2008): 44-65.

Sakenfeld, Katherine Doob. *Just Wives? Stories of Power and Survival in the Old Testament and Today.* Louisville, KY: Westminster/John Knox, 2003.

Smith, Daniel. *The Religion of the Landless: The Social Context of the Babylonian Exile.* Bloomington, IN: Meyer-Stone, 1989.

Sugirtharajah, R.S., ed., *The Post-Colonial Bible.* Sheffield: Sheffield Academic, 1998.

Vrudny, Kimberly. "Medieval Fascination with the Queen: Esther as the Queen of Heaven and Host of the Messianic Banquet," *Arts* 11:2, (1999): 36-43.

Waldman, J. T. *Megillat Esther: The Graphic Novel.* Philadelphia, PA: The Jewish Publication Society, 2005.

5

Memory, Identity and Hope: The Exile and Christian Formation

By Jessicah Krey Duckworth and Susan B. Willhauck

If I forget you, O Jerusalem, let my right hand wither! Let my tongue cling to the roof of my mouth, if I do not remember you, if I do not set Jerusalem above my highest joy. Psalms 137:5-6

This essay remembers the contributions of Bruce C. Birch, teacher, scholar, mentor and friend, and reflects on how his work informs the meaning and practice of Christian formation. We examine Christian formation as a process of coming to one's identity as a human being in covenantal relationship with the Triune God who loves the world. Identity is formed in relationship with the Triune God and shaped in community by the memory and experience of God's activity. God's love and passion for all creation orients one's identity and vocation to love of God and neighbor.

Relying on and building upon Birch's work, we explore meanings and signs of exile that paradoxically contribute to the formation of identity through the identity-negation process inherent in the exile experience.[1] Central to the exilic experience is the fear of losing one's identity through disorientation, fragmentation and grief. Further consequences of the exilic event are the experiences of abandonment, judgment and prophetic condemnation. And yet, we argue that in exilic times Christian formation takes on its most profound purpose of keeping the memory of God's activity alive and providing hope, of following the *Shema* to keep the words, to teach them and bind them as a sign and write them on our doorposts and gates. To this end we probe the stories, symbols and practices of God's people as marks of identity that endure even in the midst of exile.

Christian formation in the church requires discernment of the meanings and signs of exile. In some congregations the exilic event is obvious. In other cases is it hidden and masked. Christian formation names the reality of despair and hopelessness within the human condition and characterizes our human need and desire to remember who we are and who we are called to be. Christian formation through stories, symbols and practices mediates hope in the midst of despair through the enduring proclamation that *God remembers us* and is faithful. As a biblical scholar and educator Bruce Birch empowered many people to be in relationship with and to embody the biblical story, equipping leaders to discern signs of exile, to mediate hope in its midst and to guide God's people to deeper faith.

As our academic training is in religious education and practical theology, we tend to view the exile through that lens. In the exile Israel intentionally became a learning community, a community that is compelled to ban together to "sing in a foreign land" and to teach the stories and practices of its tradition. Practical theologians are always concerned with naming the context, so we identify the biblical exile as the deportations of Judahites beginning in the early part of the sixth century BCE. The Bible records several deportations beginning when Nebuchadnezzar exiled King Jehoiachin, his family and court officials. In these deportations, supposedly thousands were sent out from Israel into Egypt, Mesopotamia and other areas. Several different dates have been assigned as the end of the exilic period, which lasted until Babylon fell to the Persians and the Jews were allowed to return to Israel to re-build the temple (some, however, remained in diaspora). A large number of the exiles in Babylon settled on the land near Nippur. There were concerted efforts to teach and hand on the faith. Practices such as praying toward Jerusalem, circumcision, Sabbath-keeping, rites of purification and dietary observances marked Jewish identity during this time.[2] These were critical acts of *anamnesis*, the sacred remembering of their home and who they were.

During the exile, certain biblical texts were composed or edited, such as the book of Exodus, where we read of Israel's deliverance from bondage in Egypt written with the sense of urgency that came from the need to reclaim their traditions while Israel was once again held captive in a foreign land.[3] It was imperative to recall and tell the stories of what God has done. Bruce Birch often called our attention to the Exodus story as key to the formation of Israel as a moral community in which people act in response to their relationship to God.[4] The prophet Jeremiah emerged as a key figure during the exile, proclaiming the judgment of God, but also the promise of a new covenant. The book of Ezekiel, another prophet exiled to Babylon, described the destruction of Jerusalem and his visions of a renewed temple. The books of Jeremiah and Ezekiel both tell us how Judah responded "in faith and anguish" to the deportations which "reshaped Israel's life, faith and memory."[5] Second Isaiah became the harbinger of a return to Jerusalem, encouraging Israel to become a servant and to trust in God's salvation.[6] The book of Lamentations and the lament Psalms express the deep sorrow and loss of the exiled people and their appeals to God to save them.

In their influential work, *A Theological Introduction to the Old Testament*, Bruce C. Birch, Walter Brueggemann, Terence E. Fretheim and David L. Petersen refer to exile as "a deep and irreversible disruption in the life of ancient Israel." It became decisive for the faith of Israel because the community found in this event, "the workings of the inscrutable sovereign God upon whom it has staked its life.[7] The intrusions by Babylon executed the collapse of Judah.

"All that was visible and institutional, all that seemed theologically guaranteed by Yahweh's faithfulness, all that gave symbolic certitude and coherence, all that was linked to significance, identity, and security, was gone."[8] This created what educators know to be disequilibrium and cognitive dissonance, when one's mindset and very way of life are threatened. There is acute suffering. The prophets declared the nullification of covenant and temple life. Bruce Birch, a modern day prophet, wrote:

> Exile as a crisis of the spirit alongside the sociopolitical crisis is the abandonment of hope that our religious symbols retain any power or reality. Exile becomes the time when lips may open but the songs do not come; the captives are rendered voiceless. How remarkable it becomes that such a time should be the context for the creative and hopeful voices that do come forth to sing the Lord's song.[9]

Somehow Israel found a way out of no way. Actually, "ways" would be more accurate, since the many scattered communities of the displaced continued to keep their memories and hope alive. The storytelling and faith practices become subversive and defiant, as education at its most faithful always is.[10] Birch, Brueggemann, et. al. play up how extraordinary it was that the exile did not lead to despair and loss of faith. Rather, they claim, it became a "remarkable moment in the life of the Jewish community for inventive and generative faith."[11]

What is this "inventive and generative faith?" We would say that it is a faith process that summons us, the learning community, to endure and to engage in dialogic relationship with the Triune God and each other. In the face of the extreme discontinuity and fragmentation of the exile, this generative faith represents continuity and hope. As the community struggled with continuity and discontinuity, the experience of exile prompted profound questions of faith. "Where is Yahweh when we need him?" The questioning requires imagination to re-think and re-formulate one's faith—to reconstruct 'paradigms of meaning.'[12] Israel initiated that reconstruction by expressing its raw anger and sorrow in lament. They recovered a cathartic liturgical practice of "telling it like it is," naming the truth of their reality. They called upon God to do something, reaffirming that, indeed, God is one worth calling upon. In its "daring faith" Israel questions and implores Yahweh:

> Rouse yourself! Why do you sleep, O Lord ? Awake, do not cast us off forever! Why do you hide your face? Why do you forget our affliction and oppression? For we sink down to the dust; our bodies cling to the ground. Rise up, come to our help. Redeem us for the sake of your steadfast love. *Psalm 44: 23-26*

In its "daring faith," Israel demands that God be who God is supposed to be, whom they believe and know God to be. Through a tradition of protest and complaint, they move toward new hope of return and restoration.[13] Israel's identity as a community of character takes shape. It begins to understand itself in relationship with God, and capable of imitating God. In the continuing telling and re-telling of the stories they find "possibility of actual relationship to the God about whom the stories are told." Moreover, "out of this new identity, obedience to God's will can meaningfully flow."[14]

As Birch won't let us forget, the exile experience of an ancient community continues to form our identity as God's people today as congregational life is formed around memory and vision. While we cannot make a simplistic leap from one time period into another for purposes of education, we can and do engage the text as God's dynamic Word which can give energy and spirit to communities today—communities of new generations in new contexts.

Some congregations today have been shaped by an exilic experience of faithful living in a strange land. These congregations — found in El Salvador advocating for the poor and calling upon the government to act with justice, found in Rwanda working to reconcile neighbors after a brutal civil war, found in the Czech Republic where Christianity is viewed with deep suspicion, found in the United States among the Amish community in Pennsylvania or in the Pentecostal congregation serving the largest Arab community in the U.S. in Dearborn, Michigan — these congregations living in tension with the prevailing cultural winds, face the windblown feelings of cynicism and despair, isolation and abandonment, senselessness and hopelessness that arise from the experience of injustice, inequality and prejudice. At the same time these communities are knit together by the subversive and defiant stories and practices, signs and symbols that point to their identity as God's beloved.

The 'daring faith' of these communities, hoping in the midst of lament, is the living Word of exile in the world today. Using voices of lament that are simultaneously filled with daring hope and expectation for the future, congregations of exile announce a vision of "God's desire for love, justice and wholeness" not only for themselves but for the whole world.[15] The exilic congregations of today, some found in the forgotten corners of the world and some forgotten but very near, serve as the signs and symbols of exile for those congregations where the exilic event is hidden and masked.

This vision of God's desire includes those congregations that have forgotten the experience of exile. Signs and symbols of exile are not as readily apparent in congregations who don't *have* to see the nature of their social location and perspective. For these congregations the exile experience is foreign and removed, leading all too frequently to complacency and self-righteousness.

Apart from the experience of exile it is difficult to see one's need for God and without a need for God, it is easy to forget and ignore God's relationship with humanity as a whole. Birch encourages congregations who assume a white, North American, middle or upper class social location as normative to engage the witness of scripture or tradition through the eyes of another. "The task then becomes to hear and understand the different shape that our remembering takes because of social location, and to work toward finding with those differences ways of joining in the common work of the body of Christ."[16] Christian formation takes up this task urging congregations to remember, but remember in light of their own circumstances and locations.

The task then is to hear and understand the different experiences of exile by coming face to face with the stories and practices of exile in congregations of a different social location and walking together finding common ground. In such a face-to-face encounter with those congregations undergoing overt oppression and disorientation, the masked marks of exile – disorientation, suffering, brokenness and alienation – that exist within the fabric of *all* human communities are revealed. And as the revelation of a common human disorientation becomes apparent the wails and sound of lament grow. "Why do you hide your face? Why do you forget our affliction and oppression?" (Psalm 44) The need for God – who is "for us" and "for the world" is remembered collectively.

Christian formation encourages those encounters of disequilibrium and cognitive dissonance, calling congregations who fail to see the nature of their own social location into relationship with the reality of exile, into relationship with congregations who see reality differently. In this encounter identity is transformed by the memory and experience of God's activity. This memory and experience is the clear and prophetic announcement of the living Word and witness that "God remembers us". Through the witness of exilic congregations announcing God's faithfulness in the midst of exile together in partnership with those congregations that are not overtly exilic, God's love and passion for all creation orients one's identity and vocation to love of God and neighbor.

Over time the immediate stories, symbols and practices of God's people shaped in the midst of exile become identifiable as the biblical stories of exilic experiences long ago. No longer removed from one's experience, the biblical witness together with the living witness, becomes a story that is shared across space and across time. Furthermore, the shared story—once removed and distant— is now near, identifiable and particular. Once again, it is Christian formation that supports this story-telling encouraging direct engagement with the biblical witness. Birch writes, "The Christian faith is a predominantly story-oriented faith. Its real identity always has been the narrative traditions from Genesis to Jesus."[17] Congregations can support the identity-shaping practice of remembering exile by supporting the encounter with the witness of exile congregations and encouraging biblical storytelling. Together these practices will shape the memory and vision God holds for the church.

We have already explored the event of exile as an identity-negating experience that turns powerfully and remarkably into an identity-shaping encounter. And yet, as we learn from Israel's experience of exile we also encounter the prophet. Although it might seem as though the mundane task of teacher training in a congregation – equipping lay leaders for the ministry of education and formation – is the antithesis of the prophetic.

Bruce Birch has made the opposite case in his passionate commitment to prophetic leadership. "People think of a prophet as a somewhat counter-cultural, anti-establishment figure who might play an important role as an advocate of justice but is not a model for what we seek in church leadership in general."[18] Instead he argues, "we must reclaim prophetic leadership if we are to shape an adequate theology of leadership."[19] One of the leadership characteristics that Bruce identifies is the prophet's place in the tension between memory and vision, tradition and creativity.[20]

Teachers of the faith tell the story of God's faithfulness to the covenants while also pointing to the promises for us in the future. Encouragement to stand in this tension and possess a "daring faith" is what responsible teacher training needs to provide lay leaders. Inasmuch as lay leaders and teachers in the church share the memory of what God has done through the stories, symbols and practices of the faith and point toward God's yet-to-be realized vision, they embody that prophetic leadership. We must remember the past in order to imagine and hope for the future, or we will indeed wither. For in the place between God's memory and God's vision we find our identity and our prophetic voice as God's people hoping for God's vision for love, justice and wholeness in the midst of our remembering.

Sometimes biblical scholars are thought of as living and working only with dusty, ancient texts, disputing complex minutiae, aloof to the real world of ministry. Bruce Birch could not be further from this stereotype. He is keenly aware that the Bible began out of concern for the educational/formational process. As a good Methodist, following in the footsteps of John Wesley, Bruce has exhibited a life-long passion for and commitment to education from his early years in the World Student Movement to teaching adult Sunday school in his congregation. He served in theological education as professor and dean to prepare countless persons for ministry. His vision to acknowledge the call of all God's people and to equip lay people for service to the church was given reality in Wesley Theological Seminary's Equipping Lay Ministry program. Bruce Birch has not just made a mark on biblical scholarship—he has mentored and marked many church leaders. His gregariousness and "wicked" sense of humor propelled him to discover and tell all the Bible jokes (despite the groans), to portray Moses *and* Elvis *and* Santa Claus and to "take the Bible to the movies."

Like Wesley, Bruce Birch knows, teaches and preaches God's grace. His life and work exemplify that continuity of God's grace of which he wrote:

> God's graceful activity is already manifest in full measure in creation, promise, deliverance, steadfast love, forgiveness, redemption, and renewal in the pages of the Old Testament witness. It is our knowledge of God's grace from creation onward that allows us to fully understand the divine grace we see in Jesus Christ.[21]

And it is that grace in which we live and place our hope.

Notes

1. Noted practical theologian James Loder describes the human experience of negation as the work of the ego asserting one's self when facing death, denial, reduction or disregard. An excellent chapter on Loder's notion of negation called: "'Trampling Down

Death by Death': Double Negation in Developmental Theory and Baptismal Theology" by Russell Haitch can be found in *Redemptive Transformation in Practical Theology: Essays in Honor of James E. Loder, Jr.* (Grand Rapids: MI: Eerdmans, 2004): 43-68. Also see James E. Loder, *The Logic of the Spirit: Human Development in Theological Perspective* (San Francisco, CA: Jossey-Bass, 1998).

2. Ralph W. Klein, "Exile," vol. 2 of *The New Interpreter's Dictionary of the Bible* (Nashville, TN: Abingdon, 2007): 367.

3. Bruce C. Birch, Walter Brueggemann, et. al. *A Theological Introduction to the Old Testament* (Nashville, TN: Abingdon , 1999): 103.

4. Bruce C. Birch, " Divine Character and the Formation of Moral Community in the Book of Exodus," in *The Bible in Ethics: The Second Sheffield Colloquium,* ed. John W. Rogerson, Margaret Davies and M. Daniel Carroll (Sheffield ENG: Sheffield Academic Press, Ltd., 1995): 120.

5. Birch, Brueggemann, et. al., *A Theological Introduction,* 327.

6. Klein, "Exile," 369.

7. Birch, Brueggemann, et. al., *A Theological Introduction,* 319.

8. *Ibid.,* 325.

9. Bruce C. Birch, *Let Justice Roll Down: The Old Testament, Ethics, and Christian Life* (Louisville, KY: Westminster/John Knox, 1991): 283.

10. Walter Brueggemann, *The Creative Word: Canon as a Model for Biblical Education* (Philadelphia, PA: Fortress, 1982): 8.

11. Birch, Brueggemann, et. al. *A Theological Introduction,* 346.

12. *Ibid.*

13. *Ibid.,* 349.

14. Birch, *The Bible in Ethics,* 132-133.

15. Bruce C. Birch "Memory in Congregational Life," in *Congregations: Their Power to Form and Transform,* ed. C. Ellis Nelson (Louisville, KY: John Knox, 1988): 23.

16. *Ibid.,* 37-38.

17. *Ibid.,* 39.

18. Bruce C. Birch, "Reclaiming Prophetic Leadership," *Ex Auditu* 22 (2006): 10.

19. *Ibid.,* 11.

20. *Ibid.,* 18.

21. Birch, *Let Justice Roll Down,* 356.

Works Cited

Birch, Bruce C. "Divine Character and the Formation of Moral Community in the Book of Exodus," *The Bible in Ethics: The Second Sheffield Colloquium,* eds., John W. Rogerson, Margaret Davies and M. Daniel Carroll. Sheffield, ENG: Sheffield Academic Press, 1995.

_____. *Let Justice Roll Down: The Old Testament, Ethics, and Christian Life.* Louisville, KY: Westminster/John Knox, 1991.

_____. "Memory in Congregational Life," *Congregations: Their Power to Form and Transform,* Ed. C. Ellis Nelson. Louisville, KY: John Knox, 1988.

_____. "Reclaiming Prophetic Leadership," *Ex Auditu,* 22 (2006).

_____, Walter Brueggemann, et. al. *A Theological Introduction to the Old Testament.* Nashville, TN: Abingdon, 1999.

Brueggemann, Walter. *The Creative Word: Canon as a Model for Biblical Education.* Philadelphia, PA: Fortress, 1982.

Haitch, Russell. *Redemptive Transformation in Practical Theology: Essays in Honor of James E. Loder, Jr.* Grand Rapids, MI: Eerdmans, 2004.

Klein, Ralph W. "Exile," *The New Interpreter's Dictionary of the Bible*, Vol. 2. Nashville, TN: Abingdon, 2007. p. 367.

Loder, James E. *The Logic of the Spirit: Human Development in Theological Perspective.* San Francisco, CA: Jossey-Bass, 1998.

6

From the Margins: God's Strategy for Renewal?

By D. William Faupel

It is well recognized that religious movements begin on the margins of society and if successful, over time move toward the center, bringing revitalization in their wake. One sees this, for example, in the birth of Christianity, the Reformation and the Wesleyan Revival. In each case, the existing faith: Judaism, Roman Catholicism and Anglicanism were revitalized. But the effort at reform also brought into existence new traditions: Christianity, Protestantism and Methodism. Each in turn has been dynamic, sustained, and the subject of subsequent revitalization movements.

From a theological perspective, I would suggest, this process can be understood as the new movement being sent into exile where it is disciplined as one would train a child before being brought into the cultural mainstream. A more recent example of this process is the birth of Pentecostalism in 1906. It was quickly marginalized, but now one hundred years later Pentecostalism is currently having a major impact on both the faith and praxis of the rest Christendom causing some to speak of "the Pentecostalization of the Church."[1]

What is not widely recognized, however, is that Pentecostalism itself had a major revitalization movement arise within its ranks in the mid-twentieth century. Like the movements that went before it, the New Order was rejected by Pentecostalism and forced to the margins. But instead of forming a new denomination, the Latter Rain leadership followed a different strategy. They allowed their movement to die. The leaders attached themselves to the emerging Charismatic Movement, and began to working within existing denominations thereby seeking to revitalize all of Christendom.[2] In this article I shall show the distinct doctrinal and liturgical emphases that emerged during the course of the revival which fifty years later have been incorporated into mainstream Christianity.

The Revival

Like many revivals before it, The New Order of the Latter Rain began with a church fight. George Hawtin, a minister of the Pentecostal Assemblies of

Canada pioneered Bethel Bible School in Saskatoon, Saskatchewan 1935 and served as its principal until the spring of 1947 when he resigned over a policy dispute. Accepting the invitation of Herrick Holt, a pastor affiliated with the International Church of the Four Square Gospel, he opened Sharon Bible College on Holt's 1,000 acre farm just outside of North Battleford, Saskatchewan, that autumn.[3] Bringing some of Bethel's faculty and most of its student body with him, Hawtin opened his new school by calling the community to an extended period of fasting and prayer.[4] The following month, he journeyed to Vancouver, British Columbia, to hear healing evangelist, William Branham.[5] Upon returning he confessed:

> Never in my life have I ever seen anything to equal what I saw in Vancouver.... I saw the deaf receive their hearing. I heard the dumb speak.... I saw a goiter vanish. I saw sick people get up from their beds.... To my best knowledge I did not see one person who was not healed.[6]

He called the community to renew their fasting and prayer hoping revival would come to Sharon. The visitation arrived the following year. On February 11, 1948, a student prophesied that Sharon was "on the very verge of a great revival." All they had to do was "open the door" and "enter in". Hawtin responded: "Father, we do not know where the door is, neither do we know how to enter it."[7] Further instructions came via prophesy through Hawtin's younger brother, Ernest: "The gifts of the spirit will be restored to my church.... They shall be received by prophecy and the laying on of hands of the presbytery."[8] George Hawtin later recalled: "I can never begin to describe the things that happened on that day. It seemed that all Heaven broke loose upon our souls, and Heaven came down to greet us. The power and the glory were indescribable.[9]

By the time the "Feast of Pentecost" camp was held (March 30, 1948) news of the revival had spread far and wide. Milford Kirkpatrick remembered: "We never saw such a variety of cars and license plates before, from many provinces in Canada and from so many states across the border."[10] They did not leave disappointed. *The Sharon Star* reported: "People hungry to meet God had come many hundreds of miles, and God met them...the sick are being healed; the Devils are being cast out; Saints are being edified; sinners are being saved."[11]

A second camp meeting took place in July. This time "thousands of people throughout the continent who had heard of awakening" were reported in attendance.[12] People had come from as far north as Peace River, Alberta; as far west as Vancouver, British Columbia; as far east as Prince Edward Island; and from twenty states south of the Canadian border.[13] Soon people from throughout the United States and from around the world were streaming to North Battleford and taking the revival with them. Within a year, revival centers were established in every major North American city. These centers in turn were caring for churches springing up in surrounding areas as well as influencing established Pentecostal churches that had accepted the revival. By 1950 organized teams of leaders from the North American Centers were making crusades to virtually every country in the world. Within three years, every Pentecostal denomination, indeed virtually every local Pentecostal church had been impacted by the revival.

The Message of the Revival

The message of the Revival was complex. The doctrines were a new emphasis on existing Pentecostal teaching or a belief that had been briefly considered but subsequently rejected. Built upon the Pentecostal world-view, Latter Rain theology soon developed its own coherent whole.

When Herrick Holt established his orphanage, he taught that God was about to do a "new thing". Just what is not clear, but it soon was subsumed in George Hawtin's vision.[14] From his writings in *The Sharon Star*, it is clear Hawtin had a definite perception of what God was about to do. However, he seemed content to allow this plan to unfold, step by step. In general terms, he believed that God was sending a world-wide revival. As in previous moves he also believed that the revival would bring the restoration of new truth. Return from the Branham campaign in November, 1947, he gave full expression to this theme.

> All great outpourings of the past have had their outstanding truths. Luther's truth was Justification by faith. Wesley's was Sanctification. The Baptists taught the pre-millennial coming of Christ. The Missionary Alliance taught Divine Healing. The Pentecostal outpouring has restored the Baptism of the Holy Ghost to its rightful place. But the next great outpouring is going to be marked by...a demonstration of the nine gifts of the Spirit as the world...has ever witnessed before.[15]

When the revival came, "gifts of the Spirit" were restored, and other "new truths" followed. Hawtin exulted: "To be in one of these meetings is like living in another Chapter of the Acts of the Apostles."[16] As adherents reflected on their experience, they realized that internal coherence of the revival's message could be summarized in one word — "Restoration".[17] Primarily, this restoration focused on one major doctrine, the Church. The message concerned four aspects: 1) its nature; 2) its mission; 3) its worship; and 4) its authority.

The Nature of the Church

The surface reading of the primary literature suggests that instead of a coherent unifying doctrine, the revival "restored" a series of unrelated truths. Only as they are analyzed does the internal coherent structure unfold. What follows are the essential features in roughly the order that they emerged.

Fasting and Prayer

The first mark of the revival was that it was preceded by several months of fasting and prayer. Ernest Hawtin attributes this as the great factor initiating the revival. He records that Sharon was called to fasting through Franklin Hall's book: *Atomic Power with God with Fasting and Prayer*.[18] Hall asserted: "The truth of fasting is being revealed to us now that we....may receive the 'Gifts of the Spirit,' and that a mighty world-wide revival of spiritual power will sweep over the world.[19] The implication was clear. If Sharon fasted and prayed, revival would come.

The Laying on of Hands

The second restoration was "the laying on of hands". George Hawtin believed that the coming revival would be accompanied by the restoration of the gifts of the Spirit, but had confessed that he did not know how to implement it.[20] His brother's prophetic words on February 14, 1948: "They shall be received by...the laying on of hands" proved to be the catalyst.[21] The concept didn't come out of the blue. A. W. Rasmussen reports that Ernest Hawtin had been mulling the idea over in his mind for several days.[22] Furthermore, Cornelius Jaenen, contends the aspect of the Branham meetings which impressed George Hawtin most was that the spectacular healings came as Branham laid hands upon people.[23] Finally, James Watt remembers, the school had been deeply influenced by Episcopalian, J. E. Stiles' book, *The Gift of the Holy Spirit*.[24] In this book, Stiles had argued that the Holy Spirit imparted ministry gifts through the laying on of hands.

The Gifts of the Spirit

The 1948 revival was accompanied by the "gifts of the Spirit" as George Hawtin had anticipated. In his first account of the revival the April 1, 1948 edition of *The Sharon Star*, Hawtin noted: "the Gifts of the Spirit are definitely being restored to the Church."[25] Later, as he elaborated in more detail:

> I can never begin to describe the things that happened on that day.... Men and woman [sic] received the gift of healing, and immediately began to heal the sick. Discernment of spirits was given, and the influence of evil spirits was discerned, and the evil spirits were cast out. Some received the gift of faith....[26]

While the manifestation of all nine gifts was claimed, the gift of prophecy became the focus. Ernest Hawtin declared: "The Gift of Prophecy is in particular prominence."[27] The seminal understanding for this emphasis was rooted in the events which took place at the outset of the revival as they were later remembered. While Ernest Hawtin struggled on February 12, 1948, trying to decide whether he should act on his impression to lay hands on the young man, a young woman went to him "saying the same words, and naming the identical student he was to pray for."[28]

The prophecies usually contained a "word of knowledge" of past events in the person's life unknown to the person speaking, and a "word of wisdom" revealing events of future ministry. This became a standard practice and known as the act of Impartation and/or the act of Confirmation. As Raymond Hoekstra asserted, "By the laying on of hands and prophecy, gifts are imparted, and ministries are confirmed."[29] The leadership found support throughout Scripture. A key passage was I Timothy 4:14: "Do not neglect the gift you have, which was given you by prophetic utterance when the council of elders laid their hands upon you."

The Ascension Gift Ministries

The revival was barely under way when the leadership began to claim that the Ascension Gift Ministries were being reestablished. Paul N. Grubb reflected the representative view: "The revival is also a restoration to the church of the five ministries mentioned in Ephesians 4."[30] Adherents recognized that evangelists, pastors, and teachers had been operative throughout the history of the Church. The focus of their attention, therefore, was directed to the offices of apostle and prophet.[31] They took issue with those who claimed that the ministry of the apostle had ceased. They pointed out that many in the New Testament had held the title and noted that in the Ephesians passage this ministry was included among those who were to "build up the body of Christ until we attain the unity of the faith."[32]

The leadership understood the work of an apostle to be that of the missionary in its broadest sense, that is, one who establishes churches and is responsible to convey the faith to them. Paul was seen as the exemplar.

> His ministry was apostolic, which necessitated governing churches, establishing and confirming churches. He was able to preach teach, minister to the sick, discern and cast out demons, heal the sick and even work special miracles as God's gifts and graces operated through him.[33]

The prophetic ministry was seen as of second in importance to that of an apostle, proclaiming the "mysteries of God" making them plain to the Church. "It is not their voice that is heard, but it is THE VOICE OF GOD."[34] In the service of Confirmation, the Prophet speaks for God in separating persons to specific ministries.[35] Three levels of prophecy were recognized. First, there were those who had "the gift of prophecy" that functioned in the local church. Secondly, there were prophets who, like the apostles, were given authority to minister to the church at large. Finally, there were "a few prophets...

> whose ministry will be in the extraordinary use of the term. These are 'raised-up' for special purposes. They shall enter a phase of ministry such as Samuel, Elijah, Moses, and Ezekiel. There will be unusual manifestations of 'the word of knowledge' and the 'word of wisdom' in their ministry. They will not be limited in scope of ministry to just the church, but they are sent as witnesses for special purposes to the world as well.[36]

Evangelists, pastors and teachers had ministries that were much the same as those bearing similar titles in Protestant denominations. In all cases, however, they were to function under the authority of the apostles and prophets.[37] The five ascension gift ministries combined to form The Presbytery, as the leadership of the Church. Once a local church was established, it was through them that local ministries were confirmed.[38]

Elders and Deacons

Other ministries, such as elders and deacons, were recognized. Like the ascension gift ministries, these were confirmed by the Presbytery through the laying on of hands, accompanied by prophecy.[39] Local churches were under their authority. Every member of the local church was to have a ministry. These were confirmed through the laying on of hands with prophecy.[40]

The Body of Christ

In June, 1948, Hawtin took up the issue of Church Organization. In an article entitled "Local Church Government," he wrote: "No church exercises or has any right to exercise authority or jurisdiction over another church, its pastors or members."[41] The tone of the article suggested a congregational church government. In this respect it sounded very much like the pattern practiced by the Independent Assemblies of God. Indeed, the January and February 1948 issues of *The Sharon Star* carried a two-part article by A. W. Rasmussen, entitled, "Scriptural or Unscriptural Church Order," setting forth the principles of his denomination's governance.[42]

In August, 1949, Hawtin and his brother co-authored a book entitled *Church Government*, their definitive thinking on the matter. They wrote: "The Church is the most democratic of all institutions.... The believers themselves accept new members into the church, and when a member is excommunicated, the believers are the final voice in the matter." Large churches would be established in the major population centers. These "mother churches" would take responsibility for shepherding the clusters of smaller churches springing up nearby. These churches would be under the direct oversight of persons trained by the mother church. Local churches would send missionaries to establish churches in non-Christian lands. The training and support would come from the local church.[43]

In the months that followed, Hawtin gave more attention to "the Divine Pattern". As 1950 closed it was clear that he did not understand the church to be congregational at all, but rather believed it was hierarchical. Although elders and deacons had jurisdiction over local affairs, they were under authority to those called to the "Ascension Gift Ministries".[44]

The Mission of the Church

As the theology of the Revival unfolded, the mission of the church received increased attention. Its mission can be brought together into four categories: world evangelization, church unity, perfecting the saints and restoring all things.

World Evangelization

Concern for world mission was evident at Sharon from the outset. Milford Kirkpatrick recalled: "As a result of the visitation, there was a tremendous emphasis on world-wide vision."[45] In actuality, concern for world mission preceded the revival. Shortly after the Hawtins arrived in North Battleford, they established board of Global Missions.[46] The first real impetus as a direct result of the revival occurred in the meetings at Vancouver held in November 1948. Messages in tongues were given that were understood as human languages.

> Those who attended these meetings went away thoroughly convinced by experience that the Gift of Tongues is actually the gift of languages. Those possessing this marvelous gift can actually preach the gospel in foreign languages without any foreign accent.[47]

The claim had an immediate effect. Following the meeting the Swaans, left for the Fiji Islands. Shortly thereafter, others were sent to Africa, China and India.[48] Despite this, however, world evangelization did not come to the fore until the National Latter Rain Convention in St. Louis in November 1950. Thomas Wyatt brought the convention to a climax by disclosing that God had revealed to him that it was the Lord's plan to

> ...speedily dispatch apostolic and prophetic ministries to the key-cities of all foreign lands. Thousands will have hands laid upon them with a confirmation of their ministry in the Body by prophecy, and the impartation of gifts of the Spirit.... These will in turn go through the length and breadth of their own lands confirming others, and thereby, in a few short months, every nation on earth shall have received the last day message.[49]

His message sparked a ready fire. The Movement's leadership immediately began forming teams to tour overseas. Wyatt's vision became the method of world evangelization until the revival subsided.

Church Unity

In 1965, Reg Layzell, pastor of Glad Tidings Temple in Vancouver, recalled:

> Bro. George Hawtin taught under the anointing...how it would be one church in one great building in each center. No longer would the church be called by its divisive names but The Church of Vancouver, The Church of Detroit or The Church of Portland.[50]

Layzell was reflecting on the July, 1948, Sharon camp-meeting, when Hawtin suggested that a major purpose for the revival was to bring the church together.[51] In *The Body of Christ*, the authors took an oblique shot at the recently formed World Council of Churches.[52] Adherents concurred with the World Council and the Roman Catholic Church that the one universal church must have visible expression. They were convinced, however, that unity would come by the truths being restored through their revival. Christians everywhere would leave their denominations to join the emerging church. George Warnock noted:

> At the beginning it was hoped that Christians everywhere would catch the vision, and that before long the whole Body of saints would become one vital, living organism, united together in the bonds of the Spirit unto one common purpose.

As the revival progressed, it became obvious most would remain content to ignore the revival. Warnock lamented: "it is becoming apparent that only a remnant are returning to Jerusalem."[53]

Manifested Sons of God

As hope for the unity of the church narrowed to the concept of "faithful remnant," the third mission came into focus. The Revival would prepare Overcomers equipped to prepare the church and the world for Christ's second coming. The concept took on a cloak of elitism. Contrasting the revival's faithful with the universal church, Warnock suggested:

> If men choose to remain where they are in their Christian experience, then this message is not for them. Thank God that they may eat of the manna that falls from Heaven, and drink of the water that flows out of the rock, and receive healing and strength for their journey. But sorry to say, they shall die in the wilderness.

On the other hand those who chose to "arise and cross over Jordan" would join the "true church," "the Body of Christ," "The Overcomers," "The Bride," "The Sons of God." The terms that would become most popular were "The Manchild" and "Manifested Sons of God."[54] Whereas, adherents of the revival first understood these terms to be identical with the church, they came to understand them to refer to a special group who would play a critical end-time role.

> God is manifesting Himself to man in a new way...As sure as Christ ushered out the Dispensation of Mosaic Law, by a manifestation of himself in an individual "Body prepared by the Holy Ghost" (the Son of man) an offspring of the Virgin Mary, even so, He is ushering out the Dispensation of Grace by a manifestation of Himself again in a corporate "Body, prepared of the Holy Ghost" (composed of many Sons of Men), an offspring of the visible Church.[55]

The theme was introduced by George Hawtin. In an article entitled: "The Great Manifestation," published near the end of 1950, Hawtin argued that not only is it possible to experience justification and sanctification in this life, but immortality as well. Basing his understanding on Romans, he confessed:

> With shame of face I wish to make this confession: For years I taught and preached that we could never be free from the carnal nature in this life. My argument was this, though some preached such an experience, I had never seen one who possessed it, and therefore it could not be so.... This, however, does not alter the Word of God...whether or not Paul ever attained this experience does not matter. This is the experience he sought with all his might: to be rid of the carnal nature and to gain perfection, sinless perfection, to be delivered from THIS BODY OF DEATH...and to experimentally reach the glories of the eighth chapter of Romans.[56]

The Restoration of All Things

This doctrine, tied to the "Manifested Sons of God," followed closely on its heels. The phrase is taken from St. Peter's sermon following the Day of

Pentecost. The doctrine conformed closely to the premillennial understanding of the millennium. Hawtin introduced the teaching to his constituency in the November-December, 1951 issue of *The Sharon Star* in an article entitled: "Thy Kingdom Come." He opened by declaring: "The Kingdom of Heaven, the seventh dispensation, is at hand." After giving a summary of the previous six dispensations, he continued:

> And she brought forth a man-child who was to rule all nations with a rod of iron, and her child was caught up unto God and throne.' (Rev. 12:5) The man-child is the body of Overcomers that keeps his works. They are the manifested sons of God for which the whole creation groaneth and travaileth. (Rom. 8:22)....
>
> This glorious reigning-company does not include all the church. It is the Body of Christ that is being formed in this present revival; not the body of the bride, but the body of Christ who is the HEAD, the firstborn among many brothers.... It was this same glorious MAN whom Daniel, the prophet, saw: I saw in the night visions and behold, one like the SON OF MAN came with clouds of heaven.[57]

Abandoning the pre-tribulation theory he declared that these Overcomers would undergo much suffering to bring in the new dispensation. "The possessing of Kingdom of Heaven by the saints of the most high is not going to be a mere 'push-over' but through MUCH TRIBULATION we will enter it." All things would be restored to the pre-fallen state, and they, the Overcomers would rule and reign with Christ with a rod of iron.[58]

The Worship of the Church

Restoration of worship is also traced to the outset of the Revival. The concept was two-fold: 1) Worship as Sacred Space; and 2) Worship as Praise.

Worship as Sacred Space

The February 11, 1948, prophecy uttered by a young woman at Sharon declared that they "were on the very verge of a great revival" and that all they had to do was "open the door" and "enter in."[59] This image of a "closed door" with a great revival on the other side became the "key" to their understanding of worship. The community was waiting for renewal of the "latter rain" that had fallen at the beginning of the century with the Pentecostal revival. The "closed door" epitomized their conviction that the rain had ceased. George Hawtin responded by saying, "We don't know where the 'door' is neither do we know how to 'enter it'".[60] His brother Ernest provided the key. Accepting "laying on of hands" as the key that opened the door adherents believed they crossed the threshold and entered sacred space. Ernest's prophesy continued: "I would have you to be reverent before Me as never before. Take the shoes off thy feet for the ground on which thou standest in holy"[61] The very place where they had gathered became hallowed. Like Moses they were to take off their shoes.

At the Camp Meeting in July, 1948. James Watt was teaching on the meaning of the Old Testament Feasts for the Church. He noted that the Feast of

Passover had been fulfilled in the Cross, the Feast of Pentecost had been fulfilled with the Coming of the Holy Spirit, but the Feast of Tabernacles had not yet been fulfilled. The observation struck a responsive cord in George Warnock who subsequently published a book in July 1951. In the Introduction, Warnock transferred "the door" image to the exodus account, and Israel's call to "possess the land."

> The first generation that came out of Egypt by Moses failed to enter in because of unbelief, and God decreed that they should die in the wilderness.... The early generation of Spirit-filled people at the turn of the century took their journey from the blighting wilderness of denominationalism and encamped at their Kadesh-Barnea on the very door- step of Canaan—but they too failed to enter in because of unbelief...the Lord now raising up a new generation who shall be empowered to take the promised land.[62]

Using typology, Warnock developed the thesis that this Revival is the dispensational move of God. The Tabernacle became the type of the place of God's presence. The metaphor of tabernacle was merged with "body of Christ," and "heart." The Old Testament tabernacle in the wilderness was transformed into the true church and into the hearts of true believers. The "door" which Hawtin discovered, came to represent a limited access to the latter rain which was falling. Now they possessed the corresponding "key" for entry into God's overflowing presence—the Tabernacle, the dwelling place of God.[63]

Worship As Praise

The leadership of the revival believed that the dwelling place of God was a "felt" presence to be experienced in worship. Fasting and prayer followed by the Laying on of Hands of the Presbytery became the initiation rite of entry by the individual. For the gathered community the point of entry lay elsewhere. James Watt reflecting on the events of 1948 concluded: "Jerusalem is about to be made a praise in the earth.... Prepare ye your hearts."[64] "Jerusalem," for Watt, meant the restored church which was about to be made a "praise" in the earth.

The early literature abounds with such references as "Praise is the door-opener." Such scriptures as Psalm 22:3: "Thou art Holy, O Thou that inhabits the praises of Israel," were also cited repeatedly. Praise, was the "key" enabling the gathered community to "enter in" to the Holy of Holies.[65] Reg Layzell claimed God revealed this truth to him in January, 1946, two years before the revival began. At the time, Layzell was a sales manager for a large office furniture firm serving as a lay preacher on the side. He was called to hold a week of meetings at a small church in Abbotsford, British Columbia. The meetings did not go well. He started a fast and begged God for a breakthrough. The verse from Psalm 22 burst in upon his memory. It dawned on him: "God actually lives in the praises of His people."[66]

Acting on this "revelation from God" he praised the Lord silently as he announced the opening hymn, "There is Power in the Blood." At the end of the second verse, a young lady threw up her hands and began to speak in tongues.

Then another, and still another received the baptism of the Holy Spirit. He interpreted this response to be confirmation to the insight he had received that afternoon.[67] Layzell shared his revelation with the Sharon brethren. They readily accepted his message.[68]

Praise became the basis for the Latter Rain understanding of worship. What had first come forth in a somewhat spontaneous manner became institutionalized. Reflection on these experiences led to the conviction that "'praise' produces the divine presence — an 'atmosphere' in which 'supernatural' manifestations can take place."[69]

Authority of the Church

For Latter Rain adherents, authority came through submission. When adherents thought about authority in the Church, their minds were directed toward Christ, the elder brother, who in obedience to the Father "made Himself of no reputation." They were reminded that self must be crucified before being used of God.[70]

> The Church is not perfected by prayer, by the reading of the Word, nor the many other ways we have been taught. But God has set in the Church...apostles, prophets, evangelists, pastors, teachers for the PERFECTING OF THE SAINTS for the WORK OF THE MINISTRY for the BUILDING UP of the body of Christ, till we all come in the unity of the faith and the knowledge of the Son of God unto a perfect man.[71]

To submit to Christ meant to submit to those that God has set in authority over them. Beginning in North Battleford in February, 1948, adherents believed the church had been established on the foundation of apostles and prophets. Readers of *The Sharon Star* were constantly urged to follow the pattern that had been laid down by the Word of God.[72] Adherents came to understand this as a "theocratic chain of command" that came "from Christ down, not from people up." Authority came from The Father to the Son to those whom the Holy Spirit had revealed to be apostles and prophets. These divinely appointed leaders then were given the wisdom and knowledge to appoint pastors, evangelists, and teachers and to confirm them through the laying on of hands. Together, as the Ascension Gift Ministries, they appointed first Elders and then Deacons in the Local Church. Finally, came the "congregational ministries." Each rank stood in a descending order, not only having less authority, but also less direct access to God.[73]

The Significance of the New Order of the Latter Rain

From the perspective of the original stated aims of its leadership, the revival must be judged a complete failure. Far from "restoring the church," and achieving the unity of the body of Christ, it only served to bring further fragmentation. Within a few years virtually every Pentecostal denomination had rejected the revival. Repeated warnings of doom failed to materialize. Classical

Pentecostalism would go on to experience the greatest period of sustained growth in the years that followed. Internally, the new movement soon began to fragment. New centers of influence emerged that refused to submit to the chain of command linked to North Battleford. The short term missionary strategy proposed by Wyatt failed to sustain a growing network of global churches. By 1955, the New Order of the Latter Rain had ceased to function as a movement.

On the other hand, the assessment of classical Pentecostal historians, typified by Carl Brumback's classic comment that by the mid-fifties "The new Order had practically come to naught," is clearly incorrect.[74] Walter Hollenweger is accurate when judging this appraisal to be an example of "the same wishful thinking that led the traditional churches to ignore the beginnings of the Pentecostal movement."[75] As an agent of renewal, the New Order of the Latter Rain has proven to be successful. First of all, a quick check on the internet reveals literally hundreds of congregations in North American and thousands globally that identify directly with the revival.[76] More significantly, when the Charismatic Movement burst into prominence in the late 1960's, it was Latter Rain leaders rather than classical Pentecostalism that had the major influence. Richard Riss, the most prominent historian of the New Order, identified some 20 ministries that brought Latter Rain teaching and practices in the Charismatic Movement. The Charismatic Movement in turn has had much impact on worship patterns of mainline denominations in the last decades of the twentieth century. It's teaching and practices are clearly evident in the flood of independent churches that have sprung into existence both in North America and globally during the same period. Riss correctly concludes:

> Traditional Pentecostal denominations have been, to a large extent, unaware of the lasting effects of the Latter Rain Movement. However, the Latter Rain was one of several important influences upon the Charismatic Renewal of the 1960's and 1970's. Its significance in the context of World Protestantism, therefore, lies in its effects upon a growing influence in most Protestant denominations.[77]

Notes

1. Scholars estimate Pentecostal adherents are in excess of 500 million world-wide equaling the numerical strength of the rest of Protestantism, Eastern Orthodoxy and just short of the size of Roman Catholicism or 25% of Christianity. Vinson Synan, *The Century of the Holy Spirit: 100 Years of Pentecostal and Charismatic Renewal, 1901-2001* (Nashville, TN: Thomas Nelson, 2001): 450.

2. The author is currently working on a book on this revival in its historical context that will demonstrate its impact on contemporary Christianity. in a forthcoming article: *The Latter Rain: A Canadian Innovation*, the author sketches the revival's history.

3. L. Thomas Holdcroft, "The New Order of the Latter Rain," *Pneuma*, 2:2 (Fall 1980): 47.

4. George R. Hawtin, "How It Started," *The Sharon Star* (March 1, 1950): 1.

5. Richard Riss, "The Latter Rain Movement of 1948 and the Mid-Twentieth Century Evangelical Awakening," *Pneuma*, 4:1 (Spring 1982): 80.

6. George R. Hawtin, "Editorial," *The Sharon Star* (January 1, 1948): 2-3.

7. George Hawtin, "How It Started," p. 1.
8. Ernest H. Hawtin, "How This Revival Began," *The Sharon Star* (August 1, 1949): 3.
9. George Hawtin, "How It Started," p. 2.
10. Milford E. Kirkpatrick, *The 1948 Revival and Now* (Dallas, TX: The Author, n.d.): 9.
11. George R. Hawtin, "Local Church Government," *The Sharon Star* (May 1, 1948): 2-4.
12. Noel McNeill, "As of a Rushing Mighty Wind: An Assessment of North America's Pentecostal Movement," (Unpublished manuscript. Haliburton, Ont: 1964): 27.
13. George R. Hawtin, "Editorial," *The Sharon Star* (August 1, 1948): 2.
14. Cornelius J. Jaenen, "The Pentecostal Movement" (MA Thesis, University of Manitoba, 1950): 87.
15. George R. Hawtin, "Editorial," *The Sharon Star* (January 1, 1948): 3.
16. George R. Hawtin, "Editorial," *The Sharon Star* (May 1, 1948): 2.
17. Paul N. Grubb. Interview with D. William Faupel (July 1, 1976), tape cassette. D. William Faupel papers, David DuPlessis Center, Pasadena, California.
18. Ernest Hawtin, "How the Revival Began," pp. 3-4.
19. Franklin Hall, *Atomic Power with God with Fasting and Prayer* (San Diego, CA: The Author, 1946): 9.
20. George R. Hawtin, "How It Got Started," p. 1.
21. Ernest Hawtin, "How the Revival Began," p. 3.
22. A. W. Rasmussen, *The Last Chapter* (Monroeville, PA: Whitaker House, 1973): 138-144.
23. Jaenen, "The Pentecostal Movement," p. 86.
24. Stiles attacked the then common Pentecostal practice of "tarrying" for the Baptism of the Holy Spirit which was modeled on the disciples' experience in the Upper Room. He argued that the disciples had to wait until Pentecost, because the Spirit had not yet been given dispensationally. Stiles' analysis of other New Testament evidence led him to conclude that the Holy Spirit was conferred subsequently through the laying on of hands. J. E. Stiles, *The Gift of the Holy Spirit* (Glendale, CA: The Church Press, n.d.): 79-89.
25. George Hawtin, "Revival at Sharon," *The Sharon Star* (April 1, 1948): 2.
26. George Hawtin, "How It Started," p. 3.
27. Ernest Hawtin, "The Other Side of the Picture," *The Sharon Star* (November 1, 1948): 3.
28. Ernest Hawtin, "How the Revival Began," p. 3.
29. Raymond G. Hoekstra, *The Ascension Gift Ministries* (Portland, OR: Wings of Healing, 1950): 39.
30. Paul N. Grubb, *The End Time Revival* (Memphis, TN: The Author, n.d.): 34-35.
31. Paul W. Stewart and Barbara Franzen *Confirmation* [Harvest Rain Series] Book 2 (Detroit, MI: Evangel Press, 1954): 79.
32. Hoekstra, *The Ascension Gift Ministries*, p. 14.
33. *Ibid.*, p. 30.
34. Morris. R. Urgren, "The Prophet, His Ministry and Office," *The Voice of Faith* (September-October, 1950): 5.
35. Hoekstra, *The Ascension Gift Ministries*, p. 48.
36. Urgren, "The Prophet, His Ministry and Office, p. 10.
37. George R. Hawtin, "Ministries in the Body of Christ," *The Sharon Star* (January 1, 1951): 3.

38. Stewart and Franzen, *Confirmation*, pp. 76-77.
39. George R. Hawtin, "Restoration of Elders and Deacons," *The Sharon Star* (May 1952): 4.
40. George Hawtin, "Ministries in the Body of Christ," p. 3. Other ministries that Hawtin suggested include such things as the ministry of tongues, the ministry of helps and the ministry of giving.
41. George Hawtin, "Local Church Government," p. 1.
42. A. W. Rasmussen, "Scriptural or Unscriptural Church Order," *The Sharon Star* (February 1, 1948): 3.
43. George R. Hawtin & Ernest H. Hawtin, *Church Government* (North Battleford, SASK: Sharon College, 1949): 19, 26-29.
44. George Hawtin, "Ministries in the Body of Christ," pp. 3-4.
45. Kirkpatrick, *The 1948 Revival and Now*, p. 18.
46. *The Sharon Star* (April 1, 1948): 1.
47. James Watt, "Progress with God," *The Sharon Star* (December 1, 1948): 3.
48. Watt, "Progress with God," p. 3, and George Hawtin, "Editorial," *The Sharon Star* (December 1, 1948): 2. In each instance the person or couple sent to a particular field went having received a word of prophecy directing them to go. In several cases, further confirmation had come in the form that the "tongues" they spoke was the actual language spoken by the people of the country to whom they were sent.
49. "Revelation of World Evangelization Given at St. Louis Convention," *The Voice of Faith* (February 1951): 8.
50. Maureen Gaglardi, *The Pastor's Pen: Early Revival Writings of Pastor Reg Layzell*, (Vancouver, BC: New West Press, 1965): 65.
51. George Hawtin, "Editorial," *The Sharon Star* (August 1, 1948): 2
52. Paul W. Steward & Barbara Franzen, *The Body of Christ* [Harvest Rain Series], Book 3 (Detroit, MI: The Evangel Press, 1954): 5.
53. George H. Warnock, *The Feast of Tabernacles* (Springfield, MO: Bill Britton, 1951): 90.
54. *Ibid.*, pp. 119-121.
55. Grubb, *The End-Time Revival*, p. 5.
56. George R. Hawtin, "The Great Manifestation," *The Sharon Star* (November 1, 1950): 1; and December 1, 1950): 1.
57. George R. Hawtin, "They Kingdom Come," *The Sharon Star* (November-December 1951): 1.
58. *Ibid.*, pp. 2-4.
59. George Hawtin, "How It Got Started," p. 1.
60. *Ibid.*
61. George R. Hawtin, "The Great Restoration," *The Sharon Star* (May 1951): 3.
62. Warnock, *The Feast of Tabernacles*, pp. 6-7.
63. Tom Craig Darrand & Anson Shupe. *Metaphors of Social Control in a Pentecostal Sect* (New York, NY: Edwin Mellen, 1983): 125, 128.
64. Watt, "Progress with God," p. 3.
65. Darrand, *Metaphors of Social Control*, pp. 120-122.
66. Gaglardi, *The Pastor's Pen*, pp. 9-11.
67. Reg Layzell, *"Into Perfection: The Truth about the Present Restoration Revival* (Mountlake Terrace, BC: The King's Temple, 1979): 1.
68. Watt, *Progress with God*, p. 4.
69. Gaglardi, *The Pastor's Pen*, p. 152.

70. Myrtle D. Beall, "At the Cross," *The Latter Rain Evangel* [Detroit] (March 1952): 6.

71. George R. Hawtin, "Submission," *The Sharon Star* (May 1952): 7.

72. George R. Hawtin, "Submission," *The Sharon Star* (June-July 1952): 8; and George R. Hawtin, "A Letter to the Ecclesia," *The Sharon Star* (November-December, 1952): 6.

73. Richard Iverson, *Present Day Truths* (Portland, OR: Bible Press, 1975): 71.

74. Carl Brumback, *Suddenly...from Heaven: A History of the Assemblies of God* (Springfield, MO: Gospel Publishing House, 1961): 333.

75. Walter J. Hollenweger, "Handbuch der Pfingstbewegung," Vol. 2 (Th.D. Dissertation, University of Zurich, 1965): 758.

76. Ten years ago, one of my student assistants identified over 2,000 Latter Rain Church's websites in North American and hundreds more globally. I am not aware of any published statistics that has sought to identify such churches separately from Pentecostalism.

77. Richard Riss, "The Latter Rain Movement of 1948," *Pneuma* (Spring 1982): 45.

Secondary Works Cited

Brumback, Carl. *Suddenly... from Heaven: A History of the Assemblies of God.* Springfield, MO: Gospel Publishing House, 1961.

Darrand, Tom Craig & Anson Shupe. *Metaphors of Social Control in a Pentecostal Sect.* New York, NY: Edwin Mellen, 1983.

Holdcroft, L. Thomas. "The New Order of the Latter Rain," *Pneuma*, 2:2. Fall 1980.

Hollenweger, Walter J. "Handbuch der Pfingstbewegung," vol. 2. Th.D. Dissertation, University of Zurich: 1965.

Richard Riss, "The Latter Rain Movement of 1948 and the Mid-Twentieth Century Evangelical Awakening," *Pneuma* (Spring 1982): 32-45.

Synan, Vinson. *The Century of the Holy Spirit: 100 Years of Pentecostal and Charismatic Renewal, 1901-2001.* Nashville, TN: Thomas Nelson, 2001.

7

Reflections on the Use of "Exile" as a Christian Category

By Craig C. Hill

Given its enormous significance for biblical history, it might seem surprising that the Babylonian Exile is so seldom mentioned in the New Testament. That is not to say that the Exile is irrelevant to the rise of Christianity. Quite the opposite: the Exile was the decisive event shaping inter-testamental Judaism, which was itself the seedbed of the earliest church. It is impossible to imagine the birth of Christianity apart from the enduring eschatological expectations of the exilic and post-exilic prophets, not to mention the ongoing hope for the fulfilment of God's purposes sustained by the apocalyptic writings of the inter-testamental period. These sources are heavily drawn upon and widely presupposed by the New Testament authors. It is indisputably the case, as N. T. Wright maintains[1], that the early Christians saw Jesus as having fulfilled—or, more accurately, as having begun to fulfil—the promises made by God to exilic and post-exilic Israel. For example, the glorious expectation of a new covenant in Jeremiah 31:31-34 is believed by Paul, among others, to have been realized in the work of Christ (2 Corinthians 3:6; Luke 22:20 and, Hebrews 8:8-13).

Nevertheless, explicit references to the Exile are few and far between in the New Testament. Matthew mentions it three times in his opening chapter, but only in the context of his genealogy (1:11, 12 & 17). In each case, the reference is merely historical: Matthew derives no lessons from and draws no parallels to the Exile. It appears in Acts as part of Stephen's speech in chapter 7 (v. 43) as a key incident in the long rehearsal of Israel's past failures.[2] Babylon is mentioned in 1 Peter 5:13 and Revelation. 14:8; 16:19; 17:5; 18:21, but these verses are actually veiled references to Rome, a substitution found in both Jewish and Christian writers following the destruction of Jerusalem in A.D. 70. (See, for example, 2 Esdras 3:1-2: "I was in Babylon...")

Multiple reasons can be suggested to account for the paucity of such references. The first, alluded to above, is that Christians regarded themselves as living at a time when earlier hopes were being fulfilled. It would have been natural for them to regard the Exile as something past, not integral to their own religious experience. A second factor is the meaning assigned to the event in the prophetic and Deuteronomistic traditions. The Exile was not merely a human tragedy; it was punishment for Jewish disobedience—in particular, judgment for Israel's idolatry. That the church would not have widely employed this negative category in developing its self-understanding is unremarkable. Another, though probably less significant reason is the fact that the first-century church included a great many Gentiles, for whom the Exile was not part of their history.

Two other considerations complicate the above description. One is obvious: the fact that a great many exilic and post-exilic hopes were *not* fulfilled in the experience of the early Christians. For example, the hope for the (re)gathering of the people of God (Isaiah 27:13; 40:1-11; 43:5; Jeremiah 23:3; 31:7-10; etc.) is paralleled in *eschatological* passages in the New Testament (e.g., Matthew 24:31; John 11:52; 1 Thessalonians 4:15-17; etc.). Numerous other examples could be cited, the most prominent being the expectation of a future resurrection of the saints (Isaiah 26:19; Daniel. 12:2; cf. Mark 12:26; John 6:40; 2 Corinthians. 4:14; etc.). In short, many of the hopes of Judaism that arose in and because of the Exile were shared by early Christians. Consequently, the notion of Exile as a place of as-yet-unfulfilled expectation is resonant with Christian experience.

A parallel consideration concerns the New Testament's references to the status of believers in the world, where they are sometimes described as "strangers," "aliens," or "pilgrims." Two key words in Greek, *paroike•/paroikos* ("to sojourn/alien, stranger," from the verb "to live alongside") and *parepid•mos* ("refugee, pilgrim"), are rendered by the English word "exile" in some translations. The greatest concentration of such language is found in 1 Peter. The initial usage is the most interesting since it specifically mentions the Diaspora/Dispersion:

"Peter, an apostle of Jesus Christ, To the exiles [*parepid•mois*] of the Dispersion [*diasporas*]..." (1:1).

A close parallel is found in the salutation of the letter of James: "James...To the twelve tribes in the Dispersion" (1:1). This is as near as the New Testament comes to identifying the church with the dispersed Jewish community awaiting restoration.[3] The references are clearly metaphorical; neither author is actually writing to the Jewish Diaspora. Nevertheless, the use of this terminology is significant and demonstrates that some early Christians saw themselves as living in a situation in some way parallel to that of scattered Israel. The fact that 1 Peter refers to Rome as "Babylon" in 5:13 underscores this point.

1 Peter 1:17 enjoins believers to "live in reverent fear during the time of your exile ['your sojourning,' *paroikias*]." Similarly, 2:11: "Beloved, I urge you as aliens and exiles [both *paroikous* and *parepid•mous*] to abstain from the desires of the flesh that wage war against the soul." This advice is reminiscent of the first half of the book of Daniel, which was written in part to encourage Jews living among Gentiles to remain faithful to the law. The young Daniel and his Jewish com-

panions, who reject the Babylonian king's food and refuse to commit idolatry, are nevertheless raised to positions of honor. Indeed, their obedience leads ultimately to the king's acknowledgment of the God of Israel (e.g., Daniel 3:28; 4:37). Similarly, 1 Peter 2:12:

> Conduct yourselves honorably among the Gentiles, so that, though they malign you as evildoers, they may see your honorable deeds and glorify God when he comes to judge.

A majority of scholars date Daniel to the time of the Maccabean Revolt in the second century B.C.E. If this is correct, the book of Daniel demonstrates how post-exilic Jews could look back to the Exile as a model for interpreting their own circumstances. Something similar appears to be at work in the letter of 1 Peter.

The idea that Christians are in the (fallen) world but not of it is commonplace in the New Testament. For example, the author of Hebrews wrote, "For here we have no lasting city, but we are looking for the city that is to come" (13:13). Compare Galatians 6:14: "May I never boast of anything except the cross of our Lord Jesus Christ, by which the world has been crucified to me, and I to the world."

There are many practical advantages to conceiving of one's group as "aliens" or "exiles" in the world. As we saw both in Daniel and in 1 Peter, this way of thinking accentuates the differences between insiders and outsiders, substantiating the call to live according to a higher standard than that of the surrounding culture. It also underscores the group's distinctive purpose and importance, securing a higher level of self-identification and allegiance on the part of group members, especially in the face of opposition. On the other hand, otherworldliness (or, as is more often the case in the New Testament, "nextworldliness") can lead all too easily to sectarianism with all of its attending faults (disconnection from the needs of the present world, spiritual arrogance, and so on.)

It is interesting in this context to consider Jeremiah's letters to the exiles (29). Jeremiah counters not the lack of expectation of return, but the overheated and immediate expectation encouraged by some false prophets. Jeremiah instructs the exiles that God's promise of restoration to the land of Israel will indeed be fulfilled, but not until seventy years have passed (29:10). In the meantime, the prophet requires the people to "Build houses and live in them; plant gardens and eat what they produce" (v. 5).

Perhaps this is a useful word today. On the one hand, we ought not to give up on the hope of God's ultimate triumph. Let us not forget that a great many Jews became so comfortable in Babylon that they chose to remain there even after return to their homeland became possible. On the other hand, we ought not to be so eager to leave this present world that we chase after every preacher who says, in effect, "'The vessels of the Lord's house will soon be brought back from Babylon'" (v. 16). Jeremiah instructed his exiled readers to hold fast to God's promise but also, in this time-between-the-times, to "seek the welfare of the city where I [God] have sent you into exile, and pray to the Lord on its behalf, for in its welfare you will find your welfare" (v. 7).

Notes

1. N. T. Wright, *The Climax of the Covenant: Christ and the Law in Pauline Theology* (Minneapolis, MN: Fortress, 1993)..

2. Note that the original text of Amos 5:25-27 refers to "Damascus," not "Babylon." The author is deliberately paralleling Jewish rejection of Moses with present-day rejection of the "prophet like Moses," Jesus. In this way, the destruction of Jerusalem and the deportation of the people at the time of the Exile serve as an interpretive key to understanding the tumultuous events of A.D. 70.

3. The Exile and Diaspora are different things, of course, but the former is to an extent the cause of the latter, and the two ideas are often linked. For example, it was the hope of the prophet Jeremiah, writing at the time of the Exile, that God would one day "bring them [the Jews] from the land of the north, and *gather them from the farthest parts of the earth*" (31:8).

Works Cited

Wright, N.T. *The Climax of the Covenant: Christ and the Law in Pauline Theology.* Minneapolis, Mn: Fortress, 1993).

8

Who is the Stranger?
Preaching in the Diverse Church

By Lucy Lind Hogan

I have been a stranger in a strange land.
Exodus 18:3

Ultimate loyalty among the people of God's promise rests in God and not in the cultures, societies, and institutions of any one setting...one "sojourns."[1]
Bruce C. Birch

Funny things can happen when a Scandinavian from Minnesota, who grew up on meat, potatoes, and NO seasonings or spices, meets an enchilada laced with jalapeño peppers. My children would not believe how red their mother's face could get. I was truly a stranger in a strange land—my system was not prepared for such a different cuisine.

When lutefisk meets jalapeños it is one thing. But Eric Law, in *The Wolf Shall Dwell with the Lamb*, reminds us that culture is like an iceberg. When we become aware of differences, the external parts of culture—whether it is language or food, we have to realize that those are but the tip of the iceberg. What about the other 3/4 of the iceberg that lay below the surface of our awareness? What about the power dynamics, rituals, and expectations that informs the way we approach the world and others?

> The major part [of culture] is the internal part, which consists of the unconscious beliefs, thought patterns, values, and myths that affect everything we do and see. It is implicitly learned and is very hard to change.

How do those internal parts of culture help or more likely hinder, the way that we communicate and live together? And how do they affect how we communicate and proclaim the gospel? What does it mean to preach in the diverse, global twenty-first century world? How can preachers be sojourners? In this essay, in grateful thanksgiving for the teaching and writing of Bruce Birch, I will explore these questions drawing on his scholarly contributions to the religious conversation.

Sojourners and Strangers

The children of Israel had always known what it meant to be peripatetic pilgrims, sojourners, strangers in strange lands. Moses reminded them that their father, Abraham, was a wandering Aramean (Deut. 26:5). In *Let Justice Roll Down*, Bruce Birch writes that

> The sojourner (*ger*) is a resident alien; he lives in a place dependent on the hospitality of its inhabitants without full membership and rights in the community. In Genesis the role of sojourner is freely chosen as a part of the journey toward God's promise.[3]

They wandered to Egypt. They wandered through the wilderness out of Egypt. They wandered, not of their own choice, to the lands of Babylon. And in all of their travels they encountered the "other," the stranger who did not follow their God, the God of Abraham, Isaac, and Jacob.

To that "other" there were several responses. First, as Birch observed, they were to dwell in, but did not become the other, "One participates in those settings but is not captured by them".[4] Second, remembering that they too had been sojourners, they were to care for the stranger, "When you reap the harvest of your land, you shall not reap to the very edges of your field, or gather the gleanings of your harvest; you shall leave them for the poor and the alien: I am the Lord your God" (Lev. 23:22).

Yet these first two responses stand in contrast to a third approach. As they prepared to move into the land that was being given to them by God, Moses was told how they were to treat the "others" whom they encountered. They were to "utterly destroy them. Make no covenant with them and show them no mercy. Do not intermarry with them...for that would turn away your children from following me, to serve other gods" (Deut. 7:2-4).

Throughout the scriptures, therefore, we see these very different responses. We are both to care for the other, and we are to scorn and reject them. The same Jesus, who praised the Samaritan as the only one to care for the wounded traveler, also ordered away the Canaanite woman seeking help for her daughter. "It is not fair to take the children's food and throw it to the dogs" (Matt. 15:26). (Although we should note that he quickly changed his mind when he saw her faith and healed her daughter.)

How are we to live as pilgrims, sojourners, aliens? How are we to deal with those who are different from us; who have different beliefs? These continue to be significant theological questions and ones that are becoming more and more important in our rapidly shrinking world.

The Preaching Situation

We live in an increasingly multi-cultural, diverse world. The days of any sense of homogeneity in a community are certainly over. Whether one lives in California, Texas, Vermont, or Minnesota, the likelihood that all of one's neighbors are all of the same ethnic background or religion is slim. When I was growing up in Minnesota, I was going to school with the children of the people my parents went to school with. They were all named Johnson and Anderson and knew where in Norway or Sweden their grandparents or great-grandparents had come from. But now a large segment of the student population at my high school comes from Somalia. Check with your neighborhood elementary school to find out how many different languages are spoken at home by their young students. I think you will be amazed. We are truly living the Pentecost experience.

Luke tells us that as the city prepared to celebrate the Feast of Pentecost the streets of Jerusalem were bustling with people from far beyond the city walls. In the markets a plethora of different tongues could be heard. Jews from far and near had traveled to the holy city to celebrate on that morning. Therefore, when Peter and the other disciples walked down out of that upper room, a group of friends who spoke the same language and had similar backgrounds, they encountered a very different world. Filled with the power of the Holy Spirit, through their speaking, they began to work with that same Spirit to bring into being a church that would be, forever, a blend of different languages and different cultures – a potluck church if you will. The body of Christ would never be, could never be, and should never be made up of one kind of people. That is not in our "DNA". We are always strangers brought together by the Holy Spirit to be church. We are strangers seeking ways to live together as community; as the body of Christ.

Therefore, from that first day, the church, its preachers and pastors, have struggled with singing strange songs in strange lands. They have been charged by the Holy Spirit to speak so that "all would hear in their own native tongue."

The Ongoing Debate - Whose Native Tongue?

Throughout the life of the church, a crucial and unavoidable point of stasis in the homiletical conversation has revolved around the ways that a sermon is to relate to its place and time. Is a sermon to be a universal message that could be preached at any time for any group of people? Or, does a particular preacher, coming out of a particular social location try to preach to a particular group of people at a particular time in a particular place? Are sermons timeless or timely messages?

Those who argue for the former; that a sermon is to preach the universal message of the gospel truth, would claim that we are to focus on God and on the scriptures. For those who argue from this point of view, to turn one's attention to the preacher, the listeners, or the context is to obscure the point that God, not we, are the focus of the sermon. They would argue that God, our living God, was and is and is to come. God is the same now and always, and we therefore do not need alter and adjust our sermons for a particular time or particular community.

I, on the other hand, would join the argument on the side of the later. Preaching is done for a particular time, place, and people, and who we are, as preachers matters. To preach to a southern black congregation at the height of the civil rights movement in the 1960s was going to be very different from preaching to an all white, southern congregation. Likewise, it would matter, if the preacher preaching to the black congregation was white or black.

If one accepts that the time, place, and social and cultural location of the preacher and of one's listeners matters, this has profound implications for the preparation and preaching of the message. But what arguments lie behind this understanding of preaching?

Preaching and the Incarnation

First, our preaching is grounded in the incarnation, the word of God made flesh in Jesus Christ. Jesus was a man who lived and moved in a particular time and particular place. He spoke of shepherds and fishermen. He compared the Kingdom of God to yeast in flour and misplaced coins. He spoke of the things that people knew to point them to the transcendent reign of God. Jesus did not ignore or reject the world but was very much a part of the world.

Therefore, we will always be challenged to incarnate the word of God; to make the word of God come alive, giving it flesh, bones, and blood. We are to speak to people who walk particular paths, smell certain smells, and eat particular foods, whether it is lutefisk or enchiladas. Just as Jesus took bread, wine, and told us that in that everyday meal we would meet him so, too, do we lift up the everyday experiences of the children, women, and men to whom we preach and, as Mary Catherine Hilkert reminds us, to point them to the grace of God moving in their lives.[5]

Preaching and Pentecost

Second, as we have already noted when the disciples spilled out of the upper room that Pentecost morning they began to speak to the people that they encountered. Luke records Peter's speech, but clearly many of the others were speaking. The crowd was amazed that they could understand what these people could say. Many also thought that they seemed inebriated. Was that because of what they were saying or how they were saying it? Or, was it because they were so filled with joy and amazement that they seemed totally different from the hard working, over burdened, downtrodden women and men that bustled and jostled through the streets of Jerusalem?

Luke's depiction of that important moment would seem to indicate that the break of Babel was healed, not in the direction of one tongue or one language, but rather, in the direction of openness to the other. The disciples, who no doubt spoke Aramaic, were now understood by those who spoke Arsacid Pahlavi, Phrygian, and Egyptian. How strange that was. It would seem that the Holy Spirit changes the preacher and not just the listener.

Accepting the Other

Finally, as was noted earlier, woven throughout the Hebrew Scriptures is a sense of both cares for and suspicion of the other. In an effort to maintain their religious purity and faithfulness to the one true God, those who were sent into exile avoided strangers, the other. Yet the message of Pentecost would seem that those who are filled with the Holy Spirit and seek to live as the Body of Christ are sent out into the world not just to care for, but to seek out the other. We are to move beyond those messages of exclusion and rejection to those of acceptance and respect.

The message given to Moses, to destroy the other and not to intermarry, was not the message of Pentecost. They were to speak to the other in the tongue of the other. Likewise, they were not to think of themselves as aliens and strangers who were to avoid those who spoke other languages. Rather, through the amazing power of the Holy Spirit, they became like the others, speaking their languages, becoming one with them. As the hymn reminds us,

We are one in the Spirit; we are one in the Lord.
                                        Peter Scholtes

In Each Native Tongue - Timely and Local

The people of God continue to be filled by that amazing Spirit and are led to become one people. And that also continues to come with the challenges met by those who stepped out of the upper room and into the streets of Jerusalem that Pentecost day. Preachers must not only learn how to speak in the tongues of the other, they must realize the many ways that one might be an "other." Coming from a different country and speaking a different language is, as Eric Law reminded us, the tip of the iceberg. There are many more ways that one might be an "other."

Today's preachers are learning how to sing many songs. And they are asking "who is the stranger?" As this wonderfully diverse Body of Christ, we must realize that **we all** are the other, we all are the stranger. And this understanding has profound implications for those who preach.

Contra-diction: The One-For-The-Other

John McClure is one person who is exploring what it means to preach in the twenty-first century; what it means for preaching to become a conversation amongst strangers. He notes that the homiletical conversation has recently turned toward that stranger, that other. There is, he writes, an "ongoing concern of many homileticians to relate preaching to ethics and to the tasks of liberation."[6] Therefore, he puts forward what he describes as "other-wise preaching."

Drawing on the writings of Levinas and the broader philosophical conversations of critical theory, structuralism, and poststructuralism, McClure challenges preachers to give priority to "the human other," because therein lies "a site for the revelation of the Holy Other".[7] The other, the stranger, the listener, must be an integral part of the preaching life, "We will search for a form of preaching that is constantly interrupted by the proximity of the other, by an obligation to the other, and by what Levinas calls the 'glory of the Infinite' given in the fact of the other".[8] Preaching must be a "timely, embodied, face-to-face interaction ...[that both] deconstructs reason and keeps reason truly critical".[9]

In other-wise preaching, both preacher and listener are called to let go of any sense that one controls the moment, the experience, the understanding of who has the power and who is the other, the stranger. In doing so they are both opened to the realization that it is God, the Holy Other, who is present and engaging.

> Once the knower releases his or her thematizing control in the event of knowing, uncovering oneself, and becoming exposed to the other, to infinite strangeness and otherness, the knower's ability to solidify or rigidify into a table identity or position is considerably undermined.[10]

This is what is, according to Levinas, "passive, proxemic knowing...an endless adventure"[11] that is divine engagement. When we let go of our desire to control and dominate. When we turn to the other, we will finally know that it is our God who has called us together.

McClure would argue that there are those who are already engaging in "other-wise preaching." We experience this in the liberation preaching of Justo Gonzalez, and the ethical preaching of Christine Smith and Philip Wogaman.[12] But how might one characterize other-wise preaching? It is preaching that moves outward from an ethical commitment. It is preaching that "find ways to engage in a centripetal exegesis of the biblical canon".[13] Other-wise preachers listen to the textual margins and practice deconstructive critical practices; "what Walter Brueggemann calls the 'countertestimony,' to hear the 'erasure-testimony".[14] Other-wise preachers also exit the study and move out into the community engaging the other, the stranger, in conversation, Bible study, and theological reflection. Ultimately,

> the style and manner of the preacher, therefore, is not that of the self-righteous prophet or the voice of the wounded healer. It is the voice, ultimately, of *contradiction*, of *speaking across* diverse lives, across the entire field of discourse. It is a voice that gathers a community of contra-diction, that speaks, and then cares, advocates, works, and gives *across* and ultimately *beyond* the huge range of positions for living within the universe of discourse.[15]

Fish of Every Kind

So, how do we get to know those others, those strangers? Who are they? What are they like? And how does this challenge the preparation and design of the sermon? We must always remember that, as Jesus proclaimed, "The kingdom of heaven is like a net that was thrown into the sea and caught fish of every kind" (Matthew 13:47). A number of writers have sought to explore the homiletical implications.

In their book, *One Gospel, Many Ears,* Joseph Jeter and Ronald Allen encourage preachers to reflect on the variety of listeners that they are drawing into their preaching net. As they observe:

> Every time the congregation gathers for worship, many different people come from different points in life with many different needs and perspectives. The same sermon may touch people in different ways, because they are at different places in life.[16]

They seek to do two things in their book. First, they seek to sensitize preachers to some of the many ways that the people to whom they will be preaching will be different. And second, they provide the preacher with different approaches to attend to and possibly reach those different listeners.

Who are those different listeners? Jeter and Allen explore generational differences and gender differences. They also discuss the differences one will find amongst the way people learn and process information. In the net of God's reign one will find those who are prosperous and politically conservative, and those who are poor and have lost their job. And they discuss what it means to preach in a multi-cultural setting.

James Nieman and Thomas Rogers also provide preachers with a way to "speak an authentic word amid people whose unique experiences and values bring unfamiliar expectations".[17] They argue that all preachers today are challenged to reflect upon the important question, "who is my neighbor?" We are called to preach to people who are different from ourselves and this presents certain challenges.

To meet that challenge they introduce preachers to the concept of "cultural frames." Cultural frames are "a set of ways to look at any one culture".[18] The four frames that they have chosen to examine are: ethnicity, class, displacement and beliefs. How do we listen? How do we get to know the other? How to we shape our message so that we honor and respect these different neighbors? That is what their work explores.

Likewise, Thomas Troeger and Edward Everding seek to find ways that preachers might "draw upon their full humanity in order to communicate effectively with the full humanity of their congregation."[19] Theories of knowing and learning, also known as multiple intelligences, help us to take into account "all of us." Children come to know differently from adults. Some of us learn through words, others through actions, while another might learn by math or science. They observe:

> Our greater awareness of different ways of knowing affects not only our relationship to God but also our relationship to one another. We become attuned to the richness in others, their particular ways of perceiving, processing, and responding to the world. We gain a more expansive vision, one that is gracious to those who see the world in a different light from ourselves. We begin to live more faithfully not only the first commandment, but also the second commandment: to love our neighbors as ourselves.[20]

The Next Step?

I must confess—it is interesting to watch when presenting the materials from the previous authors to students in an introductory preaching course. They quickly become overwhelmed by this challenge to think about the wide range of differences presented in the potential congregation: age, gender, languages, cultures, ethnicity, learning styles, not to mention milk and meat Christians. The differences would seem to be almost as numerous as the number of people sitting in the pew. They quickly throw up their hands in despair; "Where should I begin? How can I ever hope to speak to all of these people?" Fortunately, writers such as McClure, Jeter, Allen, Neiman, Rogers, Troeger, and Everding are there to help preachers navigate this challenging but essential road. Therefore, the most important first step, as each of these authors suggest, is to help preachers understand, honor, and respond to these differences. The first step is to convince preachers that shaping their sermons for the listeners lives into the gift and challenge of Pentecost. God has invited them to make sure that they are "speaking in the native language" of each.

But what is next? Is it enough for preacher to accept the other, the stranger? Is it enough if only preachers are the ones who listen to and shape their messages for the great diversity in the Body of Christ?

Eric Law observes that, in a world that is increasingly pluralistic, diverse, and uncertain, people come to church to find homogeneity, stability and changelessness. They "want the church to be a place of refuge from the turbulent world out there".[21] Consequently, those churches, "work very hard to change in shallow water without addressing the challenges found in the deep, rushing currents" in which they find themselves.[22] Yet to change is what is demanded of us as the people of God. We are called to be sojourners in this world. We are called to speak to and live with the other, the stranger. Law writes, "We change because we are *doing* God's will in the world. We change in order to present Christ anew to a world that has changed and is still changing".[23]

The seas of change can be traumatic. Peter certainly knew that. But the good news of the Gospel is that we are called to step out of the boat of safety and sameness and into the deep of diversity—for that is where our savior is moving. We are all being called to proclaim the good news to a multi-cultural, multi-colored, multi-gifted world. And we are all called, not just preachers, to learn how to accept, to welcome, and adapt to that world.

Drawing on the image of the paralytic and his friends in the 2nd chapter of Mark, Law reminds us that, "The transformation of a church community often requires a group of faithful members who are willing to bring their community's paralysis to a place where Christ dwells, where God's grace is abundant, and where the Word is spoken and lived".[24] It would seem that for preachers and their listeners, the next step is that everyone in the Body of Christ, ordained and lay, strives to be those who accept and honor the other. Everyone should seek to be "other-wise Christians." Preachers will need to continue to seek to speak to the other, but developing that sensitivity and those skills will likewise need to become the sensitivities and skills of the entire people of God as we live in this diverse, global world - God's beloved world.

Notes

1. Bruce C. Birch, *Let Justice Roll Down The Old Testament, Ethics, and Christian Life.* (Louisville, KY: Westminster/John Knox, 1991): 111.

2. Eric H. F. Law, *The Wolf Shall Dwell with the Lamb: A Spirituality for Leadership in a Multicultural Community* (St. Louis MO: Chalice, 1993): 5.

3. Birch, op. cit., p. 110.

4. *Ibid.*, p. 111.

5. Mary C. Hilkert, *Naming Grace: Preaching and the Sacramental Imagination* (New York, NY: Continuum, 1997.

6. John S. McClure, *Other-wise Preaching: A Postmodern Ethic for Homiletics* (St. Louis, MO: Chalice, 2001): x.

7. *Ibid.*, p. 8.

8. *Ibid.*, p. 9.

9. *Ibid.*, p. 10.

10. *Ibid.*, p. 121.

11. *Ibid.*

12. *Ibid.* p. 133.

13. *Ibid.*, p. 138.

14. *Ibid.*, p. 143.

15. *Ibid.*, p. 151.

16. Joseph R. Jeter and Ronald J. Allen. *One Gospel, Many Ears: Preaching for Different Listeners in the Congregation* (St. Louis, MO: Chalice, 2002): 2.

17. James R. Nieman and Thomas G. Rogers. *Preaching to Every Pew: Cross-Cultural Strategies* (Minneapolis, MN: Fortress, 2001): vii.

18. *Ibid.*, p. 16.

19. Thomas H. Troeger and H. Edward Everding, Jr., *So That All Might Know* (Nashville, TN: Abingdon, 2008): 2.

20. *Ibid.*, p. 12.

21. Eric H. F Law, *Sacred Acts, Holy Change* (St. Louis, MO: Chalice, 2002): 7.

22. *Ibid.*, p. 19.

23. *Ibid.*, p. 27.

24. *Ibid.*, p. 78.

Works Cited

Birch, Bruce C. *Let Justice Roll Down The Old Testament, Ethics, and Christian Life.* Louisville, KY: Westminster/John Knox, 1991.

Hilkert, Mary C. *Naming Grace: Preaching and the Sacramental Imagination.* New York, NY: Continuum, 1997.

Jeter, Joseph R. and Ronald J. Allen. *One Gospel, Many Ears: Preaching for Different Listeners in the Congregation.* St. Louis, MO: Chalice, 2002.

Law, Eric H. F. *The Wolf Shall Dwell with the Lamb: A Spirituality for Leadership in a Multicultural Community.* St. Louis MO: Chalice, 1993.

_____, *Sacred Acts, Holy Change.* St. Louis, MO: Chalice, 2002.

McClure, John S. *Other-wise Preaching: A Postmodern Ethic for Homiletics.* St. Louis, MO: Chalice, 2001.

Nieman, James R. and Thomas G. Rogers. *Preaching to Every Pew: Cross-Cultural Strategies.* Minneapolis, MN: Fortress, 2001.

Troeger, Thomas H. and H. Edward Everding, Jr. *So That All Might Know.* Nashville, TN: Abingdon, 2008.

9

Playing in Exile

By Michael S. Koppel

A colleague who recently received a medical diagnosis said about her illness: "I'm learning to accept my unacceptance...." Coming to terms with unwelcome information or learning to accept our unacceptance is a prayer of the heart, a posture for living in transitional time and space. Some things in life simply come to us, not of our choice. Their arrival, though, does present us with a choice: how to respond, how then to live? My colleague experiences exile in the form of illness as separation from life as she has known it. She asks: how shall I live fruitfully in this place I really did not want to inhabit? Acceptance of such exile does not happen quickly, if it happens at all. We might choose not to inhabit this place, this land of exile, fighting our way bitterly and angrily toward the land we prefer. However, this is not a life-giving choice for ourselves or those around us, as the force set in motion by such inner war leads to deadness.[1]

As a teacher, scholar, and academic dean, Bruce Birch has exemplified the capacity to nurture qualities of hope, creativity, and renewal in the midst of exile, as the church experiences its place within a radically changing culture.[2] Bruce Birch argues that the "themes of exilic theology may offer radical and creative possibilities for singing the Lord's song in a foreign land."[3] Themes of exile emanate from prophetic voices that help communities to recognize, name, and embody strengths that ensure survival and enable vital flourishing. Bruce's personal and professional gifts for leadership among his colleagues and students reflect just such a voice of wise compassion, ever calling ecclesial and scholarly communities to remember and celebrate the many good gifts in our midst. In honor of Bruce Birch, who invites us to think about the exile experience as a source of creative possibility, I offer questions that inform this reflective essay. What contemporary pastoral theological practices might contribute to personal and community cohesion for the journey through exilic times of transition? How might we through these practices creatively navigate exile so that we work psychologically and spiritually with our pain and proactively refuse to give in to negativity and lifelessness?

The biblical theme of exile connects with contemporary narratives from the deeply personal to the expansively corporate. Separated from their homeland with its familiar symbols, structures, language, and ways of life, the Israelite people long to return. Walter Brueggemann points out that a "displaced people needed a place from which to validate a theologically informed, peculiar sense of identity and practice of life."[4] The need exists regardless of whether exile is historical or an ideological self-characterization.[5] Exile can also be other- or self-imposed, and either way contributes to pain, grief, and lament.[6] Exile is soul-altering, and without focused intent it can become soul-withering. Yet this possibility need not necessarily become destiny.

A reading of Psalm 137 offers pastoral theological clues for formative faithful living in exile. As Denise Dombkowski Hopkins believes, an allegorical reading of this Psalm can be a "dishonest response," in that it subtly negates the horrors of oppression, genocide, or Holocaust.[7] The final line of Psalm 137 sends a shockwave through us: "Happy shall they be who take your little ones and dash them against the rock!" (v.9) Anger of an oppressed people speaks.[8] Too easily might we sit in righteous judgment of this emotion, hurling accusations and epithets back at those who express such harsh words. Yet, we might also listen to these words again and attune ourselves more closely to the underlying hurt and sorrow. This is a communal lament[9] of a despondent and beleaguered community whose hurt-filled anger drives an impulse toward revenge. This anger is also hope-filled because it reflects the yearning of a community to find a way through its pain. Anger is an energized and faithful response.[10] Movement from despondency, listlessness, and hopelessness leads us through complex psycho-emotional terrain. How shall we sing the Lord's song in a foreign land? The question of despondency finds its energy in the psalm's culmination. One way through lament toward life on the other side comes in accepting the unacceptable—the situation and its accompanying emotion—as faithful refusal to submit to resignation's destructive power. A way through may be in responding differently to the oppressor's demand.

In exile, whether real or imagined, we have the opportunity to learn about ourselves as individuals and communities. Exile wrestles from us an intention more deep than we might ever imagine, and develops the capacity for resilience. How shall we sing the Lord's song in a foreign land? How shall we exist in an unknown and unfamiliar place? This essay offers threads of insight and practice for pastoral teachers, leaders, and congregations.

Play and Hoped-for Reality

What if we imagined God calling us to creative play in exile? We don't usually think of our call in these terms. Church people, including pastors and lay members, ordinarily assume an unusually serious tone about matters of faith and the challenges facing postmodern religious life. One pastor voiced reluctance to engage playfully in ministry: "I fear that people might not take me seriously." Unfortunately, we have forgotten or lost touch with the soulful rhythm of mindful play and whole-hearted work just when we need it the most. As a professor of pastoral care, I am intimately aware of the many care needs that accompany various forms of exile: older members separated from beloved homes as they move into convalescent care; families strained by job loss through economic downturns and forced to move in order to find work; and persons stigmatized and marginalized from community because of mental illnesses.

Many forms of exile threaten to unravel the web of covenant community. Still, I observe God at play in many places, ranging from the experiences of struggling congregations to stories of seminarians awakening to the delight and weight of a vocation in professional church ministry. Isn't it possible and even necessary in the midst of transitions and challenges to take faith seriously but with a playful spirit? By linking serious thought with an open heart, play attunes people to the possibility for new life even amidst hardship and calls forth remembrance of God's whimsical movement in the act of creation (cf. Psalm 104, Proverbs 8). Play strengthens muscles for vital ministry.

The vocation of Christian people and congregations in exile has something in common with the seesaw, a favorite childhood play apparatus. The deep joy of a seesaw comes from staying in motion: the movement between being balanced and off-balance. Congregations in transition build on seesaw play through practices that connect intellectual and emotional intelligence.[11]

Congregational Exile

A complex story of what it means to live as a people in exile comes from the St. Stephens Presbyterian Church.[12] Tucked away on a neighborhood street in North Highlands, California, the church's location made it difficult for people to find. Eighteen years ago, the congregation made a bold decision of faith to step out on a literal and metaphorical journey into a new land: they sold their building and purchased a piece of property in the nearby development of Antelope with a plan to construct a new, more visible, church. Between selling the previous church property and building a new campus, the congregation worshiped in a local high school gymnasium. Through ups and downs of the real estate market and mostly downs of church membership, the congregation still meets in that school gymnasium. While the dream of a new church campus has not yet been realized, the congregation's ministry continues.

St. Stephens, as a congregation experiencing the low boiling frustration of living in exile, exercises creative play each week in its corporate worship. Members faithfully set up the gymnasium with folding metal chairs, a folding table covered with paraments for the Lord's Table, and a lectern wired with a microphone system. Festive banners and decorations appropriate for the liturgical season adorn the folding room dividers. The community's identity goes underground after worship, as volunteers deconstruct the setting and place all items on a rolling platform beneath the stage in the school auditorium. Rev. Peggy Cross, pastor of this congregation for the duration of its time in transition, acknowledges that the congregation and the church elders sometimes grow dispirited by the circumstances of this temporary space and the lack of a permanent church home. Rev. Cross implements creative means of play in congregational life as a reminder of God's playful presence during this time of transition. She notes that the congregation plays in worship by making space for silence that allows attentive listening to God in a community steeped in the Reformed tradition with its reliance on the spoken word. The congregation also plays in its worship space as members bring tangible objects from creation and daily life to worship, items such as a rock, piece of fabric, a leaf, or a bird's feather the meaning of which the pastor weaves with improvisation into the day's message. The members also play while on retreats by creating artistic expressions of their lament-filled journey of faith with paint, clay, and paper that reveal joy and celebration.

Edith Roberts, one of the oldest members of congregation, describes the congregation with the words 'tenacious' and 'patient'. "We've hung in almost to the point of exhaustion.... When you look around, you can see how creative we get." Roberts also expresses the community's yearning: "We have to have a home."

The congregation in exile creates a home for others as it plays in ministry and mission. One poignant illustration comes from Vacation Bible School several years ago: A grandmother sent a letter to the program chairperson, with words of deep gratitude about the week's significance for her granddaughter: "This little seed of knowledge [standing on the promise of God's love] which you sowed deep in her heart has sustained her (and us) through a most horrible series of unfortunate events. She lost the CD you gave her and it is all she wants for Christmas. I would gladly purchase another one." As a lay leader read an excerpt of this letter to the congregation, people wiped tears from their eyes. The congregation without a home reaches out to others who yearn for a spiritual home. Through its own seesaw experience of being off-balance for these many years, St. Stephens continues to remember God's love for them as the congregation in exile reaches out to love and welcome others.

Playful Teaching

Through my pastoral theological research and writing on play, I have discovered that even a potentially interesting topic can become disconnected from lived reality. As one minister recently asked: "Can you give me a concrete example of play to help me grasp what you mean?" To capture the highlights of my research and lessons for play with leaders and congregations, I have created the following memory model.[13]

P=Purposefully Purposeless

It is not an accident that books with titles referring to a purposeful life often top the best-seller lists since people of faith want their lives and work to have significance. People want to live lives that matter, though ironically, too much emphasis on "purpose" can be counterproductive. Too much "purpose" often means bearing down, nose to the grindstone, with a grip on life that can leave little room for God's winsome spirit. Many religious people fear, of course, moving toward the opposite extreme of listless, aimless, unfocused lives and ministries. Exile presents the dual psychic challenge of disintegration and despair—as selfhood and community fragment in response to the trials associated with disconnection with a familiar space or place. A danger lurks in the effort to become overly purposeful and driven with focus on agendas to the detriment of seeing that which is occurring in this moment. Play is about *practicing incompleteness* as people recognize and come to terms with even severe limitations and begin to participate in the hoped-for future right now. This aspect of play does not surrender effort, but reframes the purpose of effort from futile exertion toward not-knowing what the creative response might be.

L=Laughter

Genuine play is often reflected in the eruption of laughter within one's self and in a community with others. Laughter is not limited to just making jokes. Who hasn't had the experience of intense deliberation or conversation breaking forth into sudden and spontaneous laughter? The Spirit catches people off-guard in these moments and shifts the focus of attention. Laughter recognizes incongruities and contradictions as it bridges divisions that could all too easily tear people apart, lightening the burden even when the challenge and journey ahead appear formidable. Laughter comes as a gift in congregations and seminary classrooms. Part of my vocation as a theological educator is to create the conditions that invite laughter into the space. Laughter born in genuine play restores the soul; might we come to revere such mystical and holy moments? These experiences erupt suddenly to welcome people back to their God-given selves in community whenever tension, preoccupation, boredom, or simply the weight of life threaten to prevail. Laughter is like a moment of soul Sabbath as it interrupts and reshapes people with renewed spirit and purpose. Standing in awe of these experiences, I also intend to model for students and others the practice of awe-filled reverence. Whimsical moments of laughter temporarily suspend the burden of exile in order to gladden the heart to spark ministries of spirit and compassion.

A=Awareness

Practicing intellectual, emotional, and spiritual play in classrooms and congregations can help stir awareness of which we are what we are called to do. Flashes of insight come as participants together increase awareness of the many possibilities for ministry that might otherwise go unrecognized, and are all the more needful in personal and communal experiences of exile. As a pastor and educator, one of my goals is to foster an environment of trust that allows for growth of this awareness. Through meaningful conversation about matters that touch and trouble the heart, people recognize an essence or spirit beyond, beneath and containing them that the biblical text references as the Spirit of the Risen Christ in community. Emmaus-type moments happen frequently in theological classrooms and congregations when leaders stay flexibly open to new ideas, ask questions without predetermined answers and thus enliven curiosity, and cooperatively ask ethical questions of themselves and others. Walking and waking to awareness also makes space for tension, disagreement, and conflict as people deliberate and struggle together seeking to follow God's imaginative vision for ministry. Such occasions can at once be fleeting and life-changing.

Y=Y (representation of the special Hebrew name of God revealed to Moses at the burning bush that cannot be spoken aloud or written and is translated in the Bible as LORD)

At the center of play lies a hope for the way I hope pastoral leaders and members of congregations encounter the presence of the Holy. This ineffable Presence can infuse congregations and classrooms in sudden or surprising ways, in the dance of ideas or the serenade of emotions. Sometimes the communal response is reflective silence while at other times it may be an "uh-huh" or "Amen." One wonders whether the Presence is playing with us or whether we are playing in God's Presence. Play can unfold in a variety of ways in God's presence; prayer is one such way. As it takes both verbal and non-verbal expressions, prayer opens our being to the Presence.

My passion for play is grounded in the conviction that a playful spirit of teaching and learning in seminary classrooms leads to creative pastoral leadership in congregations experiencing major transition as well as more stable communities. The members of St. Stephens Presbyterian Church in North Highlands, California struggle with the challenges of life in-between and exemplify a spirit of forbearance. Many congregations face similar struggles and live in places of exile. Religious leaders and congregations in exile face a choice: How, then, will we sing in a strange land? How will we play in this place?

As response to the call, we exercise playful imagination as a means to nurture life, even as we recognize the potentially immense suffering of exile. A cinematic example of this comes in the 1997 film, "Life is Beautiful." Actor and director Roberto Benigni depicts a man helping his young son survive a Nazi concentration camp through creative play. Play-acting becomes a practice of soul survival, an alternative and life-giving response to the imminence of death. In authentic play, we exhort with Paul's words to pray without ceasing, aware all the while, even as we play, of the real-world trials we encounter. In classrooms and congregations, through speech and in action, in exile and at home, play becomes a sacred act of prayer that draws people closer to the heart of God.

Notes

1. Ann Belford Ulanov, *The Unshuttered Heart: Opening Aliveness/Deadness in the Self* (Nashville, TN: Abingdon, 2007): 37.

2. Israel's exilic experience gives rise to voices that also witness to the "capacity for hope, creativity, renewal, and survival of the faith community." See Bruce C. Birch, *Let Justice Roll Down: The Old Testament, Ethics, and Christian Life* (Louisville, KY: Westminster/John Knox, 1991): 281.

3. *Ibid.*, p. 285.

4. Walter Brueggemann, *An Introduction to the Old Testament: The Canon and Christian Imagination* (Louisville, KY: Westminster/John Knox, 2003): 22.

5. *Ibid.*

6. Denise Dombkowski Hopkins and Michael S. Koppel, *Grounded in the Living Word: Hebrew Bible and Pastoral Care Practices* (Grand Rapids, MI: Eerdmans, 2009). See biblical and pastoral expansion on these themes in chapter 6.

7. Denise Dombkowski Hopkins, *Journey Through the Psalms*, revised and expanded (St. Louis, KY: Chalice, 2002): 92.

8. For a theological analysis on this point, see Andrew Sung Park, *From Hurt to Healing: A Theology of the Wounded* (Nashville: Abingdon, TN, 2004).

9. Hopkins, *Journey Through the Psalms*, p. 91.

10. See Carroll Saussy, *The Gift of Anger: A Call to Faithful Action* (Louisville, KY: Westminster/John Knox, 1995).

11. See Daniel Goleman, *Emotional Intelligence* (New York, NY: Bantam, 1995).

12. This community is the shaping and calling congregation of the author.

13. For expanded reflection and analysis on this topic, see Michael S. Koppel, *Open-Hearted Ministry: Play as Key to Pastoral Leadership* (Minneapolis, MN: Fortress, 2008).

Works Cited

Birch, Bruce C. *Let Justice Roll Down: The Old Testament, Ethics, and Christian Life.* Louisville, KY: Westminster/John Knox Press, 1991.

Birch, Bruce C. et. al. (eds.). *A Theological Introduction to the Old Testament.* 2nd Ed. Nashville, TN: Abingdon, 2005.

Brueggemann, Water. *An Introduction to the Old Testament: The Canon and Christian Imagination.* Louisville, KY: Westminster/John Knox, 2003.

Goleman, Daniel. *Emotional Intelligence.* New York, NY: Bantam,1995.

Hopkins, Denise Dombkowski. *Journey Through the Psalms.* St. Louis, MO: Chalice Press, 2002.

_____ and Michael S. Koppel. *Grounded in the Living Word: Hebrew Bible and Pastoral Care Practices.* Grand Rapids, MI: Eerdmans, 2009.

Koppel, Michael S. *Open-Hearted Ministry: Play as Key to Pastoral Leadership.* Minneapolis, MO: Fortress, 2008.

Park, Andrew Sung. *From Hurt to Healing: A Theology of the Wounded.* Nashville, Missouri: Abingdon, 2004.

Saussy, Carroll. *The Gift of Anger: A Call to Faithful Action.* Louisville, Kentucky: Westminster/John Knox, 1995.

Ulanov, Ann Belford. *The Unshuttered Heart: Opening to Aliveness/Deadness in the Self.* Nashville, TN: Abingdon, 2007.

10

The Exile Question of African Americans: "Lord, How Come We Here?"

By William B. McClain

For almost thirty years, Bruce C. Birch has been a colleague and friend as we have taught together at Wesley Theological Seminary in Washington, D.C. And for almost thirty years, he has wrestled with the meaning of wilderness and exile in the experience of the Hebrew people in the scriptures: How do a people cope with being torn from their land, torn from what is meaningful and familiar to them, and how can a Psalm-loving people of Zion sing their Zion's song in a strange land – especially when they feel that the God of their song has abandoned them? And Birch's biblical scholarship and wrestling with these questions and ones related to the Exodus and Exile of the Hebrew people has led to significant and numerous publications cited in the extensive bibliography printed at the end of this volume, Probably even more significant is the lasting learning and impressions left on the hearts and minds of thousands of students who have sat in his classroom and struggled with the texts of the Hebrew Bible and the questions and sometimes even the answers Birch has offered as he has explored ways these ancient texts have meaning and application in the contemporary world.

Conceived in 2007 and realized in April of 2008, Dr. Emilie M. Townes, the Andrew Mellon Professor of African American Religion and Theology and Associate Dean of Yale Divinity School, issued an invitation to about 100 or so African-American scholars of African American Religion to gather for four days of guided conversation at Yale. The Conference was called *Middle Passage Conversations on Black Religion in the African Diaspora*. We were formed into panels to discuss eight questions, one each in segments of four hours guided by a moderator. The questions were framed in a somewhat sophisticated fashion, such as: "What makes a body Black in the USA?" "When will we be able to stop pleading our case that we are human?" "How does history and memory shape us as a diasporic people?" "Is freedom always conditional?" "What are the sounds of freedom that fuel your work?" Also in Spanish to include Spanish-speaking Blacks was the question: "*Como a historia e a memoria nos forman como as pessoas de diasporia?*"[1]

But in truth, it was the ancient Exile question of the African Diaspora: **"Lord, how come we here?"** that under girded the discussion. For the great corporate issues of our society — poverty, pollution, global warming, racial profiling, gender discrimination, hospitality to strangers, sexual abuse and harassment, utter economic greed, international violence of war, anarchy, race, and national priorities – are not primarily political matters; they are rooted profoundly in our attitude toward God: the derelictions and the delinquencies of our human communities.

It is the question that we can pose for insight and meaning of worship and spirituality from an African-American perspective that is relevant for all. It is a simple question in the idiom of the people who first raised it that way. I believe this question can be spoken again in this way, even in the twenty-first century, for two reasons: 1) because God speaks to our human experience and not to our affectations; and 2) because the profound expressions of African people, and in particular, African-American people who raised it in this profound grammatical way, were shaped in a terrible time of uprootedness and transition. It is exile, if you will.

They raised this question as the Africans' first encounter with God in America came — when they were struggling to bridge the communication gap and the cultural gap between themselves and their captors. The language patterns they developed were a hybrid of their native language(s) and that of the host society. Just as the host language was imperfectly understood, so was the Africans' sense of being and purpose confused by their arrival in a new and alien land, exiled, if you will, to an unfamiliar place. They were strangers in a strange land.

How come we here? is a very logical question for the Africans to rise in this new setting. Forcibly torn from their homeland and the routine of their settled lives in their own villages and towns without their consent; ripped from all that is familiar; herded on death ships like cattle to come to America to be slaves to their capriciously cruel captors; auctioned off in the marketplace – not even as human beings – but merely as property to be bought, owned and used; stripped of every vestige of their dignity and respectability; kin separated from kin, tribe separated from tribe, sons and daughters separated from mothers and fathers, and all separated from the place of spiritual and human meaning in their lives, forced to work for free from what my mother used to call "from kin to can't – from the time you can see until the time you can't see;" in this strange land to which they were brought to bear these unusual and heavy burdens, the spiritual strivings and wrestlings begin, the exile question is raised; i.e., the soul's inquiry into the worth, meaning and purpose of their lives. **"Lord, how come we here?"** is asked in an effort to bridge the communication gap. The spiritual implications of the question are vast indeed.

The spiritual strivings of these transplanted Africans began long *before* and continues long *after* the so-called "Magnolia Missions" of white Christians to convert them to Christianity had a chance to plant the heretical notion that these Africans had no identity and were cursed and ordained by God to be but "hewers of wood" and "drawers of water." Even though they were stripped of everything of their former lives and left with nothing else of their prior selves but a mere gossamer of their spiritual identity, these involuntarily depersonalized expatriate souls used this last fragile fiber of faith – half-forgotten and therefore half-remembered – to ponder the most piercingly profound and perennial of spiritual questions: **"Lord, how come we here?"**

The spiritual implications of the question would take on ever-increasing significance as the developing African-American experience unfolded in the complex, diverse, and human relationships that make that experience unique. Clearly, the question: **how come we here?** is much easier to *explain* than it is to *answer*. That requires the complete acceptance of God's inscrutable agenda, by faith alone. The obvious answer is that we are here because God has chosen to bring us here. But it is the "why" behind the divine choice that we truly long to understand. We know by faith that in the Divine Scheme "all things work together for good," but what we do not know, and cannot know, is, the "all things." We see through a glass darkly and perhaps dimly, and that is because we are mortal and our human vision is limited. We will see more clearly when our vision is improved by a level of faith we have not yet achieved.

In the meantime, life has to be lived and confronted on a daily basis, for survival itself is the first condition of "survival-for-what?" If we are not here when the glass is cleared and the revelation is made, then we will never know **"how come we here?"**

In an effort to deal with the "meantime," African Americans have struggled with this spiritual question and have labored to appropriate the meaning of suffering and their experience of pain with expressions of soulful soliloquies, songs, sayings, sermons, and shouts; but also dances, confessions, poems, raps, and other forms of spiritual responses. All are a part of the "stuff" that forms and informs African-American spirituality. All are a part of what makes the African-American experience of worship the soulful passionate experience that it is. This is what we explore in depth and detail in a course I have offered for several years: "Preaching and Worship in the African American Tradition(s)."

All are a part of what my late teacher, Howard Thurman at Boston University, used to call their "life's working paper." For in a real sense it is made up of the creative combination of what a people are in their many and various parts and how they react to the process of living. There are the personal and deep longings of every African American (even among those who act it out in rage and strange and utterly destructive behavior) to be simply viewed and received just like everybody else — as who they are – and to be free to be themselves on their own terms: just "one of God's children" with strengths and weaknesses, gifts and limitations, and all of the rest of the characteristics common to the human lot. And, yet again, African Americans are tied to others who share a common heritage, history and hope, and who look and are like themselves and sing and shout, pray and die, even though sometimes in a different mien.

Although they were attracted to the stories of the Hebrew people who suffered similar bondage and oppression, Exodus and Exile, the oracles and pronouncements of the eighth-century prophets and their denunciation of social injustice that Professor Birch plumbs the depths in his classes and his writings, and the dreams and visions of a beloved community that would come about because of the teachings, compassion, passion, and the resurrection of Jesus of Nazareth as the *Christus Victor.* Professor Vincent Wimbush is right when he says "... In their spirituals and in their sermons and testimonies African Americans interpreted the Bible in light of their own experiences."[2] Yes, they identified by faith with the Hebrew heroes and heroines, and especially with the long-suffering, but ultimately victorious and conquering, nail-driving, fearless Prophet of Galilee who identified with them as "the disinherited," as Thurman so often used the description.[3]

It would be unfair and untrue to simply paint the picture of African-American worship and African-American spirituality — or the worship and spirituality of any people — as only a life of struggle and merely a response to suffering. There is always within its very fiber a fierce and abiding sense of justice and what is right, and a response to the active presence of **grace** and even **"grace upon grace,"** (especially among Wesleyans and Methodists of whatever stripe)**,** as they ponder the question, **"Lord, how come we here?"** In doing so, they incorporate into their struggle for meaning the notions of justice, freedom and love.

In its many facets and in so many different ways, African-American spirituality as expressed in worship identifies its suffering with Moses and the Hebrew children and their struggle and suffering and the Hebrews who insisted that any Pharaoh who holds the children in bondage must let God's people go — by whatever means the Lord chooses! For as so many faithful African Americans put it: "You are God *all by yourself!*" This means that even if God has to roll back the waters of the Red Sea and drown Pharaoh's army, or cause "Jordan to stand still," God's children have to get to the Promised Land of freedom. This unquestioned notion of freedom is at the heart of any form of African- American spirituality that is true to its African roots. And for Methodists of any stripe, this is true to their Wesleyan heritage. For them it is the unquestionable, uncontestable, undebatable, orthodox, and dogmatic belief that the act of the liberating of God's people is an amazing act of divine grace.

African-American spirituality is also a response to God's act of grace. We hear it in the classical and traditional prayer of the Baptist deacon and the old-fashioned steward [an officer still maintained in the Black denominational Methodist churches – and even in some African American United Methodist Churches; I did as pastor of Union United Methodist Church in Boston for ten years – even when the national church abandoned the office]. As I tried to point out in an earlier work I wrote, *Come Sunday: The Liturgy of Zion*: It does not matter at all that this same prayer was prayed last Sunday or Wednesday night at prayer meeting or at any number of other worship settings. It is still the African American response to grace and one of the answers to the spiritual question: **"Lord, how come we here?"**

The African Americans who remained in The Methodist Episcopal Church had to face this question in a different way and at a different time. Some of the African-American Methodists in Philadelphia departed with Richard Allen and others to form the African Methodist Episcopal Church because of the racism and mistreatment they experienced at Saint George's Methodist Episcopal Church. This was their spiritual and denominational answer to the predominantly white and Mother Church. The African Methodists in New York City who had similar experiences were soon to follow and establish themselves as The African Methodist Episcopal Zion Church. The southern African Americans waited until after the Civil War and then they got permission in New Orleans at The Southern Methodist General Conference in 1866 to form themselves into a separate denomination in Jackson, Tennessee in 1870.[4]

Left were those African Americans who saw staying as a statement and an act of freedom also. They said: "To leave is an act of freedom; but to stay is also an exercise of freedom." But they were in a dilemma, for then there were two questions: How do we respond to the answer that the majority whites come up with when they answer their question: "What shall we do with those Black people who stayed in the church and will not go away?" And then the perennial question: **"Lord, how come we here?"**

Well, as John Graham put it in his account of the 1939 General Conference when the split church of the North and South over slavery came back together: "The Negro became the 'sacrificial lamb' on the altar in order that the union could be consummated."[5] While they decided to organize the church into geographical areas, at the same time they established a racially segregated jurisdiction of the church called "The Central Jurisdiction" and placed essentially all African Americans in that jurisdiction.[6] As James P. Brawley, former President of Clark College tells it, and he was one of the Black delegates to that General Conference: "...Delegates arose, after the voting to sing 'We Are Marching to Zion,' the Negro delegates remained seated and some of them wept."[7]

One of the responses to grace and the question: **"Lord, how come we here?"** has come in the form of that creative and the imaginative prayers of the laity. In the words of one of the stewards or one of the other prayer warriors as they come before the throne of grace, knee-bowed and body bent:

> We thank you that you watched over us all night long while we slumbered and slept in the very image of death. Early this morning you touched us with the fingertip of love... I want to thank you that when I rose this morning, my bed was not my cooling board and my sheet was not my winding cloth. Through your goodness and mercy you have seen fit to leave us here to pick and choose our own praying ground. We thank you for protecting us from dangers, seen and unseen. We thank you for leading us from one good degree of grace to another..."[8]

We hear the African-American response to the experience of grace as the people gather, whether there be two or three or two or three thousands, singing and praising God and shouting about "Your grace and mercy brought me through, living each moment all because of you. I want to thank you and praise you, too. Your grace and mercy brought me through." Some quietly with reverence in their hearts and thanksgiving within the very depths of their grateful souls, give thanks for this miraculous pouring out of this matchless, unfathomable, unspeakable and amazing grace. Some others may even quietly wipe away the tears of joy. It is their own response to the question, **"Lord, how come we here?"** But some of the people cannot be quiet, nor can they be still. They can contain themselves no longer. To avoid the "rocks crying" out in response to the presence, reality, and manifestation of God's overwhelming grace, they shout and scream out as if their whole selves — mind, soul, spirit, and body — have been taken over, possessed by an unseen controlling force beyond the ability of any human eyes to perceive. Their responses are passionate, and their emotional outpourings are often tears of joy, praise and thanksgiving, sometimes unintelligible as if it came from another world, and some even dance between the pews and in the aisles. Their uncontrollable screams, shouts and chants begin decipherably and crystal clear: "Hallelujah! Thank you, Jesus! Praise the Lord! Hallelujah!" Not everyone, but some said: **"Lord, that is how come we here!"**

Notes

1. The oral and visuals of the presentations of these panels can be seen on the internet: http://www.yale.edu/divinity/video/middlepassage.shtml.

2. Vincent Wimbush, "The Bible and African Americans," *Stony the Road We Trod: African American Biblical Interpretation,* Cain Felder, ed., (Minneapolis, MN: Fortress, 1991): 86.

3. See Howard Thurman, *Jesus and the Disinherited* (Nashville, TN: Abingdon, 1949). It is reported that Martin Luther King always carried a copy of Thurman's book with him in his briefcase along with his Bible as he traveled. Thurman was a tremendous influence on King, and especially during his doctoral studies at Boston University where Thurman was Dean of Marsh Chapel at Boston University.

4. They were later to change their name from "Colored" to "Christian Methodist Episcopal Church in 1956.

5. Quoted in my book, *Black People in the Methodist Church: Whither Thou Goest?* (Nashville, TN: Abingdon, 1984): 75.

6. I say "essentially, "because there were a few Black churches such as Union Methodist Episcopal Church in Boston, Massachusetts where I served for ten years, a few churches in New York and a few churches in the West which were not a part of the Central Jurisdiction.

7. James P. Brawley, "Methodist Church from 1939," *Central Christian Advocate* (October15, 1967): 4.

8. William B. McClain, *Come Sunday: The Liturgy of Zion* (Nashville, TN: Abingdon, 1990). See also Frederick Hilborn Talbot, *African American Worship: New Eyes for Seeing*

(Lima, OH: Fairway, 1998): 72-73 for a version of this prayer heard in the A.M.E. Church. There are many variations on this classical African American prayer with denominational and doctrinal nuances and emphases, e.g. whether it is a deacon in Baptist circles or stewards and others in Wesleyan churches.

Works Cited

Brawley, James P. "Methodist Church from 1939." *Central Christian Advocate* (October 15, 1967): 4.

Talbot, Frederick Hilborn. *African American Worship: New Eyes for Seeing*. Lima, OH: Fairway, 1998.

McClain, William B. *Black People in the Methodist Church: Whither Thou Goest?* Nashville, TN: Abingdon, 1984.

_____*Come Sunday: The Liturgy of Zion*. Nashville, TN: Abingdon, 1990.

Thurman, Howard. *Jesus and the Disinherited*. Nashville, TN: Abingdon, 1949.

Wimbush, Vincent. "The Bible and African Americans." *Stony the Road We Trod: African American Biblical Interpretation*. Cain Felder, ed. Minneapolis, MN: Fortress, 1991.

11

Black Abolitionists: Faithful Voices in Exile

By Beverly Eileen Mitchell

In my study of Black abolitionism I have been inspired by the fight of Black abolitionists not only against slavery, but also their tireless struggle for the recognition of the dignity of peoples of African descent. However, as I continue to explore the legacy of these freedom fighters, I have come to see that the lessons they taught expand farther and wider than I had originally thought. Not only have they taught me about the early fight for freedom in the context of white supremacy, but they have also taught me lessons regarding the value of education as a tool against oppression, the importance of political power in the fight for equality, and most recently, the nature of prophetic witness in the context of exile.

The Exodus has been a prominent theme in the history of African-American religion and also in current Black theological reflection. Early on African Americans identified themselves with the enslaved Hebrews, and came to believe that just as God delivered the Hebrew slaves from their Egyptian oppressors, God would also liberate them from their American captors and deliver them into a Promised Land – or at least a rightful place in America. The other notable experience of the Hebrews, later the Israelites, was their exile into Babylonian captivity. But the experience of exile is not something people readily wish to remember. Yet, the Babylonian exile is also an experience with which African-Americans could also resonate in a profound way. Instead of an exodus deliverance first, and then a painful exile, as the ancient Israelites experienced, African Americans knew the exile before any hope of divine deliverance in an exodus. The devastating journey to slavery in the New World was the Exile for those of African ancestry.

Black abolitionists have something to teach all of us about life in exile. They exercised leadership in a community engaged in the task of forging a new identity after being stamped with strange-sounding names, held captive in a hostile environment, and forced to perform back-breaking labor for no wages until their bodies gave out or they escaped on foot to a free state. Undoubtedly, they, like their enslaved brothers and sisters, struggled with the question of theodicy, but they learned in that struggle how to sing the Lord's song in exile. Even though the Atlantic Slave Trade thrust Black Africans into involuntary exile in the New World, the exiled slaves encountered the Christian gospel, embraced its liberating message, and some among them bore a fearless witness that would trouble the conscience of Christian America. African Americans and non-African Americans, Christians and non-Christians alike, can now reflect upon the witness of those freedom fighters as they transformed their experience of unjust suffering into an occasion in which God could be encountered. In turn, these freedom fighters were empowered to speak a prophetic word of judgment and justice in the name of the Lord. .

Involuntary Exile

Sometimes economic, social, and/or political realities make it necessary for groups to flee their homeland and start life anew in another place. If one is "fortunate" in such a situation, one can depart the land of one's birth voluntarily. Often, however, exile is involuntary. Certainly that was the case with Africans during the Middle Passage. There are not many written accounts of survivors of the Atlantic slave trade, but there are extant accounts of the transport of African captives from their slavers. Even these secondhand accounts from captors leave no doubt that the forced departure of African men, women, and children on slave ships to the New World was, as John Hope Franklin has put quite boldly, "a veritable nightmare."[1] Even in less egregious circumstances, abrupt departure from one's homeland to a foreign land would evoke a sense of alienation, isolation, and fragmentation. But in the case of African slaves, this pain was compounded by the *manner* of exile – a journey of horrors steeped in injustice and dehumanization.

Prior to boarding a slave ship, some captives were forced to march their way to the coast from the interior of Africa. Others were bound and taken on long rides on river canoes to meet the waiting slave ships.[2] Slavers warehoused the captives in filthy holding cells until a full cargo was ready to depart. Once aboard the slave ship, the nightmare reached even greater proportions. Male slaves were manacled and shackled together, unable to position themselves comfortably, as they lay pressed together in their own filth, hardly able to breathe.[3] The chains and shackles often cut into the flesh of their wrists and ankles, as the slaves tried to lessen their discomfort. Under heavy guard by crewmen poised at strategic locations throughout the ship to prevent escape and mutiny, the slaves were forced to live in the cargo area for weeks and months in conditions unfit even for animals.[4] Those slaves that survived disease, suicide attempts, brutality, and attempted revolts landed on the shores of the New World, where they were prepared for auction. Bereft of family, homeland, and bodily liberty, it was not entirely certain whether and for how long they would survive. It is even less conceivable that they could sing *any* god's song in this foreign land. However, progeny of the survivors of the Middle Passage did come to sing the song of the God of Abraham, Sarah, Isaac, Rebecca, Mary, and the Son of Man, Jesus.

Success in Evangelization

By the fires of revivalism during the first and second Great Awakenings, Blacks were converted to Christianity in large numbers. The form of Christianity was "experiential, revivalistic, and biblically oriented."[5] What made the evangelical Christianity of camp meetings appealing to Blacks, in contrast to the arid, catechistically-oriented Anglican missionary efforts of the Society for the Propagation of the Gospel in Foreign Parts, was that the former method of evangelization placed much emphasis on the importance of having a dramatic conversion experience. For the slaves, evangelical Christianity meant conversion of sinners, extension of church membership, and reformation of society.[6] As African Americans struggled with the incongruity of the message of the gospel of freedom and the proclamation of that same gospel by slave holders, the slaves were able to find meaning and value for their lives and maintain their confidence that the Christian God did not condone their enslavement. Despite the fact that they shared many of the same doctrines, beliefs, and rituals, whites and Blacks held fundamentally different views about God's will for Black people and about the meaning of the presence of Blacks in America.[7] Evangelized Blacks whose faith aroused resistance to slavery were disturbing prophetic witnesses. These witnesses pricked the conscience of white Americans as they rebuked not only the political hypocrisy of slavery in the land of the free, but the religious hypocrisy of a slaveholding nation shaped by the Judeo-Christian principle of the sacredness of human life made in the image of God. Black abolitionists constantly raised the specter of this double hypocrisy; thereby, troubling the waters of political and religious unity. The opposition of Black evangelicals to slavery, colonization, and the moral depravity inherent in a slavocracy lead them to pursue the end of slavery with the means available to them.[8] These freedom fighters, who embraced the Good News of Jesus Christ, operated under the unassailable conviction that faithful discipleship and an answered call to ministry necessarily included the work of abolitionism. In fact, abolitionists such as James Pennington, Henry Highland Garnet, and Samuel Ringgold Ward could not conceive of a Christian ministry that did *not* involve participation in the abolitionist movement.

Singing the Lord's Song

In *Singing the Lord's Song*, Bruce Birch explains what "singing the Lord's song" means. It involves articulating God's word in a time when our accustomed way of life is coming apart."[9] It demands confidence that the last word has not been spoken in a context of upheaval and apparent disaster.[10] Birch wrote this text in the context of affluent communities of faith in the United States in the late twentieth century. The Word of the Lord in that context calls for one kind of response. Speaking the Word of the Lord in the context of exiled Black Africans in nineteenth century America called for a different kind of response. For Black Christians who worked for abolition, the message for the Black community of that time was one of hope, rather than resignation and despair. It focused on empowerment in its mission, not constant awareness of the condition in which they had found themselves and were sent to sing.[11]

The evangelicalism that shaped Black abolitionists allowed them to "sing," not only praises to God, but also emboldened them to call for repentance. Evangelical Christianity forged an identity for the Black community, strengthened their prophets for bold witness, and perfected their praxis with a notion of servanthood. God was praised because God the Liberator was seen as faithful. Implicit trust was placed in God despite the calamity of slavery. Although the Israelites under Babylonian captivity were called to repentance for their failure to remain faithful to God in the Promised Land, African Americans did not attribute their exile and captivity to sins of their own making. They understand that in this instance, they were the sinned against. However, they also accepted their dependence upon God and sought to be pruned of anything that would hinder God's work in them. Their fight for liberty and the restoration of their dignity as full human beings was neither fueled by hatred nor by retribution. Black slaves, fugitive slaves, and freeborn Blacks who encountered the gospel message and were stirred by the fires of revival formed a new community that gave them an identity as a people of God. They clung to the knowledge that they were saved, sanctified, and filled with God's spirit. They embraced the call to challenge America to repent from slavery, abandon "negro-hate," and live up to the ideals promulgated in the founding documents of this nation. The challenge of faithful witness in the context of exile was borne in a spirit of humility, for the One that the abolitionists followed was Jesus, the ultimate Suffering Servant. In the Negro Spirituals sung in the context of slave worship, Black evangelicals did not affirm a high and mighty Christ the King, but the lowly Jesus their Friend. Their identity with the "man of sorrows, acquainted with grief," ensured that their pursuit of freedom and justice was grounded in the manner of a *theologia crucis*, not a *theologia gloriae*.

Faithfulness in Exile

As Black abolitionists fought not only for the liberation of African American slaves, but also the recognition of their dignity, they called upon the Christian church of America to repent of its captivity to an economic system of human bondage and an institutionalized ideology of white supremacy; and they gave this call for repentance in the manner of the prophets of old. In his famous *Appeal*, David Walker wrote:

> Can anything be a greater mockery of religion than the way in which it is conducted by the Americans? ... Will the Lord suffer this people to go on much longer, taking his holy name in vain? Will he not stop them, PREACHERS and

all? O Americans! Americans!! I call God – I call angels – I call men, to witness, that your DESTRUCTION is at hand, and will be speedily consummated unless you REPENT.[12]

Fellow abolitionist James Pennington saw slavery as "more hideous than ever" after his conversion. He maintained, "... I saw [slavery] now as an evil under the moral government of God – as a sin not only against man, but also against God. The great and engrossing thought with me was how shall I now employ my time and my talents so as to tell most effectively upon this system of wrong?"[13] This new way of seeing led Pennington to employ his time and talents to abolitionism *as a ministry of the gospel*.

Pennington's co-laborer in the abolitionist movement, Henry Highland Garnet, charged that the cries of the oppressed had gone unheard and that slavery had become more powerful as the Church stood by idly. He sharply criticized the Church for the false prophetic witness of "priests of the church," and the prohibition it placed upon Blacks against reading the Bible. Garnet contended that the Church's failure to heed the cry of oppression in the land amounted to a "national tragedy."[14]

Fellow preacher and abolitionist Samuel Ringgold Ward also leveled a sharp critique of the American church, as he named preachers as the most corrupt because of their leadership responsibilities. Yet Ward believed that the American church *could* be reformed if it understood clearly its choice with regard to the "Negro problem" in America:

> [The question] is neither whether some men have wisely or unwisely pleaded this cause nor whether their measures were commendable or not; nor merely, what shall be done with the Negro. It is, shall religion, pure and undefiled, prevail in the land; or shall a corrupt, spurious, human system, dishonouring to God and oppressive to man, have the prevalence?[15]

In the resolute manner of Joshua, who offered a similar choice as he stood before the Israelites ready to enter the Promised Land, Ward maintained that white Christian America could choose to worship the God of the Christian faith or another god, but a choice was required of them.

Black abolitionists like Ward, Pennington, Garnet, and Walker, working alongside white abolitionists, could have despaired at the enormity of the task of bringing an end to slavery. Fortunately, they did not. When the Civil War ended, and Reconstruction failed, the succeeding generations of Black activists could have given up. However, they did not. There were those who followed the example set by Black abolitionists who persevered in exile, long after memories of their ancestral homeland faded from consciousness. Because of their trust in the God who delivered the Hebrews out of Egypt, Black abolitionists learned to sing the Lord's song in exile, and their children's children have learned to sing that song as well.

Notes

1. John Hope Franklin, *From Slavery to Freedom: A History of Negro Americans*, 5th ed. (New York, NY: Alfred A. Knopf, 1980): 41.
2. Beverly Eileen Mitchell, *Plantations and Death Camps, Religion, Ideology, and Human Dignity* (Minneapolis, MN: Fortress Press, 2009): 24; as quoted from Vincent Harding, *There Is a River, The Black Struggle for Freedom in America* (New York, NY: Harcourt Brace, 1989): 3.
3. Mitchell, p. 25; as quoted from Marcus Rediker, *The Slave Ship, A Human History* (New York, NY: Viking, 2007): 72.
4. Mitchell, p. 25; as quoted from Vincent Harding, *There is a River*, p.11.
5. Albert J. Raboteau, "The Black Experience in American Evangelicalism, The Meaning of Slavery," *African American Religion, Interpretative Essays in History and Culture*, Timothy E. Fulop & Albert J. Raboteau, eds. (New York, NY: Routledge, 1997): 91.
6. Raboteau, "The Black Experience in American Evangelicalism, p. 91.
7. *Ibid.*, p.98.
8. *Ibid.*, p. 100.
9. Bruce C. Birch, *Isaiah 40-55: Singing the Lord's Song* (Nashville, TN: Abingdon, 1981): 25.
10. Bruce C. Birch, *What Does the Lord Require? The Old Testament Call to Social Witness* (Philadelphia, PA: Westminster, 1985): 86-87.
11. Birch, *Isaiah 40-55, Singing the Lord's Song*, p. 27.
12. *David Walker's Appeal, To the Coloured Citizens of the World, but in particular, and very expressly, to those of the United States of America* [1830]. "Introduction," by James Turner (Baltimore, MD: Black Classic, 1993): 63.
13. Beverly Eileen Mitchell, *Black Abolitionism, A Quest for Human Dignity* (Marynoll, NY: Orbis Books, 2005): 66; as quoted from James W.C. Pennington, "The Fugitive Blacksmith; or, Events in the History of James W.C. Pennington," *I Was Born a Slave: An Anthology of Classic Slave Narratives*, vol. 2, [1849-1866], Yuval Taylor, ed. (Chicago: Lawrence Hill, 1999): 139-140.
14. Beverly Eileen Mitchell, *Black Abolitionism*, p. 73; as quoted from Henry Highland Garnet, "An Address to the Slaves of the United States of America," Buffalo, New York, 1843, in "Appendix of Selected Speeches and Writings of Henry Highland Garnet," in Earl Ofari, *"Let Your Motto Be Resistance!" The Life and Thought of Henry Highland Garnet*. Boston: Beacon, 1972): 146.
15. Beverly Eileen Mitchell, *Black Abolitionism*, p. 84; as quoted from Samuel Ringgold Ward, *Autobiography of a Fugitive Negro: His Anti-Slavery Labours in the United States, Canada, and England* [1855]; reprint (Eugene, OR: Wipf and Stock, 2000): 72.

Works Cited

Birch, Bruce C. *What Does the Lord Require? The Old Testament Call to Social Witness*. Philadelphia, PA: Westminster, 1985.

_____ *Isaiah 40-55, Singing the Lord's Song*. Nashville, TN: Abingdon, 1981.

Franklin, John Hope. *From Slavery to Freedom: A History of Negro Americans*. 5th ed. New York, NY: Alfred A. Knopf, 1980.

Harding, Vincent. *There is a River: The Black Struggle for Freedom in America*. New York, NY: Harcourt Brace, 1981.

Mitchell, Beverly Eileen. *Black Abolitionism, A Quest for Human Dignity*. Marynoll, New York, NY: Orbis Books, 2005.

_____ *Plantations and Death Camps, Religion, Ideology, and Human Dignity*. Minneapolis, MN: Fortress, 2009.

Ofari, Earl. *"Let Your Motto Be Resistance!": The Life and Thought of Henry Highland Garnet*. Boston, MA: Beacon, 1972.

Pennington, James W. C. *I Was Born a Slave: An Anthology of Classic Slave Narratives*, vol. 2, [1849-1866]. Yuval Taylor, ed. Chicago, IL: Lawrence Hill, 1999.

Raboteau, Albert J. "The Black Experience in American Evangelicalism: The Meaning of Slavery," *African American Religion, Interpretative Essays in History and Culture*. Timothy E. Fulop & Albert J. Raboteau. eds. New York, NY: Routledge, 1997. pp. 90-106.

Rediker, Marcus. *The Slave Ship: A Human History*. New York, NY: Viking, 2007.

Turner, James. "Introduction," *David Walker's Appeal: To the Coloured Citizens of the World, but in Particular, and Very Expressly, to Those of the United States of America* [1830]. Baltimore, MD: Black Classic, 1993.

Ward, Samuel Ringgold. *Autobiography of a Fugitive Negro: His Antislavery Labours in the United States, Canada, and England* [1855]. reprint. Eugene, OR: Wipf and Stock, 2000.

12

Pastoral Reflections on Exile and Hope

By Mary Clark Moschella

Lost among the many better-known writings of Bruce C. Birch is a brief but telling article he wrote in 1983, "Biblical Faith and the Loss of Children."[1] In this article, Birch mines the biblical narrative for pastoral resources that can address one of the most painful experiences of emotional exile imaginable—the loss of a child. The reader soon learns that this is not a theoretical exercise for the scholar; it is instead a searching response to Bruce Birch's personal and familial experience of losing a daughter, Christine, at age three, to lymphocytic leukemia. Writing a dozen years out of the whirlwind of this life-changing loss, Birch offers some pastoral wisdom on the nature of God and the ways in which God can be engaged in the midst of such tragic losses. This wisdom is made more compelling because it is woven into the poignant story of the Birches' loss, a story generously shared with readers. In spite of the sense of utter parental sorrow that this story evokes, it is a story that moves in the direction of hope.

Exile, suffering, and loss are human experiences that none of us fully escape. Those experiencing diverse forms of exile—political, cultural, or personal—may seek solace from communities of faith. In the throes of grief, people often ask, "Where is God in this?" or, "How could God let this happen to me?" A raft of contemporary literature in pastoral theology attempts to address these questions and provide means of grace for those who mourn.[2] Authors who focus on complicated loss, miscarriage, and stillbirth help elucidate the intricacies of the particular emotional exile that accompanies the loss of children.[3] Communal and contextual approaches to pastoral theology and care remind us of the power of the laity to listen, to understand, and to bring healing and growth to persons and groups who grieve.[4] In an interesting way, Bruce Birch's article anticipates some of these recent offerings. Birch achieves this by sketching out three significant biblical emphases that he found helpful in the midst of his own experience of emotional exile in losing Christine. These three emphases or "aspects of God" are described as: God as hearer, God as life-giver, and God as sufferer.[5]

The first of the three biblical aspects of God that Birch describes is that of

"*God as hearer.*"[6] Pastoral theologians have long emphasized the importance of listening as a form of care, recognizing the need that sufferers have to cry out—to express the pain of loss and all of the accompanying emotions that may arise in the face of it. Expressing such emotions helps to externalize grief, to "get it out" rather than keep it bottled up inside. This common wisdom is aptly conveyed in a saying: "When you tell someone your troubles, you give a piece of them away." It is a relief to tell one's story of loss and grief, especially when the loss is untimely or traumatic or both, as in the case of a child's death. A good listener can help the sufferer articulate and understand the contours of this particular grief, this specific sensation of what Birch refers to as the "offense" of death.

In his description of God as hearer, Birch emphasizes God's capacity to endure human expressions of emotion, citing the Psalms of lamentation. God can handle the human outcry of sadness, anger, or despair. We can cry these emotions out to God, without fear of retaliation. God gets our grief. Perhaps the Psalmist's cry in Psalm 22, echoed by Jesus himself in Gethsemane, is the best biblical evidence for this: "My God, my God, why hast thou forsaken me?" Many pastoral counselors would concur that crying out in this way is actually a form of faithfulness, a form of staying in relationship with God even while protesting the offense of a child's death. Furthermore, the full airing of grief can give way, as it does in the Psalms, to expressions of praise, confidence, or trust that God will respond.[7] When the experience of grief can be shared and not censored, a space is opened up for the anticipation of hope and help.

What Birch adds to this pastoral wisdom, I think, is a call for the *public* expression of such pain in the context of a worshipping community. In citing the "gutsy and honest" expressions of anger and bitterness found in the Psalms, he reminds us that psalms are public songs of lament, lament that can and should be uttered aloud in the presence of the wider congregation. Worship, rather than being a polite and formulaic experience, ought to create a space where people can be open with each other, where sufferers can reveal their woundedness, so that hurts can be exposed and healing words spoken.[8] If pastoral counseling is restricted to private encounters between a pastor and individual congregants, the pain of loss is kept largely hidden from the community, and members of the community lose out on the chance to minister to one another through compassionate listening. This approach also compounds the suffering of grievers who may start to feel that their emotions are somehow wrong or shameful, and can only be taken care of behind the closed door of the pastor's study. Both those who are grieving and their communities of faith forfeit the opportunity to experience God's grace in its fullness when the expression of grief is so restricted.

In recent years, pastoral theologians have caught up with Birch's insight, emphasizing the role of the faith community in the work of pastoral care. While in the middle years of the twentieth century, pastoral ministry in the United States was often understood as an individual form of counseling that only trained and authorized clergy could offer to parishioners, this paradigm has now given way to a more communal model, wherein the members of congregations share in the work of pastoral care.[9] Indeed, the unique role of the congregation is now emphasized as crucial to the healing and support of persons through the long-term processes of grief and mourning.[10] As laypersons learn how to listen, hear, and bear expressions of pain in the faith community, greater avenues for help and healing are opened up. When people are allowed to cry out openly, the shame of suffering alone is not added to the pain of the original offense of death, especially the death of a child.

In a lovely little book on mourning, pastoral theologian Allan Cole Jr. describes five faith practices that promote good mourning. They are: church membership, worship, reading scripture, serving others, and prayer.[11] It is not surprising that all of these practices are linked to the faith community in some way. Cole is explicit about the importance of moving through the process of mourning in a context of connection to other persons of faith. While being alone is also an important part of mourning, we who mourn need to share our experiences, emotions, practical needs, and spiritual questions with fellow and sister sojourners in the life of faith. The success of support groups, both secular and religious, also bears witness to the benefits of mutual sharing. When human beings stand near to each other in their grief, they help to embody the notion of God as hearer.

The second theme that Birch lifts up from the scriptures is that of *"God as life-giver."* In the Hebrew Bible narrative of the Exodus, the people's deliverance from bondage is experienced as a gift from God. It is an unexpected new birth that comes in a dramatic moment at the sea, when death seemed the only reality. "Exodus was a sign of God's gift of life despite death, beyond death, in the midst of death. One can give praise for life as God's gift even when the life of a child is ended prematurely, as was our daughter's," Birch writes. "The three years of her life are a gift which her death cannot erase."[12] This is a stunning recognition of God as life-giver, an embrace of the blessing of this one unique life, however brief and fleeting.

Similarly, Birch lifts up the central New Testament symbol of salvation: the resurrection of Christ. He points out that the terrible aloneness of death is not denied or skipped over in the crucifixion of Jesus. The hope of resurrection for Birch is that this death is not the final word. Birch and his wife, with the help of their friends gathered in a house church in Iowa, decided to write a service of thanksgiving for Christine's life, because they did not want her death to be the final word, "obscuring all that she had been in life."[13]

Reflecting on God as life-giver through these images in both the Hebrew bible and the New Testament offers a needed word of hope to those who mourn. Cognitive approaches to healing alert us to the importance of the ways we think about our experiences. If we focus our attention solely on the death and loss of a loved one, we can obscure the very real gift of that person's life. We can also miss out on the new life that God continues to give every new day.

Given that the loss of a child is one of the most painful experiences imaginable, mourners need breaks from constant suffering. Reflecting on these biblical passages and symbols of faith in a life-giving God may help mourners see some of the goodness and beauty of life, even in the midst of death. Recalling the wonder of the one particular child who was given and whose life cannot be erased challenges the erroneous idea that death is the final word in life.

This last insight can get tricky for caregivers. If we try to cheer people up when they are grieving, through pat reminders of God's goodness, the effort will almost always fail. This might even lead grievers to feel worse, to feel unfaithful as well as bereft. However, if caregivers and friends are willing to listen to the totality of a mourner's experience, it is likely that we will hear in it both anguish and a yearning for life to go on. Sharing stories, memories, or pictures of the one who has died helps provide mourners the space in which this yearning for life and joy can find voice. New understandings of God as the giver of life and love may then dawn upon the mourner, spontaneous and unbidden. Such thoughts make way for the return of hope and the lessening of suffering.

The third and final aspect of God that Birch lifts up in his article is that of God as sufferer. This idea is found in God's words to Moses, "I have seen the affliction of my people. I have heard their cries. I know their sufferings."[14] Birch points out that the Hebrew verb translated as "know" indicates God's interaction with and experience of our human suffering.[15] A God who shares our sufferings is one who enters into the experience of loss, who weeps with us, and affirms life even in the midst of death. More evidence of God as sufferer is found in the New Testament where "the divine Self shares our ultimate aloneness in pain and death in the form of the cross."[16] Knowing that God knows our suffering, "is acquainted with grief," helps us rest assured that we ourselves are known by God, understood, and connected to God in the midst of loss and grief.

Shared suffering is a theme in theologian Serene Jones' story of attempting to offer pastoral care to a woman who had just miscarried. Out in the backyard in a driving rain, the woman, Wendy, wanted Jones to help her bury the remains of her pregnancy—"pieces of tissue, bloody, unrecognizable."[17] This they did, amidst tears and mud, while Jones tried to come up with a prayer: "Please God, receive this, our will, broken; our hope, lost; our body, ruptured; our blood, poured out; our womb, a grave."[18] Jones goes on to describe the exquisite suffering the evening entailed, for even as she tried to care for Wendy, administering soup and wine, Jones herself was recalling her own too-recent experiences of two miscarriages in the last year. The particular pain of miscarriage, for Jones, includes the utter pain of losing the child one longs for, and at the same time, experiencing one's own body becoming a grave. "This death-site was inside us, deep in us. It was in a place even unknown to our own eyes, in a cavern from which we had believed a future would spring forth but from which only loss had issued."[19]

Serene Jones tells of her own grief pouring out later that night, as she tried to wrestle with a divine mystery: "What happens in the Trinity, when, on the cross, the Son of God dies?"[20] She goes to say:

> We are told that the grief of this event is unlike any other known to us. Our ancient theologians tell us that we can't extrapolate from our experience to it, for it is part of the divine mystery; it stretches beyond human imagination. Yet what is it that we cannot imagine? The whole of Trinity, we are told, takes death into itself. Jesus doesn't die outside of God but in God, deep in the viscera of that holy tripartite union. Because the union is full, no part of God remains untouched by this death. . . . If this is true, then, yes, God becomes quite literally the site of dying. The Trinity is a grave, a dank tomb of death.[21]

Jones is struck with the recognition that the Trinity bears death inside but does not die; this God is bereft but yet alive. She reflects back on her experience of shared grief with Wendy. "And there with us," she adds, "the most blessed gift of all, the dark, miscarrying, aching Trinity that held us."[22]

Experiencing God as sufferer is a balm for us. In grief, we long to know and be known by one who is like us, one who has felt the precise kind of loss and emptiness that we ourselves feel. In the case of miscarriage, it is comforting to believe that God knows what it is like to become in Godself a grave. God knows what it is like to lose a pregnancy or a child, what it is like to be bereft, and yet to live.

Bruce Birch has helped call attention to the blessings of understanding God as hearer, God as life-giver, and God as sufferer. These biblical ideas do not take away the feeling of emotional exile that we may feel in the face of death, especially a death that is untimely or sudden or both. The offense of death remains. Yet the suffering of those who mourn can be mitigated, over time, through the support of faith communities that offer unqualified acceptance of grief. When a worshipping community can support the honest public proclamation of lament, and hold the bereaved in the safety of a shared sacred space, a healing process begins. When the great symbols of Christian faith, such as Exodus and resurrection and Trinity are made available in stories, hymns, and artwork, and through theological reflection, they become resources that people can draw upon during times of loss or crisis. When these symbols reveal a God who suffers with us and yet lives, a path through exile to hope opens up. The death of a child is not forgotten, but it is not allowed to obscure the gift of life, either.

Finally, we all have to face the tragedy of death—our own and those of people we love. Birch's searching reflection remains a helpful resource, a story that touches us and reminds us of many similar stories. This piece is only one among many enduring scholarly gifts that Bruce C. Birch has given to the wider church. We are grateful for this little article that tells a poignant first person story of exile, leans into the scriptures, and illuminates a path toward hope.

Notes

1. Bruce C. Birch, "Biblical Faith and the Loss of Children," *The Christian Century* (October 26, 1983): 965-7.

2. For example, see Allan Hugh Cole Jr., *Good Mourning: Getting Through Your Grief* (Louisville, KY: Westminster John Knox, 2008); Kenneth R. Mitchell and Herbert Anderson, *All Our Losses, All Our Griefs: Resources for Pastoral Care* (Louisville, KY: Westminster John Knox, 1983).

3. See Nadine Pence Frantz and Mary Stimming, eds. *Hope Deferred: Heart-Healing Reflections on Reproductive Loss* (Cleveland, OH: Pilgrim, 2005); Roslyn A. Karaban, *Complicated Losses, Difficult Deaths: A Practical Guide for Ministering to Grievers* (San Jose, CA: Resource Publications, 2000).

4. See Leonard M. Hummel, *Clothed in Nothingness: Consolation for Suffering* (Minneapolis, MN: Augsburg Fortress, 2003): 113–122; Earl E. Shelp and Ronald H. Sunderland, *Sustaining Presence: A Model of Caring by People of Faith* (Nashville, TN: Abingdon, 2000); and Ronald H. Sunderland, *Getting Through Grief: Caregiving by Congregations* (Nashville, TN: Abingdon, 1993).

5. Birch, *Biblical Faith*, 966–7.

6. *Ibid.*, 966.

7. For more reflections on this issue, see Denise Dombkowski Hopkins, *Journey Through the Psalms*, (St. Louis, MO: Chalice, 2002): 105-126.

8. *Ibid.*

9. Nancy J. Ramsay, ed. *Pastoral Care and Counseling: Redefining the Paradigms* (Nashville, TN: Abingdon, 2004).

10. Sunderland, *Getting Through Grief*, 114-115.

11. Cole Jr., *Good Mourning*, 74–92.

12. Birch, *Biblical Faith*, 966-7.

13. *Ibid.*, 967.

14. Exodus 3:17.

15. Birch, *Biblical Faith*, 967.

16. *Ibid.*

17. Serene Jones, "Rupture," *Hope Deferred: Heart-Healing Reflections on Reproductive Loss*, Eds. Nadine Pence Frantz and Mary T. Stimming (Cleveland, OH: Pilgrim, 2005): 48.

18. *Ibid.*

19. *Ibid.*, 53.

20. *Ibid.*, 61.

21. *Ibid.*, 62.

22. *Ibid.*, 65.

Works Cited

Birch, Bruce C. "Biblical Faith and the Loss of Children," *The Christian Century* (October 26, 1983): 965-7.

Cole, Allan Hugh Jr. *Good Mourning: Getting Through Your Grief*. Louisville, KY: Westminster/John Knox, 2008.

Frantz, Nadine Pence, and Mary Stimming, eds. *Hope Deferred: Heart-Healing Reflections on Reproductive Loss*. Cleveland, OH: Pilgrim, 2005.

Hopkins, Denise Dombkowski. *Journey Through the Psalms*. St. Louis, MO: Chalice, 2002.

Hummel, Leonard M. *Clothed in Nothingness: Consolation for Suffering*. Minneapolis, MN: Augsburg/Fortress, 2003.

Karaban, Roslyn A. *Complicated Losses, Difficult Deaths: A Practical Guide for Ministering to Grievers*. San Jose, CA: Resource Publications, 2000.

Mitchell, Kenneth R. and Herbert Anderson, *All Our Losses, All Our Griefs: Resources for Pastoral Care*. Louisville, KY: Westminster/John Knox, 1983.

Ramsay, Nancy J., ed. *Pastoral Care and Counseling: Redefining the Paradigms*. Nashville, TN: Abingdon, 2004.

Shelp, Earl E., and Ronald H. Sunderland. *Sustaining Presence: A Model of Caring by People of Faith*. Nashville, TN: Abingdon, 2000.

Sunderland, Ronald H. *Getting Through Grief: Caregiving by Congregations*. Nashville, TN: Abingdon, 1993.

13

"How Can We Sing the Lord's Song in a Foreign Land?" Narrative Collapse in Small Churches

By Lewis A. Parks

Although three out of four congregations in America have less than 100 in weekly worship, the public status of these congregations is less than enviable. They are the scapegoat for the decline in mainline denomination membership numbers. Church growth consultants find them ornery; conflict mediators find them cantankerous. They are the object of nostalgia by a generation that finds no compelling contemporary use for them. They are scolded for having empty cupboards when the all important Seeker comes bearing 24/7 needs. Their everyday-ness bores academic theologians.

Small churches internalize this barrage of criticism. How could they not? The most telling symptom of the pressure on small churches today is that many of them have become existential by default; that is, they live totally immersed in the presence of immediate concerns such as paying the oil bill, securing some minimum form of pastoral leadership, and staying open for one more year. There has been a loss of institutional memory, a shrinking of corporate confidence, and a diminished capacity to plan into the future.

I use the term "narrative collapse" to name what is going on in small churches today. It is a term heard wherever narrative has become the core template for ordering experience in disciplines as diverse as epistemology, history, ethnography, feminist studies, medicine, therapy, biblical studies, spirituality, and congregational studies. Narrative collapse can be described variously as: (1) a condition where a person or group is overtaken by experiences that are not "storyable," that do not make sense in terms of their existing narrative resources; (2) a condition where a person or group experiences a severe blow to the essential everyday confidence that things have a way of working out and that the text of one's life is intact; and (3) a condition where a person or group is under the spell of a domineering power's story about them instead of being the authors of their own story.

Psalm 137 takes us into the throes of a narrative collapse, the People of God in Exile. It was written during the Exile (587-539 BCE) or shortly after the return to Judah. The pain is still raw. The voice is the voice of a wounded corporate personality, now first person plural (we wept, we remembered, we hung our harps), now first person singular (if I forget, if I do not remember, if I do not see). There is a consensus among scholars that this psalm of lament falls into three divisions. Verses 1-4 convey the grief of a people plucked out of their homeland, verses 5-6 lift up the act of remembering as a practice of resistance, and verses 7-9 confess a rage and channel a desire for revenge on the captors.[1]

Grief, memory, rage – this is not the emotional environment most of us associate with the typical small community of faith. I do not claim that most small churches have experienced the extremes of deprivation that the original subjects of Psalm 137 suffered, or even that small churches are in the same league of agony as many of the corporate exiles who have taken solace in this psalm through the centuries. But I would argue that there are repressed truths about life in small churches and one of the most important of these is the condition of narrative collapse. Psalm 137 can help to bring the truth of narrative collapse to consciousness as well as point a way forward. Leaders of worship in small churches like the Levite musicians who likely wrote this psalm are in the best position for translating this new information into practices for transformation in small churches.

Grief

> By the rivers of Babylon—
> there we sat down and there we wept
> when we remembered Zion.
>
> On the willows there
> We hung up our harps.
>
> For there our captors
> Asked us for songs,
> And our tormentors asked for mirth, saying,
> "Sing us one of the songs of Zion"
>
> How could we sing the Lord's song
> in a foreign land?[2]

You don't have to look very hard to see the signs of a dislocated people in many contemporary small churches. On the macro level it begins with a dissonance between geographic location and population shifts. At one point small churches were at the center of their communities, doubling as schoolhouses when needed, hosting meetings of township supervisors and Boy Scouts, tolling the steeple bell to mark the rhythms of the week or honor the passing of a community figure. But the bell is silent now and its contribution is forgotten. The bell's weight contributed to the deterioration of the steeple which had to be dismantled to the level of the roofline and capped off in a makeshift manner, as if to serve as a conspicuous warning sign against hubris posted at the base of the fallen Tower of Babel.

If located in a city the small church may be hemmed in by busy streets, public spaces, and buildings where people work or shop but do not live. If located in small towns it may find itself surrounded by older homes converted to low rent apartments, fast food restaurants, and gas stations. If located in a rural setting it may find itself suddenly surrounded by a commuter development where the average house has more square feet of usable space and two times the economic value of the church building it dwarfs.

As you zoom in closer to many small churches the suspicion grows of being in a time warp. There are obvious hindrances to hospitality: lack of directional signs, scarce parking, steep steps, narrow doors, poor lighting, and make-do restrooms. There is the 1950s décor: speckled carpet, faded cantaloupe walls on which hangs Warner Sallman's *Head of Christ*, and 110 amp receptacles hard to find. And not to be forgotten, there is the ever present clutter of donated bric-a-brac: home organs, discarded pulpits, replaced pews, and over-sized family Bibles. No clean lines and minimalist décor of the shopping mall here, no sports stadium bells and whistles, and no plush seats with cup holders of movie theatres.

If an anthropologist were to observe the people who congregate in these small churches, that anthropologist would notice several distinctions from public gatherings elsewhere: the disproportionate number of older persons, the reluctance to segregate the children and teenagers, the generous flow of laughter and tears, the easy mix of small talk and intimate sharing, the quick and complete surrender to favorite hymns.

And always, always, if the anthropologist is attentive, there is the self-deprecation, telltale remarks that this particular expression of the gathered People of God has been tested and found wanting. People in small churches regularly apologize for an imagined sin of omission, the failure to become what their critics said they should. They have internalized demeaning stories foisted on them by domineering powers.

So here they are out of place, out of date, and out of sync, small churches surrounded by the modern world with its symbols of status and power, exiles in Babylon. Congregations remember their brighter days just as the People of God remembered their home in Judah. "The geographical strangeness of the land, with its systems of canals between the Tigris and the Euphrates – the "rivers of Babylon"—may have exacerbated the grief when Jerusalem was remembered."[3] And then the captors add insult to injury; they command the exiled People of God to put on a happy face, get out their musical instruments, and entertain their captors with some indigenous music –a favorite sport of colonial powers, sadism with subtlety.

For some time it has been apparent to me what "singing for our captors" means for small churches. It means: embody the nostalgia projected upon them by those who have dismissed their contemporary religious significance. Be for them the "little brown church in the vale."⁴ Elicit their childhood memories. Be the October picture on their calendars. Fill them full of warm, fuzzy sentiment so they are immune to encounters with the Holy One.

"Sing us one of the songs of Zion," the captors demand. But something stirs inside the exiles. They do not stand to gather their harps hanging on the willows. They do not lift their eyes to assemble or clear their throats to sing. The captors sense it is time to back down and they do. There is self-evident power in such acts of quiet defiance. Imagine a leader of a small church interrupting the dismissive caricature of a critic: "you really have no idea what goes on here, do you?"

Memory

> If I forget you, O Jerusalem,
> Let my hand wither!
>
> Let my tongue cling to the roof of my mouth,
> If I do not remember you,
> If I do not set Jerusalem above my highest joy.

The heart of Psalm 137 is found in these middle verses. "As painful as it is for the people to remember Jerusalem (v. 1), it would be more painful for them not to remember, for these memories offer hope, indeed life, amid the pain (vv. 1-4) and devastation of exile (vv. 7-9)."⁵ The only chance the exiled People of God will have to play their harps or sing their songs again is if they actively remember Jerusalem.

In the language of narrative analysis there are *counter stories* to the official stories told about one by the domineering powers. They lie within the personal and collective memories of victims, a wellspring of "disqualified knowledge" (Michael Foucault)⁶ waiting to nourish acts of protest, reframing, and transformation.

Leaders of small churches who want to see transformation in their congregations could not take a better first step than to begin an intentional search for those counter stories. Although much is made of small churches living in the past, clinging to their history, and hiding behind mantras against change, the truth is there has been a narrative collapse in most small churches. No one is trying to recover "what really happened" in *either* a classical or deconstructionist voice. No one is trying to reconstruct a credible account of religious vitality. No one is pressing to get behind the constricted version of small church history as a chronicle of pastoral leadership, the evolution of property, or a collection of unrelated but endearing anecdotes.

Leaders in small churches will not stop with the benign anniversary booklet edition of their history, but will gather oral history from long term members and former pastors. They will sift through church documents: minutes, deeds, attendance books, worship bulletins. They will read the architecture and interpret the artifacts of the building. They will reconstruct a timeline of the congregation's story in the context of larger developments in nature, society, and the church universal. Their passion is to remember the past more faithfully than they have remembered it recently under the influence of their critics. They are searching for the counter stories that favor a more open ended future. Let me point to five species of those counter stories.[7]

Counter stories of origin

In the official version of the congregation's origin, the one offered by the denomination, the congregation's existence is typically described as a "creation out of nothing." A village of secular recipients is suddenly blessed by the appearance of some heroic circuit rider on horseback who will bring the word that gives birth to faith. But there are stories of organized house churches and other expressions of indigenous corporate faith that predate the circuit rider's appearance and sustain the nascent congregation over the weeks or months until the circuit rider returns.

Counter stories of family character

Judicatory administrators who would like to close small churches and frustrated pastors who would like to get away from them employ a favorite label; they will say that a given church has become nothing but a Family Chapel. Images of clan censorship and dysfunctional family scripts fly to the surface; end of discussion. But there are stories where persons from dominant families of a congregation clearly understand that their faith may call them to order their loves differently. And there are other stories that hint at a quiet evolution from various distortions of clan or biological family to the life-giving generosity of a surrogate family of faith.

Counter stories of community connection

The story of devolution is well established: small churches which were once central to the populations they served have been left behind by those populations. Their disappointment at the dislocation eventually gives way to defensiveness. Their confident interface with the community at large is replaced by self-absorption. The organism is cutting itself off from the environment that might have sustained it. But this story is forty per cent fact and sixty percent projection. There are counter stories that show that a congregation's efforts to insinuate itself into the life of the community at large is as much a matter of personal connections and inspired leadership as it is a matter of the location of the building.

Counter stories of creativity

For small churches under a more connectional rather than congregational type of governance, there has been a steady erosion of local control over the last century as the denominations to which they belong have developed large centralized bureaucracies. These bureaucracies have standardized everything from the official logo to the credentialing of clergy. They have capitalized on group rates, and regulated local fairness toward underrepresented groups. Since small churches are least likely to have the voice or clout to talk back in this setting, they may settle into a resigned passivity. Even when judicatories want to give them more autonomy, as many today do, they do not respond. All the more reason for the leaders of those small churches to bring to memory their own stories of bold decisions, of extraordinary labor, and of members staking personal assets to rekindle the native entrepreneurial spirit.

Counter stories of growth

The prevailing official story is that small churches have quit growing. They no longer receive new members by birth (since they have no members of a child-bearing age), by transfer (since no one would leave a full-service church to attend them), or by confession of faith (since a receptive population has moved elsewhere). Small churches cherish an equally unhelpful story about themselves. They explain their growth in the past by the success of "good, old fashioned" revival services that they wish could be brought back. Behind the stereotyping from above and the nostalgia from below there are stories of local church growth that really do help. Like the ones that reveal a sequence of belonging, behaving, and believing rather than the reverse.[8] Like the ones that come about because of organic rather than forced sharing of faith. And like the stories where the corporate congregation adopts a person in a vulnerable condition.[9]

"If I forget you, O Jerusalem" – but the psalmist does not forget. And in that tenacious clinging to distant but real things a space is created for alternatives to the passivity of resignation.

Rage

Remember, O Lord, against the Edomites
The day of Jerusalem's fall,
How they said, "Tear it down! Tear it down!
Down to its foundations!"
O daughter Babylon, you devastator!
Happy shall they be who pay you back
What you have done to us!

Happy shall they be who take your little ones
And dash them against the rock!

It would be convenient to stop at verse six as do some of the renderings of Psalm 137 in the Psalters used in liturgy. Contemporary exegetes struggle with verses 7 through 9, and while repelled by the image of dashing children to the rocks, they generally try to rescue two values from the ashes.

The first is a discipline of self-awareness: the recognition that the anger of the victim must find expression. It is a necessary component of grief and a healthy form of objectifying rather than internalizing oppression. The second is a discipline of self-control: the practice of submitting such anger to a higher authority. "... [T]here is no evidence that the psalmist did act out the expressed desire for revenge. Rather the psalmist expresses these feelings to God in prayer (v. 7) and apparently leaves them with God. Thus the cycle of violence is broken by the psalmist's honesty with God...."[10]

Leaders of small churches need both disciplines. They need a spark of righteous indignation, a gritty claim of the worth of the small church as seen by God rather than by its critics, detractors, and cultured despisers. A little more anger and a little less psychic numbing is the first step to any transformation in many small churches today. But this discipline of self-awareness must be joined to a discipline of self-control. The anger should not be wasted on household feuds or rudeness toward visiting judicatory leaders. It should be surrendered to God—"be angry but do not sin" (Eph 4:26)—and channeled toward specific action plans for transformation. Success is the best revenge and gives rise to the songs of mirth like the ones the tormentors could demand but not extract (137:3).

Notes

1. J. Clinton McCann, "The Book of Psalms," *The New Interpreter's Bible*, vol. 4. Leander E. Keck, et al., eds. (Nashville, TN: Abingdon, 1996): 1227.

2. *New Revised Standard Version of the Bible*, copyright 1989, by the Division of Christian Education of the National Council of the Churches of Christ in the United States of America.

3. McCann, 1227.

4. From William S. Pitts, "The Church in the Wildwood" (1864).

5. McCann, 1228.

6. Michael White and David Epstein explore the potential of Foucault's analysis of knowledge and power for the healing of individuals in their book, *Narrative Means to Therapeutic Ends* (New York, NY: W. W. Norton, 1990). In this essay I am trying to show its relevance to the corporate confidence of small churches.

7. The specific counter stories that gave rise to the generic examples in the paragraphs that follow may be found in an unbound collection of several hundred congregational stories written and collected as part of the Small Church Project of the Making Connections Initiative sponsored by a grant from the Lilly Foundation, Wesley Theological Seminary, 2006-2008.

8. It is a helpful distinction emphasized by Robert E. Webber among others. See *Ancient-Future Evangelism: Making Your Church a Faith-Forming Community* (Grand Rapids, MI: Baker, 2003): 55-87. This distinction is validated in recent attempts to uncover the social and group dynamics of the house churches which were the dominant form of church for the first three centuries. See Joseph H. Hellerman, *The Ancient Church as Family* (Minneapolis, MN: Fortress, 2004): 216-225.

9. Carl S. Dudley introduced the metaphor of adoption to explain growth in small churches. See *Effective Small Churches in the Twenty-first Century*. (Nashville, TN: Abingdon, 1978, 2003): 60-65. For contemporary accounts of such a formation process with its character of an adoption and its sequence of belonging, behaving, and believing see Anne Lamott, *Traveling Mercies: Some Thoughts on Faith* (New York, NY: Pantheon Books, 1999): 46-55; Richard Lischer, *Open Secrets: A Memory of Faith and Discovery* (New York, NY: Doubleday, 2001): 212-216; and Heidi B. Neumark, *Breathing Space: A*

Spiritual Journey in the South Bronx (Boston, MA: Beacon, 2003): 47-48.
  10. McCann, 1228.

Works Cited

Dudley, Carl S. *Effective Small Churches in the Twenty-first Century*. Nashville, TN: Abingdon, 1978, 2003.

Hellerman, Joseph H. *The Ancient Church as Family*. Minneapolis, MN: Fortress, 2004.

Lamott, Anne. *Traveling Mercies: Some Thoughts on Faith*. New York, NY: Pantheon, 99.

Lischer, Richard. *Open Secrets: A Memory of Faith and Discovery*. New York, NY: Doubleday, 2001.

McCann, J. Clinton. "The Book of Psalms," *The New Interpreter's Bible, vol. 4*, Leander E. Keck, et al., eds. Nashville, TN: Abingdon,1996.

Neumark, Heidi B. *Breathing Space: A Spiritual Journey in the South Bronx*. Boston, MA: Beacon, 2003.

Webber, Robert E. *Ancient-Future Evangelism: Making Your Church a Faith-Forming unity*. Grand Rapids, MI: Baker, 2003.

White, Michael, and David Epstein. *Narrative Means to Therapeutic Ends*. New York, NY: W. W. Norton, 1990.

14

The Gospel for an Uprooted People: Perspectives on the Fourth Gospel

By Sharon H. Ringe

All of the communities whose deepest beliefs and longings came to expression in the New Testament lived under the canopy of the Roman Empire. Some perceived that canopy as a sheltering tent that allowed them to thrive and grow. Others experienced it as a reason to be afraid for their well-being or even for their lives. Between those extremes, the New Testament documents reflect a continuum of ways of negotiating life under Roman rule, depending on local circumstances and the theological traditions on which they relied. For all of these communities, the Jesus-tradition—the gospel—was refracted through their reality. It had to be "good news" in the specificities of their lives, or it would not be good news at all.

The Synoptic Gospels give us a lens into Jesus' ministry (albeit with the filters of the lives of their communities and the traditions that fed into them), and we see what seems to have been Jesus' effort to proclaim by word and deed God's "empire" (*basileia*) as a counterpoint to the economic, social, and political suffering in early first century Palestine under the Roman *basileia*. The Fourth Gospel tells the Jesus story, but more fully shaped by the community's life and theological reflection. That is not to say that we see nothing of Jesus' own story in the narratives, the chronology and geography, and even the teachings recorded there, but the foreground is the "so what?" question: How does this story touch and impact our lives?

The differences between the Fourth Gospel and the Synoptics are so dramatic that they suggest a different "family tree" connecting that Gospel to the time of Jesus. The Gospel itself claims the unnamed "disciple whom Jesus loved" as its source of authority. Scholarship is rich with arguments in favor of that being either a model or ideal disciple or one or another of the named followers of Jesus, including John of Zebedee, who actually has little more than a bit-part in the Gospel narrative. Within the Gospel itself, though, three persons are said especially to be loved by Jesus, and those three are the family from Bethany:

Mary, Martha, and Lazarus (11:5). Without arguing for one or another of those as the Beloved Disciple whose memories form the bedrock of this Gospel, the aggregate suggests that the Gospel has come from a community whose connection to Jesus goes back to the earlier community of his followers based in the Jerusalem suburb of Bethany. The heirs of that community, if they were still in the area as tensions built up and erupted into the Roman Jewish War of 66-70 C.E., would certainly have been among the many driven from the Jerusalem area in its wake, whether by direct expulsion or because of the general social and economic collapse the war provoked.

Where they ended up is also up for debate. Several details in the Gospel suggest that we are dealing with a community whose core was Jewish. First, Jewish festivals serve as a temporal framework for the events of Jesus' public ministry, and those events reinterpret the traditional festivals. That would make sense only if people were familiar with the festivals and if that way of marking time were important to them. Like expatriates from the U.S. on the fourth Thursday of November who suddenly crave turkey and the singing of "We Gather Together to Ask the Lord's Blessing," members of the Johannine community compelled to live far from their place of origin would have treasured the affirmation of the calendar they knew and loved, integrated now with the new core identity story they claimed. Second, the fact that separation from the synagogue community would appear as a threat (9:22; 12:42; 16:2) means that being part of the congregation was important to them. While that would not have been the case for all Jews, the synagogue came to be especially important for Diaspora groups for whom interpreting Torah in their new situations was essential to their life as Jews. Third, the vocabulary of the Gospel is clearly Greek (and in fact several puns crucial to the story like *semeion*, which is "sign" and "pole" or "standard" in the Greek translation of Num. 21:8-9, and *an•then*, which can mean either "again" or "from above" [3:3, 7], work only in Greek), but the grammar and sentence structure is Semitic. This hybridity suggests a community with roots in that language context, and likely with continued exposure to it as well as to the Greek of the surrounding culture. (Think, for a modern example, of the "Spanglish" that has evolved in the Hispanic communities of North America.) Taken together, such details point to a location of John's community in a city of the Diaspora with a sizeable Jewish population, such as Ephesus or Alexandria.

The Fourth Gospel tells us little about the economic status of the community. Surely as "uprooted people" (to use a term that avoids the legal distinctions among such categories as "exiles," "refugees," "asylum seekers," or "internal refugees") they were not among the economic elites. Missing from this Gospel is the Synoptics' emphasis on "the poor," though the narrative does include people who are ill, people with disabilities, and other marginalized groups. We get the sense that the struggles and pains of the community come from directions other than the abject poverty and destitution conjured up by pictures of refugee camps in modern sub-Saharan Africa. Think rather of the eastern European

Jewish *shtetls* of the Lower East Side of New York City. People lived close together to be surrounded by a familiar language and culture (and of ways to meet religious requirements, such as kosher markets)—a place of comfort in a strange land.

Given the importance of internal cohesion in such immigrant communities, one can only imagine the pain generated by tension and divisions within them. It is clear that some such thing is happening for John's community, though the exact nature of the tension is less clear. Two clues to the tension are the expressed caution about expulsion from the synagogue (mentioned above) and the often hostile references to "the Jews" (*hoi Ioudaioi*)—clearly a sub-group of the religio-ethnic group usually meant in modern usage of this term—who struck fear into the hearts of the Johannine community and, in the narrative of the Gospel, into the heart of Jesus as well (see, for example, 7:1-13).

Throughout the second half of the twentieth century, the consensus among scholars was that some formal decree expelling Christians from the synagogue had been promulgated, probably by the Council at Javneh, using the prayer called the Eighteen Benedictions (especially the twelfth, which invoked a curse on "heretics" that emphasized the "followers of the Nazarene"). That consensus was modified with the recognition that there was not a sufficiently coherent structure of Judaism in the final third of the first century to have allowed for any such system-wide decrees to be recognized. Many scholars settled instead for the assumption of a local policy that may have been particular to John's community. An equally, if not more likely possibility, is that it was the Johannine community that initiated the tension when the larger community declined to follow them in their devotion to Jesus and to the healing, transformative power that they experienced when they gathered around those memories and experienced Jesus' presence. When the larger synagogue congregation could not follow them in their devotion to Jesus, they *felt* rejected, which in time would have escalated into feeling they had been forced out. They then set about rereading their religious traditions to demonstrate that they were indeed the ones who were being faithful to those traditions, and not the synagogue. The report in 11:31 of a pastoral call by "the Jews" on Mary and Martha at the time of their brother's death supports the suggestion that if we could get the synagogue leaders' version of what happened, expulsion of the Christians would not be in the picture. Eventually it would be, of course, as recriminations and hostilities moved in both directions between the increasingly separate church and synagogue, but that would be part of subsequent history.

What, then, were the issues and concerns of daily life and of the faith journey of such a doubly-uprooted community to which the Gospel would need to respond? And how did the Fourth Gospel accomplish that task, such that it could be recognized as "good news"? The two dimensions of their uprootedness need to be looked at separately—first, what seems to address the physical and cultural dislocation, and second, what additional issues come into play with the tensions between this subgroup and the surrounding Jewish community, and how are they countered by the good news of John.

Though all of the New Testament was written in *koine* or "common" Greek more at home in the market place than in formal literature or academic writing, this Gospel goes a step further with its hybrid language that reflects the bi-cultural situation of the community. The fluidity with which the Greek of their Diaspora context and the rhythms of their Semitic roots are interwoven would reflect daily practice, as some in the household faced outward and interacted with Gentile neighbors, but then return to those—principally the women and children—whose world was more limited.

A similar blend can be seen in the attention to geographical details of the community's place of origin (like the Sheep Gate Pool in Jerusalem, for example) on the one hand, and the centrality of Wisdom traditions in the Christology of this Gospel on the other. The first of these characteristics served to evoke precious memories of a place and a home now lost, and the second reaches into the immediate religious surroundings for themes, values, and tropes that they would have come to know in their new home. While Wisdom literature goes deep into the traditions of the Hebrew Bible, it appears to have flourished especially during the Second Temple period, when issues of identity and lifestyle essential to Judaism were increasingly negotiated in Diaspora contexts.[1]

In those contexts the public economic, social, political, and religious institutions of Jewish society no longer functioned, and the center of life shifted to the household, which was the sphere in which women held the greatest influence and power. The image of God functioning as a female presence (Ms. Wisdom—*sofia* is a grammatically feminine word) both made sense in people's experience of how life was managed and drew on philosophical traditions and religious expressions (stories of various goddesses) shared by the surrounding societies. At the same time, such overtures of enculturation evoked concern from religious leaders, who emphasized the integration of Wisdom with the traditional language and theology of Jewish monotheism. The *logos* hymn of John 1:1-18 echoes hymns to Wisdom in Proverbs and the Wisdom of Solomon (among others), and follows Philo's lead in referring not to Wisdom but the Word (*logos* a grammatically masculine word in Greek, and therefore easier to connect to the man Jesus) to affirm the divine power that "became flesh" in him.

While such details of language and philosophical and cultural images and references were ways this Gospel addressed the physical uprootedness of the Johannine community, the more difficult task remains to see how the Gospel met the needs generated by the second level of dislocation, namely their tension with their Jewish neighbors. Using such techniques as keying the events of the narrative of Jesus' public ministry to the traditional Jewish festivals would have helped the community find language to affirm their faith catalyzed by Jesus as a coherent expression of the religion of Judaism. Still, however, both social and theological challenges would have remained.

The community's feelings of exclusion from the synagogue congregation would have torn the fabric of the whole *shtetl*, not just of the worshipping congregation. Neighbor would have drawn away from neighbor, and even families would have been divided over their view of Jesus, but more dramatically over the loyalties it entailed. Once again, the author drew on a trope and set of traditions from the surrounding culture to address the need for reliable supporters to accompany the members in times of danger and loneliness.[2]

Motifs of friendship developed especially in chap. 15 came to satisfy that need, with the affirmation that "No one has greater love than this, to lay down one's life for ones friends" (15:13). Jesus' sacrificial death clearly has shaped the translation of the Greek verb *tithēmi* as "lay down." The verb is broader in meaning, however, from the root-meaning of "put" or "place," and encompassing the meaning "appoint" as well, as the verb is translated in 15:16. The point is not to glorify martyrdom, but rather to speak of the commitment and solidarity shared by friends that no hardship or threat can dislodge. Where families and inherited communities are strained, friendship as a commandment and guiding rule for the community can see folks through the crises that come.

The way the Fourth Gospel speaks of the Holy Spirit addresses the same threat of isolation and loneliness in the community's doubly-uprooted context. The Spirit in John is identified by two terms that fit with the somber judicial tone of "witness" and "testimony" that characterize this Gospel from the beginning (see for example 1:6-7, 19-23; 3:11; 4:39, etc., as well as 15:26-27). The first of these terms is the "Spirit of truth" and the second the "Paraclete" (*paraklētos*) or "Advocate." The first of these terms links the Spirit and Jesus, who identifies himself as the truth (14:6), and now continues in the witness of the community. The latter term has always challenged translators. In English, it has been read as "Comforter" (KJV), "Helper" (NKJV), "Counselor" (RSV, NIV, New Living Bible), "Advocate" (NRSV), or simply transliterated as "Paraclete" (NJB). Other modern Western languages show a similar range of choices. The Greek word is made up of the participial form of the verb "to call" and the preposition "beside," and thus means one who has been summoned or called to the side of another—literally, an "advocate," or, by extension, a helper or legal representative in a trial or other arena of judgment. It too links Jesus and the Spirit, for this Spirit will be sent in Jesus' "name" (14:25) and on his behalf (15:26). The Spirit is also called "another Advocate" (14:16), implying that Jesus himself has held that role in the community while he has been with them. The same accompaniment that sustained the community of Jesus' followers will be theirs as well in the scary post-resurrection time of Jesus' physical absence. Just as the Word became flesh in Jesus as the first Advocate, so now the "other Advocate" also takes on flesh in the lives of the other believers who live out their friendship with one another as they put their lives on the line, even to the death if need be.

Finally, if the Johannine community was experiencing itself uprooted from the synagogue congregation, which was the way they knew themselves to be part of the people of God, then most likely their biggest fear was that if they were separated from the synagogue, they would also be separated from God. How could that connection be sustained without inclusion in the physical expression of God's people? They found the solution to that problem also in the traditions about Jesus' own unbreakable connection to God (10:38; 14:10-12). In the farewell discourse on the night of Jesus' arrest, that connection is extended to include Jesus' followers and their descendants in the community (17:21). The "knot" of mutual in-dwelling—of Jesus in God, of God in Jesus, of Jesus in the believers, and of them in one another—can only grow tighter when one attempts to pull it apart. Uprooted though they be, they will be safe, and that is good news indeed.

Concluding Reflections

I have concluded this essay while listening to the news of the people of New Orleans fleeing hurricane Gustav, which is threatening their city again, just three years after the devastation wrought by Katrina. The front page of today's *Washington Post* (September 1, 2008) also carried news of refugees fleeing floods in India and the aftermath of an earthquake in China's Szechwan province. Farther back in the paper was a report on the continuing tragedy of exile and death for thousands in Darfur. Under the guise of a discussion of the current economy were hidden the stories of families dislocated by plant closings and malfunctions of the global systems of food-distribution. The reality of uprootedness in all of its forms is a fact of life in the twenty first century, as it was in the first. Bruce Birch has always supported my own bent to follow Karl Barth's instruction to read with the Bible in one hand and the newspaper in the other as I have been today, so it seems to me especially appropriate that this study of the Fourth Gospel as directed to an uprooted people should be offered in thanksgiving to Bruce for years of mentoring, friendship, and teaching. May God bless!

Notes

1. For a discussion of these roots of the Wisdom traditions, see Sharon H. Ringe, *Wisdom's Friends: Community and Christology in the Fourth Gospel* (Louisville, KY: Westminster John Knox, 1999): 29-45.

2. For a discussion of biblical and Hellenistic example of friendship traditions, see Ringe, pp. 64-74.

For Further Reading

Carter, Warren. *John and Empire: Initial Explorations.* London, ENG: T & T Clark, 2008.
_____, *John: Storyteller, Interpreter, Evangelist.* Peabody, MA: Hendrickson, 2006.
_____, *The Roman Empire and the New Testament: An Essential Guide.* Nashville, TN: Abingdon, 2006).
Dube, Musa W., and Jeffrey Staley, eds. *John and Postcolonialism: Travel, Space, and Power.* Bible and Postcolonialism,7. London, ENG: Continuum, 2007.
Levine, Amy-Jill, and Marianne Blickenstaff, eds. *A Feminist Companion to John,* vols. 1 & 2. Cleveland, OH: Pilgrim, 2003.
Lozada, Francisco, and Tom Thatcher, eds. *New Currents Through John: A Global*

Perspective. Atlanta, GA: Society of Biblical Literature, 2006.

O'Day, Gail R. "The Gospel of John: Introduction, Commentary, and Reflections." *The New Interpreter's Bible*, vol. 9. Nashville, TN: Abingdon, 1995.

Reinhartz, Adele, ed. *God the Father in the Gospel of John*. Atlanta, GA: Society of Biblical Literature, 1999.

Ringe, Sharon H. *Wisdom's Friends: Community and Christology in the Fourth Gospel*. Louisville, KY: Westminster John Knox, 1999.

15

Art in Theology-Land
by Deborah Sokolove

The visual arts have been in exile from the majority of Western churches for nearly half a millennium. In the early years of the Reformation, statues were beheaded, stained glass windows smashed, and church walls whitewashed of any trace of art. While not all of the Reformers were iconoclasts, the insistence that faith comes by hearing made the visions of painters and sculptors suspect. In the sixteenth century, no longer in demand for images of Jesus and the saints to place above altars and in side-chapels, artists in Protestant countries began to find both their subject matter and their patrons outside the church. By the late nineteenth century, even Roman Catholic churches rarely commissioned new art, instead buying mass-produced plaster copies of pseudo-Baroque statuary.

In the five hundred years since Martin Luther nailed his 95 theses on the door of the Wittenburg church and Michelangelo painted the ceiling of the Sistine Chapel in Rome, the world of art and that of the church have become largely foreign territory to one another. Over time, the subject matter of art changed from visualizing the sacred stories to the celebration of royal marriages and political victories, and then to recording the activities and impressions of ordinary life. By the early twentieth century, artists such as Kazimir Malevich, Marcel Duchamp, Hans Arp, and Man Ray were questioning the underlying premises of art itself, asking audiences to accept canvasses painted entirely white or black, found objects, or chance arrangements of bits of torn paper, as art.

The emergence of Abstract Impressionism, Pop Art, Performance Art, and Conceptual Art, to name but a few of the many movements and styles that proliferated in the second half of the twentieth century, redefined art more as a process than a product, more as a way of thinking than as particular kinds of objects. These new definitions of art are not generally understood or accepted outside of those museums, galleries, schools, critics and artists who together constitute what Nicholas Wolterstorff calls "the institution of high art."[1] This lack of comprehension in the population at large includes large parts of the

Christian community, who are suspicious of art not only on theological grounds, but also because of the reputation of licentiousness and anti-authoritanism cultivated by many artists. The rift between the art world and the Church which began in the sixteenth century is exacerbated four hundred years later by the antagonism towards religion in general, and Christianity in particular, that seems endemic in the contemporary art world. As art historian James Elkins writes,

> ...religion is seldom mentioned in the art world unless it is linked to criticism, ironic distance, or scandal. Art critical of religion is itself criticized by conservative writers, and it is noted with interest by art critics, but sincerely religious art tends to be ignored by both kids of writers. An observer of the art world might well come to the conclusion that religious practice and religious ideas are not relevant to art unless they are treated with skepticism.[2]

Some attempts to bridge the gap between the art world and the church world are made from time to time, but generally have only limited success. Among the *avant garde* artists in the early twentieth century, Emile Nolde and Georges Rouault are often praised because of their genuine Christian faith. Following World War II, Father Marie-Alain Couturier commissioned works by Matisse, Chagall, and other important artists for several modern churches and chapels built in France. Similar efforts were made in the United States, resulting in the chapel designed by Louise Nevelson at St. Peter's Lutheran Church in New York City and Marcel Breuer's remarkable chapel at St. John's Abbey in Collegeville, Minnesota. More recently, Friedhelm Mennekes attempted to reinvigorate the triptych tradition by inviting 50 world-renowned artists to create temporary installations in the apse at St. Peter's Parish in Cologne, Germany.[3]

Despite these and other efforts, the world of art and the world of theology have generally misunderstood one another for a long time. In recent years, however, a surprisingly large number of artists have begun to seek a way to integrate their Christian faith with their artistic practice, and many Christian seminaries, churches, and other bodies have begun to reach out to them with invitations to participate in exhibitions, residencies, workshops and other programs. Christians in the Visual Arts (CIVA), founded in 1979 to "consider the place of the Christian artist in the Church and in the world"[4] lists about 150 supporting institutions and organizations and approximately 1500 individual members in its most recent directory.

When artists come to theological seminaries, many are looking for a theology of art that sees their calling as vital to the church. Hoping to be welcomed home from their long exile, they instead find themselves in theology-land, a foreign country where their visions and methods are often suspect, their discipline misunderstood, their contributions undervalued. In the land of theology,[5] artists learn the foreign language of systematic theologians, biblical scholars, preachers, and ethicists. In turn, they teach the theologians to read the language of color, line, and form, to see how ideas are embodied in pictures, sculptures, and even buildings.

It used to be a commonplace to think of the world of ideas as a great conversation, in which Plato and Aristotle conversed easily with Aquinas and Shakespeare. Those who attempted to join—or even listen in on—this conversation were assumed to have a reasonable familiarity with the paintings of Leonardo, the sculpture of Michelangelo, the music of Bach and Beethoven, and the fiction of Tolstoy and Dostoevsky. Education, it was thought, meant having enough exposure to this conversation that one might eventually have something useful to add to it. Well into the twentieth century, educated gentlemen, and even ladies, were often expected not only to converse on a wide range of intellectual topics, but to play the piano, sing on key, write poetry, and turn out reasonably accomplished watercolor renditions of flowers or landscapes.

If there ever was a time when such well-rounded individuals could converse knowledgably on topics as diverse as philosophy, biology, physics, theology, and art, that time came to an end some time in the middle of the 20th century. It has become increasingly difficult to keep up on the current questions and developments in more than a very few disciplines or fields of knowledge. Each one has developed its own traditions, its own vocabulary, its own view of history, its own way of understanding the world.

Neither the arts nor theology are exceptions to this increasing specialization and, frequently, mutual incomprehension. The possibility of such incomprehension is all the greater because each group thinks it has a pretty good understanding of the others' field. After all, everyone who has ever gone to church thinks they know something about Christianity. Art, on the other hand, has so many definitions that it is easy for everyone to think they are talking about the same thing, when in fact they carry very different understandings of what art is or is not. As artists have begun to enter theological seminaries as students, artists-in-residence, and even faculty members, both they, and the theologians whose schools have begun to change because of the presence of these artists, have many opportunities to explore these differences of vision and understanding.

One such opportunity is found in the study of history. From the first century onward, the history of the church and the history of Western art are deeply intertwined. For instance, church historians may consider the theological differences between the twelfth century Abbot Suger's theology of light and theological understandings of the fourteenth century mystic Julian of Norwich. While studying the same period of time, artists may look at the changes in figural representation from the stained glass images at St. Denis to the innovations of Giotto. For fifteen hundred years, the focus may differ, but the overall landscape of history looks about the same. The paintings and sculptures that artists study in the course of their education were made, for the most part, for cathedrals and abbeys and private chapels. Artistic styles changed along with theological understandings, the unchanging golden backgrounds of medieval Madonnas turning into the local hillsides and farms seen outside the windows of Renaissance Annunciations, as the focus moved from Christ's eternal divinity to his earthly incarnation.

However, when confronted with the way Protestant church historians understand the events of the sixteenth century, an artist may feel like an exile, sojourning in a very strange land. To those who have learned history through the lens of art, the terrain seems vaguely familiar and the people seem to be speaking words they understand, but nothing fits easily into the categories they have learned in art school. For artists in theology-land, what they know as the late Renaissance suddenly has become the Reformation. Here, people artists have learned to see as heroes are cast as villains, their enemies renamed as magisterial reformers, and the great artistic achievements of the past are brushed off as vanity and idolatry.

Consider, for instance, the year 1517. In Wittenberg, Martin Luther nailed his 95 theses to the church door, sparked in part by the sale of indulgences by Johann Tetzel. In Rome, Michelangelo was working on the Medici tomb in the church of San Lorenzo and Raphael was appointed as one of three architects for the new St. Peter's Basilica. Leonardo da Vinci had been working for the Pope, also, but he was not getting any good commissions so he left for a better job in France.[6] The artists who worked for the Pope needed money, not just to live, but to buy things like lapis lazuli to grind into paint and marble to carve into statuary, and to pay the many assistants and workmen it took to complete the massive undertakings that the Pope had commissioned. It was partially in order to pay the artists that Tetzel was selling indulgences.

Raphael, Michelangelo, Leonardo: these, of course, are the great names of the High Renaissance, the men who defined what art should look like and how artists should think of themselves for the next 400 years. Before the Renaissance, artists had been thought of as craftspeople, no better than cabinetmakers or saddlers, and, like them, largely anonymous. In the sixteenth century courts of the Medici, however, both in Florence and in Rome, artists were received as gentlemen, as philosophers, as poets. Art, now a noble calling, was no longer mere decoration, but revelation. Artists, no longer simple tradesmen, were now touched with genius.

For an artist who has internalized this version of history, it comes as a great shock to be asked to think of Tetzel not as the one who helped the Pope pay the great masters, but as a cynical seller of fraudulent promises of heaven. And while Luther is known to have been rather moderate about the art in churches, art school tends to paint Calvin, Zwingli and the other iconoclastic leaders of the Reformation as Philistines, unable or unwilling to see the importance of the paintings whitewashed out of view, the statues hidden away or destroyed, and stained glass knocked out of window frames.

However, what the artists learn in the strange world of theology-land is that the Reformers were reacting to the abuse of power and the venality rampant among the clerical hierarchy and the oppression of the common people. From the church historians, artists discover the superstition, bordering on idolatry, with which images were treated, and that this reverence was manipulated by the powerful in order to keep the people in ignorance and poverty. Heads now spinning, they read Martin Luther's assertion that:

Christians are to be taught that if the pope knew the exactions of the pardon-preachers, he would rather that St. Peter's church should go to ashes, than that it should be built up with the skin, flesh and bones of his sheep. . . . [and] that it would be the pope's wish, as it is his duty, to give of his own money to very many of those from whom certain hawkers of pardons cajole money, even though the church of St. Peter might have to be sold.[7]

Since artists, too, have a tradition of concern for the underdog and a passion for social justice, once they are made aware of the hardships imposed on ordinary folk by the ostentatious excesses of Pope Leo X, they find themselves in agreement with Martin Luther. And so Christian artists agonize, unable to reconcile what they learned in art school with what they learn in the seminary. They struggle to reconcile their understanding of God's preferential option for the poor with their equally passionate awareness that art is a good gift of God, given for the benefit of humankind.

Looking for a guide through the complicated terrain of history and ethics, the artists-in-exile may turn from history to theology. Unfortunately, often here, too, the assumptions about the purpose and processes of art are often radically different than what they learned in art school. Indeed, it turns out that theologians, for the most part, do not address art systematically. When theologians do talk about art, it is usually in the context of aesthetics, where the essential subject matter is beauty and its relationship to God. Frequently, when theologians want to take art seriously and begin to construct a theology of art, there is an underlying assumption that beauty is the point or purpose of art. Thus, Alejandro García-Rivera can write:

> [W]hat would happen if we took the visual seriously in theology? … [I]f this potential is to be explored, the elements of a theology of art need to be discerned. Such theology must not be sidetracked by philosophical considerations of what art is or is not. It must concentrate on a theology of the human person for at the heart of the mystery of Beauty is the human capacity to experience it. What art is or is not will follow from this, not the other way around [italics in original].[8]

The problem with this approach is that for contemporary artists, beauty is only one of many possible attributes of art, not part of its irreducible core. Arthur C. Danto, Johnsonian Professor of Philosophy Emeritus at Columbia University and art critic for *The Nation*, points out that beauty is very rarely the point of art today. Discussing the controversial *Sensations* exhibition at the Brooklyn Museum in 1999, he writes that those who disapproved of the show

> …pretty much to a person condemned the art, and were certain that they were being put upon. But they were ready to see it as a First Amendment rather than an aesthetic matter, and in this they were perhaps more right than someone would have been who hoped that through argument one would at last see the beauty. It is not and never was the destiny of all art to be seen as beautiful.[9]

Danto examines the notion that good art is necessarily beautiful, tracing the philosophical definition of art from the ancients into modern times. Noting that beauty often was the point of much art in the past, he finds the connection between artistic goodness and beauty understandable, even if mistaken. However, following David Hume, Danto points out that people do not always agree on what is beautiful. Hume argued that this might be due to poor reasoning or inadequate education. Writing about a hundred years before Monet's *Luncheon on the Grass* raised questions about the definition of art at the 1863 Salon des Refusés, Hume notes that artistic goodness often requires explanation if it is to be appreciated.[10] While Hume, like his predecessors, assumed that this artistic goodness was linked to beauty, Danto argues that this is a false assumption.

> A lot of what prevented people from seeing the excellence of early modern paintings were inapplicable theories of what art should be.... Matisse's *Blue Nude* is a good, even a great painting—but someone who claims it is beautiful is talking through his or her hat.[11]

Danto's understanding that beauty is beside the point of much contemporary art is commonplace of art education. Indeed, within many art circles, beauty is seen as somewhat suspect, both frivolous and meaningless. Art, I was taught, is visual philosophy, a way of making sense of and commenting on the world through visual means. Beauty might or might not be a by-product of such a statement, but its absence or presence was considered completely irrelevant.

For many artists, the paramount virtue of art is truth, or meaning. This definition is, of course, not universally agreed upon, nor is the devaluation of beauty. That lack of universality is exactly the point—artists today may or may not be interested in beauty, and the excellence of any given artwork may lie more in its truthfulness or meaning than in its aesthetic appeal. Indeed, much very good contemporary art is intentionally ugly, and for theologians to declare it beautiful is to distort the meaning of the word beyond any useful definition.

Many artists today are looking for a way to be good artists according to the standards of good art at this time in history, as well as to faithful Christian witnesses in their calling as artists. Unfortunately, it often seems to them that unless art strives for beauty, it is unwelcome in theology-land. If excellent art is to return to the churches, seminaries, and other places where Christians gather, the church needs a theology of art that takes into account art that is not, and is never meant to be, beautiful. Such a theology of art would help reconcile awareness of God's preferential option for the poor with the deep intuition that the practice and presence of art is vital for the spiritual health of God's people, rich and poor alike. Such a theology of art would wrestle with the reality that for many, art is less about making beautiful things than it is a way of knowing, a disciplined journey along a path that leads the wandering exile home to God.

Notes

¹"A striking feature of how the arts work in our society is that there is among us a cultural elite, and that from the totality of works of art to be found in our society a vast number are used (in the way intended by the artist or distributor) almost exclusively by the members of that elite. I shall call those works our society's *works of high art*. The works of Beethoven, of Matisse, of Piero della Francesca, are examples. Correspondingly, our society's *institution of high art* consists of the characteristics, arrangements and patterns of action pertaining to the production, distribution, and use in our society of those works of art [italics in original]." Nicholas Wolterstorff, *Art in Action: Toward a Christian Aesthetic* (Grand Rapids, MI: Eerdmans, 1980): 22.

²James Elkins, *On the Strange Place of Religion in Contemporary Art* (New York, NY: Routledge, 2004): 15-16.

³Friedhlem Mennekes, *Triptych: Modern Altarpieces at St. Peter's, Cologne* (Frankfurt, GER: Insel Verlag, 1995): 7.

⁴"Christians in the Visual Arts", *CIVA 2007-2008 Directory* (Wenham, MA: CIVA, 2008): 2.

⁵In this essay, I am using the term "theology" rather broadly. While I understand that this generalization glosses over the very real differences among, for instance, biblical interpretation, systematic theology, and pastoral counseling, it is in order to encompass all the various fields generally taught in theological seminaries without having to list each of them whenever I want to make a contrast between the theological and the artistic disciplines. On the other hand, my use of the words "art" and "artist" generally refers to what are often called "visual art," such as painting, drawing, sculpture, and the like, and those who produce works in these media. Sometimes, however, I will refer to the arts more generally. When that is the case, it should be clear from the context.

⁶"In the Papal court in Rome Leonardo had trouble with insolent German craftsmen, and received no major commissions for paintings comparable to those already carried out by Raphael and Michelangelo. Nevertheless, he did throw himself into Leo X's project to drain the Pontini marshes south of Rome. To this purpose he executed an extremely detailed drawing of the relevant terrain." Frank Zöllner, *Leonardo Da Vinci: 1452-1519* (Köln, GER: Taschen, 2000): 86.

⁷Martin Luther, "Disputation of Doctor Martin Luther on the Power and Efficacy of Indulgences," §50, 51, *Works of Martin Luther*, vol.1, *Project Wittenberg*, Adolph Spaeth, L.D. Reed, Henry Eyster Jacobs, et al., trans. & eds. (Philadelphia, PA: A. J. Holman, 1915): 29-38. http://www.iclnet.org/pub/resources/text/wittenberg/ luther/ web/ninetyfive.html.

⁸Alejandro García-Rivera, *A Wounded Innocence: Sketches for a Theology of Art* (Collegeville, MN: The Liturgical Press, 2003): x.

⁹Arthur C. Danto, *The Abuse of Beauty: Aesthetics and the Concept of Art* (Chicago, IL: Open Court, 2003): 36.

¹⁰"In many orders of beauty, particularly those of the finer arts, it is requisite to employ much reasoning in order to feel the proper sentiment; and a false relish may frequently be corrected by argument and reasoning." David Hume, Section One, *Enquiry*

Concerning the Principles of Morals, quoted in Danto, op. cit, 35.
[11] *Ibid.*, p. 37.

Works Cited

Christians in the Visual Arts: 2007-2008 Directory. Wenham, MA: CIVA, 2008.

Danto, Arthur C. *The Abuse of Beauty: Aesthetics and the Concept of Art.* Chicago, IL: Open Court, 2003.

Elkins, James. *On the Strange Place of Religion in Contemporary Art.* New York, NY: Routledge, 2004.

García-Rivera, Alejandro. *A Wounded Innocence: Sketches for a Theology of Art.* Collegeville, MN: The Liturgical Press, 2003.

Luther, Martin. *Works of Martin Luther,* vol.1. *Project Wittenberg,* Adolph Spaeth, L.D. Reed, Henry Eyster Jacobs, et al., trans. & eds. Philadelphia, PA: A. J. Holman, 1915.

Mennekes, Friedhlem. *Triptych: Modern Altarpieces at St. Peter's, Cologne.* Frankfurt and Liepzig, GER: Insel Verlag, 1995.

Wolterstorff, Nicholas. *Art in Action: Toward a Christian Aesthetic.* Grand Rapids, MI: Eerdmans, 1980.

Zöllner, Frank. *Leonardo Da Vinci: 1452-1519.* Köln, GER: Taschen, 2000.

16

"Hallowed be thy Name!": The Theological Significance of the Avoidance of God's Name in the New Testament

By R. Kendall Soulen

Christian theologians sometimes look for clues about the character of divine revelation by examining Jesus Christ's own characteristic patterns of speech as portrayed by the Gospels. In recent decades, many theologians have found such a clue in Jesus' practice of beginning prayer with the address, "Father!" while others have pointed to his practice of teaching about the kingdom of God in parables. Today, these two features of Jesus' speech are often made the starting point of theological study.

In contrast, theologians have paid comparatively little attention to a third feature of Jesus' speech as portrayed by the Gospels. This third feature testifies in an especially powerful way to the inexpugnable bond that unites Jesus with the faith, memory, and hope of Israel. Hence reflection on it is a fitting way to honor the exceptional contributions of Bruce Birch, who throughout his rich career of teaching and writing has taught so many to recognize and love the Israelite dimensions of Christian faith.

The practice I am referring to is Jesus' custom of avoiding the direct use of God's name, the Tetragrammaton, in favor of the use of "buffer language" or pious circumlocution that takes the place of the name itself. An example comes from Mark's account of Jesus' trial before the high priest.

> Again the high priest asked him, "Are you the Messiah, the Son of the Blessed One?" Jesus said, "I am; and 'you will see the Son of Man seated at the right hand of the Power,' and 'coming with the clouds of heaven.'" (Mark 14:61-62)

Here both the high priest and Jesus use circumlocutions in place of the Divine Name. "The Blessed One" and "the Power" are not traditional designations for God that stand independently in their own right, such as "God" or "the Holy One of Israel," but stand-in names used in place of the Divine Name. Jesus and the high priest use different buffer names, but they have no difficulty understanding each other. Each understands the other to be using a veiled reference to the deity whose name is the Tetragrammaton.

The example from Mark is interesting because it shows that the practice of using pious circumlocutions in place of the Divine Name was standard practice in Jesus' day. Indeed, the first century CE appears to have been a time when piety for the Divine Name was especially pronounced and widespread among different streams of Judaism. Josephus calls the Tetragrammaton "the hair-raising name" and reports that he was forbidden from pronouncing it in the presence of non-Jews. The Qumran sectarians prescribed banishment for those who pronounced the name. Scribes responsible for copying the Scriptures accorded special treatment to the Divine Name by differentiating it from the surrounding words of scripture through the use of special orthography. The writings of the New Testament are themselves saturated with forms of speech that show the impact of a reverent reticence to use the Divine Name. In 1917, a German biblical scholar named Julius Boehmer catalogued every instance of such speech in the New Testament and found well over *one thousand* instances in all.[1]

It is not surprising, therefore, that the Gospels should portray Jesus as displaying reverence for the Divine Name in his speech to and about God. Such practice was typical of the day. Nevertheless, we may ask if Jesus' way of appropriating this very Jewish tradition contains a special message of its own. Granted that Jesus here conforms to a standard practice of his day, does he still give this practice a distinctive twist or emphasis that contains a message of significance for Christians today? And if so, is this twist or emphasis echoed in other parts of the New Testament?

I believe the answer to both questions is "Yes." In Jesus' own practice, the avoidance of God's name is linked to an eschatological longing for *God* to declare God's name, as only God can do. The human use of God's name is to fall silent in order to make room for God's use of God's name. According to other New Testament witnesses, this is precisely what God has accomplished in the life, death, and resurrection of Christ Jesus, and what God will yet accomplish through Christ in the future.

A key witness for this understanding of the theological significance of the avoidance of God's name in the New Testament is the opening of the Lord's Prayer. "Our Father in heaven, hallowed be thy name!" This petition models reserve in the use of God's name, in keeping with Second Temple practice. God's name is referred to but not actually used, whether in the invocation (where "Our Father" appears in place of the name), or in the petition itself (where "thy name" stands alone, without the name itself). At the same time, a reserved posture toward the human use of God's name is linked to a desire for *God* to *hallow* or *sanctify* God's name. This linkage is not directly obvious, because Jesus formulates the petition in the passive voice: "*hallowed be* thy name." Logically, the passive voice leaves the *agent* of the desired action unspecified. And in fact, Christians down through the centuries have frequently supposed that Jesus is here praying that God's people or the church or creation sanctify God's name. It is more likely, however, that Jesus here employs what is sometimes called the "divine passive," where the passive voice is used to speak of God while avoiding the direct mention of God. Thus, Jesus' use of the passive voice is another expression of his reserve before God's name! In content, the first petition amounts to a plea that *God* now act to fulfill God's oft-repeated promise, "Then you shall know that I am the LORD!" (Exodus 16:2; Jeremiah 24:7; Ezekiel 36:11 etc.). That is, Jesus calls upon God to manifest God's character as YHWH, so that, in turn, God's character and dominion will at last be perfectly acknowledged by Israel, by the nations, and indeed by all creation.

In the first petition of the Lord's Prayer, then, Jesus links human *reserve* in the use of God's name with the desire that God sanctify God's name, as only God can do. When we turn to other aspects of Jesus' teaching, we find that they are consistent with this characteristic emphasis. Jesus' reserve in the use of God's name reappears in Jesus' teaching on oaths (Matt 5:33-37; cf. 23:23). Rather than employ oaths that allude to God by circumlocution (e.g., swearing by the gold on the altar of the temple), Jesus' disciples are to avoid oaths altogether in favor a simple "Yes" and "No." And it reappears again in Jesus' frequent use of the divine passive in his teaching about God's coming reign.

"Blessed are those who mourn, for they will *be comforted"* Matt 5:4)

"Blessed are the peacemakers, for they will *be called* children of God" (v.9)

"Do not judge, so that you may not *be judged"* (Matt 7:1)

"Do not fear. Only believe, and she will *be saved"* (Luke 8:50)

"Take heart, son; your sins *are forgiven"* (Matt 9:2)

"All who exalt themselves will *be humbled*, but all who humble themselves will *be exalted"*(Luke 18:14)

In these passages, Jesus points away from what humans can do toward what God alone can do. He does so even at the simplest rhetorical level, by avoiding direct reference to God. At the same time, Jesus confidently gestures toward the advent of God and God's reign. Ignatius of Antioch once wrote, "Whoever has the word of Jesus for a true possession can also hear his silence"[2] The silence of Jesus, we might say, includes the restraint he shows before the invocation of God and God's name. By exercising this restraint, Jesus opens up room, as it were, for God to glorify God's name as only God can do. The countless divine passives that punctuate Jesus' teaching recapitulate the great divine passive at the heart of the Lord's Prayer: "Hallowed be thy name!"

When we turn to other portions of the New Testament witness, we find a similar pattern: reserve before God's name is linked to the eschatological hope that *God* will now at last sanctify God's name once and for all. But we also see the appearance of the belief that God has already begun to realize this hope in "the things concerning Jesus of Nazareth." A prime example of this appears in Phil 2:5-11.

> v. 5 Let the same mind be in you that was in Christ Jesus,
> v. 6 Who, though he was in the form of God,
> did not regard equality with God as something to be explo,
> v. 7 but emptied himself, taking the form of a slave, being born in human likeness.
> And being found in human form,
> v. 8 he humbled himself and became obedient to the point of death— even death on a cross.
> v. 9 Therefore God also highly exalted him and
> gave him the name that is above every name,
> v. 10 so that at the name of Jesus every knee should bend,
> in heaven and on earth and under the earth,
> v. 11 and every tongue should confess that Jesus Christ is Lord,
> to the glory of God the Father (Phil 2:5-11).

A similar pattern appears in the Gospel of John in Jesus' "I am" statements. Here, it is true, Jesus is portrayed as assuming a more active role in relation to God's name than in the Philippians passage, insofar as Christ himself now actively employ the Divine Name in his own solemn self-declaration. Yet even here the priority of "the First Person of the Trinity" remains visible. This is evident from the curious but inescapable fact that even in Christ's self-declaration, he is portrayed as continuing to employ a circumlocution for the name in place of the name itself. ("I am" alludes to the Tetragrammaton by way of Exodus 3:14-15 and Deutero-Isaiah, but is not the Divine Name itself). It is also evident when Jesus' "I am" statements are understood against the background of other references to God's name in the Gospel of John. For example, in John 17 Jesus prays:

> "I have made *your name* known to those whom you gave me from the world....
> Holy Father, protect them in *your name that you have given me*, so that they may be one, as we are one (John 17:6, 11b).

While Jesus here ascribes to himself an active role in making the name known, he repeatedly emphasizes the fact that the name in question is *God's* name ("your name"), and that this name has been *given* to him. Thus once again God's activity, and Jesus' receptivity, is emphasized.

A final example comes from the opening of the Book of Revelation. This example is important, because it indicates that human reserve before God's name, and hope for God's own *self*-naming, remains a feature of Christian *hope for the future*. Rev. 1:4-8 opens and ends with the formula "He who is and who was and who is to come." In vs. 8, the formula is expanded to read:

> "I am the Alpha and the Omega, says the Lord God, who is and who was and who is to come, the Almighty"

John of Patmos, the author of this baroquely intricate verse, manifests reserve before God's name by alluding to God's name *indirectly*, by means of a threefold circumlocution (Alpha and Omega, Lord God, and "who is and who was and who is to come"). At the same time, he does so in order to hold forth the hope of God's own authoritative self-naming, which will be consummated in the future ("who is *to come.*"). As the Book of Revelation unfolds, it is made clear that God consummates his self-naming in and through the coming of Christ Jesus. Christ himself, however, in his identity as the slaughtered lamb, is portrayed in the Apocalypse as himself *silent* (Rev 5:6, 8 *passim*).

In sum, the avoidance of God's name in the New Testament, while consistent with the practice of Second Temple Judaism, has a distinctive theological resonance of its own. The human avoidance of God's name expresses the eschatological longing that *God* sanctify God's name, a longing that turns to joy in the confidence that God has begun to do precisely this in Christ Jesus. But here, as elsewhere in the New Testament, the dynamic of "already but not yet" continues to apply. God has already begun to declare God's own name in Christ, as Jesus' "I am" statements in the Gospel of John attest. At the same time, Christians continue to await God's climactic self-naming in Christ's return and the consummation of creation, as Phil 2 and the Book of Revelation also testify.

The conclusion I draw from this considerations is that the practice of avoiding the direct use of God's name has a permanent significance for Christians, precisely for theological reasons that go to the heart of the gospel itself. By abstaining from the direct use of God's name, and by the use of various circumlocutions in its place, Christians express their longing that God consummate God's hallowing of God's name in Christ. We remain impatient with the human use of God's name, and long for God to hallow it as only God can do. *Maranatha*, come Lord Jesus.

Notes

1. "Das Neue Testament is von der jüdischen Scheu vor dem Namen und vor der Person Gottes geradezu durchtränkt, ohne dass die Exegeten das bisher zur Kenntnis nahmen." Julius Boehmer, *Die neutestamenliche Gottesscheu und die ersten drei Bitten des Vaterunsers* (Halle, GER: Richard Mühlmann.1917), 2-3. For treatment of the Divine Name during the Second Temple period, see Sean M. McDonough, *YHWH at Patmos* (Tübingen, GER: Mohr Siebeck, 1999).

2. Ignatius, *Epistle to the Ephesians* 15:2 (Billingham, WA: Libronix Digital Library System, 2.1, 2002).

Works Cited

Boehmer, Julius. *Die neutestamenliche Gottesscheu und die erstern drei Bitten des Vaaterunsers.* Halle, GER: Richard Mühlmann, 1917.

Ignatius. *Epistle to the Ephesians.* Bellingham, WA: Libronix Digital Library System, 2.1, 2002.

McDonough, Sean M. *YHWH at Patmos.* Tubingen, GER: Mohr Siebeck, 1999.

17

Some Thoughts on the Exodus and the Exile

By Josiah Young

This well-known Spiritual attributed to African-Americans enslaved in the nineteenth century CE exemplifies many liberation theologians' assertion that "God sides with the oppressed":

> *Go down Moses*
> *Way down in Egypt land*
> *Tell old Pharaoh*
> *To let my people go.*

Exodus 11: 4-6 is at the heart of this Spiritual. The Lord tells Moses that He "will go throughout the land of Egypt" and destroy the Egyptians' firstborn, regardless of who they are. YHWH will destroy "the firstborn of Pharaoh who sits on his throne . . . the firstborn of the female slave who is behind the mill, and all the firstborn of the livestock." A great cry will ring "throughout the whole land of Egypt, such as there has never been or will ever be again." During this annihilation, not a dog will growl "at any of the Israelites—not at people, not at animals—so that [one] may know that the LORD makes a distinction between Egypt and Israel" (Exodus 11: 7-8). True to His word, YHWH "struck down all the firstborn in the land of Egypt" indiscriminately. None of the firstborn, including those of the "prisoner who was in the dungeon," survived, "and there was a great cry in Egypt, for there was not a house without someone dead" (Exodus 12: 29-30).

Pharaoh released the Hebrew people from slavery after this plague of death. Was it necessary, though, for YHWH to kill the Egyptians' firstborn? Is it not true that the firstborn of *the female slave who is behind the mill* is an oppressed person? Why is the Exodus theology only concerned with the deliverance of Israel rather than with the deliverance of all the slaves in Egypt land? Perhaps an answer has to do with those who edited the Exodus material in the exilic period. The "school," Gerhard Von Rad claims, was comprised of the "intelligentsia:

the priests, the prophets, and the whole civil service subordinated to the court."[1] Maybe their basic concern was to discredit other religions rather than to uphold the liberation of all oppressed people.

Ludwig Feuerbach argues in his book *The Essence of Christianity* that YHWH's role as liberator and guardian of Israel results from "the historical definition of the specific nature of the religious consciousness." According to Feuerbach, *all* religious consciousness reflects human experience and is nothing more than that. What makes Israel's religion different from all others is the "fact" that Israel's religious consciousness "was circumscribed by the limits of a *particular*...national interest."[2] For Feuerbach, "Israel made the wants of his national existence the law of the world and deified even his political vindictiveness under the dominance of these wants."[3] Feuerbach's speculation is troubling. Could it be that YHWH's championing of Israel and cruelty to Ham's descendents (Egypt and Canaan specifically) stem from an ancient desire to deify *an* interpretation of history?

Leviticus 25 is another reason I wonder about the ancient intentions behind the Exodus theology. In Leviticus, the Lord instructs Moses to tell His chosen people to release all Hebrews who having fallen on hard times became servants. Israel is to release them from servitude every fifty years (at the jubilee), and must not ever abuse them as YHWH had "brought them forth from the land of Egypt" (Leviticus 25:55). He instructs Moses to tell His people that they may, however, enslave *the aliens residing with* them. Israel may keep these foreigners and their children born in Hebrew land "as a possession" inheritable by Israel's children. Israel may treat *them* "as slaves; but as for [the] fellow Israelites, no one shall rule over the other with harshness" (Leviticus 25: 44-46).

Leviticus 25 is but one biblical example of slavery *within* Israel. One finds other examples in Exodus, in which the Lord sanctions the Hebrews' enslavement of other "Hebrews" after He had liberated Israel from Egypt. In Exodus 21:1-6, for instance, YHWH instructs Moses to tell His people to enslave a Hebrew bondsman for only six years. The masters are to manumit their bondsmen in the seventh year, and his wife is to be set free too if the master enslaved them together from the first year. If, however, the Hebrew master gives his slave a wife who has children in the course of six years, then the woman and the children are to remain in bondage. The man can go free in the seventh year; but if he stays, out of declared love for his master as well as his family, then the Hebrew patriarch must "bring him before God" and brand the slave—"bore his ear through with an awl"—to mark his permanent bondage.

Exodus 21: 20-21 holds that a Hebrew "slaveowner" who "strikes a male or female slave with a rod and" causes the slave to die "immediately...shall be punished. But if the slave survives a day or two, there is no punishment; for the slave is the owner's property." These verses indicate that YHWH ordains slavery within Israel. How, then, does one who believes that slavery *anywhere* is unacceptable accept a theology that sanctions it? Perhaps one does not have to if the verses from Exodus and Leviticus uphold a culturally specific theology that the Exile shaped indelibly.

The Israelites deported to Babylonia belonged to the "upper stratum." The rest of the Israelites— the non-deportees ("the farmers and vinedressers and especially the serfs")—remained in Judah. The well-organized deportees kept close contact with the stay-at-homes, according to "Jeremiah's letter to the exiles, to which the latter in turn replied."[4] The exiled Jewish elite revised and expanded both "the Pentateuch and the Deuteronomistic History" in the light of this time of great crisis.[5] Such ancient editorial work goes along way toward accounting for the Hebrew Bible's "final form."

Literary critic Regina Schwarz assesses this redaction in her book *The Curse of Cain: The Violent Legacy of Monotheism*. She argues that the redactors forged an "identity agonistically," and so excluded "'Others' memories and other memories."[6] In no sense, then, can one hold that the canon reflects all there was to say about "God." The exclusion of "certain books" from "the official store meant that the communities attached to them were left out, too."[7] Gerhard Von Rad suggests Schwartz may be correct. He writes that the "lower strata" left in Jerusalem and Judea "may have adopted cultic forms which had already gained a foothold in Judea and Jerusalem in the later period of the monarchy." King Josiah "had not succeeded in abolishing" this tendency.[8] Could it be that some of the Leviticus- aliens—who had no "jubilee" rights—upheld a theology the redactors discredited?

According to Von Rad, prophets such as Jeremiah sided with the deported "intelligentsia" and thus "opposed the claim for precedence made by those who remained on in the country. They were the bad figs, the exiles the good ones (Jer. 24:1ff.)."[9] Jeremiah's condemnation of bad figs theology is very harsh:

> Is Israel a slave? Is he a homeborn servant? Why then has he become plunder? The lions have roared against him, they have roared loudly. They have made his land a waste; his cities are in ruins, without inhabitants.... Have you not brought this upon yourself by forsaking the Lord your God while he led you in the way (Jeremiah 2: 14-17)?

The prophet continues:

> On every high hill and under every green tree you sprawled and played the whore. Yet I planted you as a choice vine, from the purest stock....Though you wash yourself with lye and use much soap, the stain of your guilt is still before me, says the Lord GOD. How can you say, "I am not defiled, I have not gone after the Baals?" Look at your way in the valley; know what you have done—a restive young camel interlacing her tracks, a wild ass at home in the wilderness, in her heat sniffing the wind! Who can restrain her lust? None who seeks her need weary themselves; in her month they will find her. (Jeremiah 2: 20-25).

If "some Israelites and Judeans" practiced human sacrifice "as a means of fulfilling the law requiring the giving of the firstborn to God (Ex 22.29-30)," then such harsh language was warranted.[10] In general though, as Regina Schwartz argues, the "delimiting of biblical narratives that was intended to separate the endorsed, official memories from others in order to demarcate the community, courted a palpable risk: closing the text against not only contemporary Others but the Others of the future, that is, of excluding future generations and their own (future) memories." According to Schwartz, however, one cannot standardize *memories*. The attempt to do so—to claim, "this is our memory and thou shalt have no other memories"—is often done "coercively."[11] Coercion results in a hegemony that arouses a hermeneutics of suspicion. One who thinks about the texts differently from the ways in which one's catechism had taught one causes him or her pain: It is discomforting to doubt what one had assumed was the unadulterated truth.

For many years, I did not question the theology of the exilic and post-exilic periods. I was afraid to do so as I did not want to be a bad fig (still don't); and I did not want anyone to undermine my deepest theological convictions. As was, and is, common among many black Christians who have never been Jewish, I saw myself as one of the Hebrew "children" oppressed by Pharaoh: *Lord, wasn't that hard trials, great tribulations, I'm bound to leave this land!* One day, a colleague of mine, a Jewish rabbi, told me, with much exasperation, that my appropriation of the Exodus narrative in the form of a gospel tune (*Oh Mary don't you weep.... Pharaoh's army drowned in the Red Sea*) was inappropriate. "That is not *your* story," she said. "It is *mine*." She was right.

I appropriated the Exodus theology to argue that "God" sides with *all* of the oppressed. Now, it does not seem correct to preach that and to write liberation theologies to that effect while using texts that appear to undermine the claim. Inevitably, a parishioner or a student is going to point out that the Tenth Plague is akin to genocide and that the Patriarchs' voice, the intelligentsia's perspective, comes through loud and clear in both the Pentateuch and the Deuteronomistic History. Eventually, someone is going to ask, "How do you, professor, reconcile the Tenth Plague and the brutal invasion of Canaan with the apocatastatic theology you commend to us? Is the Creator whose Son died so that all creatures will have eternal life the *same* YHWH (or Elohim), who favors the elite, permits slavery, destroys Israel's nemeses, and undermines theological diversity within Israel? I am grateful that I had already agonized over such questions before the questioners put me on the spot. My advice to them is the same advice I have given myself: Acknowledge the contradiction publically, from the pulpit if you feel you have to be theologically transparent. Teach those in your charge that the Bible mirrors our post-modern day conflicts.

What I mean is that the questions we raise about the ancient texts reflect the questions we put to ourselves regarding our relationships to others and the character of the world in which we live. Something Feuerbach wrote seems appropriate here: "Whatever is God to a man, that is his heart and soul; and conversely, God is the manifested inward nature, the expressed self of a man—religion the solemn unveiling of a man's hidden treasures, the revelation of his intimate thoughts, the open confession of his love-secrets."[12] One must ask oneself: Do I believe that God loves everyone and wants nothing but his or her well-being and salvation? Does my theology reflect that belief without excluding *all* of the dead, *all* of the living, and *all* who are to come? The song says,

> *Thus said the Lord, bold Moses said,*
> *Let my people go.*
> *If not, I'll smite your firstborn dead.*

Let *my* people go: The old song has come to signify the decimation of the non-elect— *from the firstborn of Pharaoh who sat on his throne to the firstborn of the prisoner who was in the dungeon, and all the firstborn of the livestock.* Do we who teach seminarians and serve local churches dare to question such theology, especially if we are capable of advancing theologies that uphold life and justice for all? I think some of us do, and should.

Notes

1. Gerhard Von Rad, *Old Testament theology*, vol. 1 (New York, NY: Harper & Row, 1962): 82.
2. Ludwig Feuerbach, *The Essence of Christianity* (New York, NY: Prometheus Books, 1989): 120, emphasis added.
3. *Ibid.*, 120.
4. See Von Rad, p. 80.
5. Israel Finkelstein & Neil Asher Silberman, *The Bible Unearthed: Archaeology's New Vision of Ancient Israel and the Origin of Its Sacred Texts* (New York, NY: Touchstone, 2002): 296.
6. Regina M. Schwartz, *The Curse of Cain: The Violent Legacy of Monotheism* (Chicago, IL: The University of Chicago, 1997):146.
7. *Ibid.*, p. 146.
8. Von Rad, p. 82.
9. *Ibid.*, pp. 82-83.
10. *The New Oxford Annotated Bible*, Michael D. Coogan, ed. (Oxford, England: Oxford University, 2001): 1090.
11. Schwartz, p. 146.
12. Feuerbach, 12-13.

Works Cited

Feuerbach, Ludwig. *The Essence of Christianity.* New York, NY: Prometheus Books, 1989.
Finkelstein, Israel & Neil Asher Silberman. *The Bible Unearthed: Archaeology's New Vision of Ancient Israel and the Origin of Its Sacred Texts.* New York, NY: Touchstone, 2002.
New Oxford Annotated Bible, Michael D. Coogan, ed. Oxford, ENG: Oxford University, 2001.
Schwartz, Regina M. *The Curse of Cain: The Violent Legacy of Monotheism.* Chicago, IL: The University of Chicago, 1997.
Von Rad, Gerhard. *Old Testament Theology.* vol. 1. New York, NY: Harper & Row, 1962.

The Publications of Bruce C. Birch

Compiled by
Eleanor Marshall Gease and
Howertine Farrell Duncan

BOOKS AND BOOK-LENGTH WORKS:

1976   *The Rise of the Israelite Monarchy: The Growth and Development of 1 Samuel 7-15.* Society of Biblical Literature Dissertation Monographs. Missoula: Scholars Press.

With Larry L. Rasmussen. *Bible and Ethics in the Christian Life.* Minneapolis: Augsburg Press.

1978   With Larry L. Rasmussen. *The Predicament of the Prosperous.* Philadelphia: Westminster.

1981   *Singing the Lord's Song: A Study of Isaiah 40-55.* New York: Women's Division, United Methodist Board of Global Ministries.

1985   *What Does the Lord Require? The Old Testament Call to Social Witness.* Philadelphia: Westminster.

1989   *Singing the Lord's Song: A Study of Isaiah 40-55.* Revised edition. Nashville: Abingdon.

With Larry L. Rasmussen. *Bible and Ethics in the Christian Life.* Revised and expanded edition. Minneapolis: Augsburg/Fortress.

1991   *Let Justice Roll Down: The Old Testament, Ethics, and Christian Life.* Louisville: Westminster/John Knox.

1992   *To Love As We Are Loved: The Bible and Relationships.* Nashville: Abingdon.

1993   *Bibel und Ethik im christlichen Leben.* Heidelberg: Chr. Kaiser/Guttersloh.

1997   *Hosea, Joel, Amos: The Westminster Bible Companion.* Louisville: Westminster/John Knox.

1998	"The Books of 1 and 2 Samuel: Introduction, Commentary and Reflection," *The New Interpreter's Bible*, vol. 2. Nashville: Abingdon, 947-1383.
1999	With Walter Brueggemann, Terence Fretheim, and David Petersen. *A Theological Introduction to the Old Testament*. Nashville: Abingdon.
2000	General Editor with Charles Foster. *Steward: Living as Disciples in Everyday Life, Participant's Manual*. Nashville: Abingdon.
2004	With Lewis A. Parks, *Ducking Spears, Dancing Madly: A Biblical Model of Church Leadership*. Nashville: Abingdon.
2005	With Walter Brueggemann, Terence Fretheim, and David Petersen. *A Theological Introduction to the Old Testament*. Revised edition. Nashville: Abingdon.
2006	With Walter Brueggemann, Terence Fretheim, and David Petersen. *A Theological Introduction to the Old Testament*, Korean translation by Joon-Hee Cha. Seoul: Preaching Academy.

EDITED VOLUMES:

1994-2002	Old Testament Editor, *The New Interpreter's Bible: A Commentary in Twelve Volumes*. Nashville: Abingdon Press.
2008	Editorial Board, *The Discipleship Study Bible*. Louisville: Westminster/John Knox Press.

CHAPTERS IN BOOKS:

1980	"Global Hunger: New Images for the Powerful," revised version, *Saving the Family Farm*. Catherine Lerza, editor. New York: Women's Division, Board of Global Ministries, United Methodist Church, 35-38.
1981	"Shalom: Toward a Vision of Human Wholeness," *Living Simply*. S. Crean, H. Ebbeson, editors. New York: Seabury, 79-86.
1983	"The Covenant at Sinai: Response to God's Freedom," *Social Themes of the Christian Year: A Commentary on the Lectionary*. D. Hessel, editor. Philadelphia: Geneva Press, 142-148.
1985	"Biblical Theology: Issues in Authority and Hermeneutics," *Wesleyan Theology Today: A Bicentennial Theological Consultation*. Nashville: Kingswood Books, 127-133.
	"The WORD and the Words," *Scripture: The WORD Beyond the Word*. New York: United Methodist Women's Division, 1-8.

1986	"Biblical Hermeneutics in Recent Discussion: Old Testament," *A Guide to Contemporary Hermeneutics. Major Trends in Biblical Interpretation.* Donald K. McKim, editor. Grand Rapids: Wm. B. Eerdmans, 3-12.
	"Choosing the Fast," *Gleanings: Hunger Meditations for Lent.* St. Andrews Press, 75-76.
	"Nimrod," "Number," "Pelican," etc. *The International Standard Bible Encyclopedia,* vol. 3, G. W. Bromiley, editor. Grand Rapids: Wm. B. Eerdmans.
1987	"Biblical Faith and the Loss of Children," *On Moral Medicine. Theological Perspectives in Medical Ethics.* Stephen E. Lammers and Allen Verhey, editors. Grand Rapids: Wm. B. Eerdmans, 516-519.
1988	"Between Memory and Vision," *Disciplines 1989.* Janet Bugg, editor. Nashville: Upper Room Books, 77-83.
	"The Meaning of Wealth: Covenant Community and Economic Responsibility," *Report: Eighteenth North American Conference on Christian Philanthropy.* New York: NCC Commission on Stewardship, 217-230.
	"The Meaning of Wealth: Economic Resources as the Gift of God's Creation," *Report: Eighteenth North American Conference on Christian Philanthropy.* New York: NCC Commission on Stewardship, 203-216.
	"The Meaning of Wealth: Wealth, Poverty and Biblical Faith," *Report: Eighteenth North American Conference on Christian Philanthrophy.* New York: NCC Commission on Stewardship, 231-246.
	"Memory in Congregational Life," *Congregations: Their Power to Form and Transform.* C. Ellis Nelson, editor. Atlanta: John Knox, 20-47.
	"Nature, Humanity, and Biblical Theology: Observations Toward a Relational Theology of Nature," *Ecology and Life: Accepting Our Environmental Responsibility.* Wesley Granberg-Michaelson. Waco: Word Books, 143-150.
	"Old Testament Narrative and Moral Address," *Canon, Theology and Old Testament Interpretation: Essays in Honor of Brevard S. Childs.* G. M. Tucker, D. L. Petersen, R. R. Wilson, editors. Philadelphia: Fortress, 75-91.
	"Scorpion," etc. *The International Standard Bible Encyclopedia,* vol. 4. G. M. Bromiley, editor. Grand Rapids: Wm. B. Eerdmans.
1989	"I and II Samuel," *The Books of the Bible.* Bernhard Anderson, editor. New York: Scribners, 127-140.
1990	"Jesus Christ is Our Peace," *Disciplines, 1991.* Tom Page, editor. Nashville: Upper Room Books, 208-214.

1991 "To Love As We Are Loved: Biblical and Theological Reflections on Human Sexuality," *Teaching Human Sexuality: A Collection of Resources for Teachers and Leaders*. Cecile A.Beam, editor. Nashville: General Board of Discipleship.

1992 "Exegeses: A New Heart and a New Spirit; The Valley of Dry Bones; God's Spirit in Our Hearts," *A New Heart and a New Spirit: Stewardship Worship Resource*. Indianapolis: Ecumenical Center for Stewardship Studies, 16-21.

"Memory in Congregational Life," *Thinking About Children and Families*. Congress on Children and Families, Scripture Union and the Bible College of New Zealand, 77-88.

1993 "Jesus Christ is Our Peace," *Disciplines, 1994*. Tom Page, editor. Nashville: Upper Room Books, 204-210.

1995 "Divine Character and the Formation of Moral Community in the Book of Exodus," *The Bible in Ethics. The Second Sheffield Colloquium*. J. Rogerson, M. Davies, M. D. Carroll R., editors. Sheffield: Sheffield Academic Press, 119-135.

"Memory in Congregational Life," *Communion, Community, Commonwealth. Readings for Spiritual Leadership*. John S. Mogabgab, editor. Nashville: Upper Room Books, 67-76.

"Unlikely Vessels, Trying Circumstances," *Disciplines, 1996*. Nashville: Upper Room Books, 181-187.

1996 "One Story or Two Stories," *Talking About Genesis: A Resource Guide*. Public Affairs Television. New York: Doubleday, 30-31.

1998 "Looking Toward the Promised Land," *The Upper Room Disciplines, 1999*. Nashville: Upper Room Books, 305-311.

2000 "Samuel," "Saul," *Eerdman's Dictionary of the Bible*. David Noel Freedman, editor. Grand Rapids: Wm. B. Eerdmans, 1161-1162 and 1170-1171.

2001 "Old Testament Ethics," *The Blackwell Companion to the Hebrew Bible*. Leo G. Perdue, editor. Oxford: Blackwell, 293-307.

2002 "How Shall We Sing?" An essay in *My America: What My Country Means to Me by 150 Americans from All Walks of Life*, Hugh Downs, editor. New York: Scribner, 31-32.

2003 "Integrating Welcome Into the Seminary Curriculum," *Graduate Theological Education and the Human Experience of Disability*, Robert C. Anderson, editor. New York: Haworth Press, 23-32.

2005 "The Arts, Midrash, and Biblical Teaching," *Arts, Theology, and the Church: New Intersections*, Kimberly J. Vrudny and Wilson Yates, editors. Cleveland: Pilgrim Press.

2006 "Ark of the Covenant," *The New Interpreter's Dictionary of the Bible*, vol 1. Ed. by

K. D. Sakenfeld, et. al. Nashville: Abingdon Press, 263-269.

"Creation and the Moral Development of God in Genesis 1-11," *"And God Saw That It Was Good: Essays on Creation and God in Honor of Terence E. Fretheim*, Word and World Supplement Series 5. St. Paul, MN: Word and World: Luther Seminary, 12-22.

2007 "Ethics in the OT," and "Hosea, Book of," *The New Interpreter's Dictionary of the Bible*, vol. 2. Ed. by K. D. Sakenfeld, et. al. Nashville: Abingdon Press, 338-348, 894-900.

"Impairment as a Condition in Biblical Scholarship," *This Abled Body: Rethinking Disabilities in Biblical Studies*, Hector Avalos, Sarah J. Melcher, and Jeremy Schipper., editors. Atlanta: Society of Biblical Literature, 185-195.

2008 "Forward," *Biblical Figures in the Islamic Faith*, Stephen Vicchio. Eugene, OR: Wipf & Stock, xxxi.

"Introduction," and "Introduction and Notes on 1 and 2 Samuel," *The Discipleship Study Bible*, Louisville: Westminster/John Knox, xi-xiii, 365-461.

2009 "Notes for the Book of Isaiah." *The Wesley Study Bible*. Nashville, TN: Abingdon Press, 813-893.

ARTICLES:

1971 "Conservatives and Costs Pressure Church-Related Colleges," *Christian Advocate* 15 (December 23): 9-10.

"The Development of the Tradition on the Anointing of Saul, 1 Samuel 9:1-10:16," *Journal of Biblical Literature* 90:55-68.

1973 "Black Theology Means Liberation For All," *Christian Advocate* 17 (June 21): 13-14.

1975 "The Choosing of Saul at Mizpah," *Catholic Biblical Quarterly* 37 (October): 447-457.

"Hunger, Poverty, and Biblical Religion," *The Christian Century* 92 (June 11-18): 593-599.

1977 With Larry L. Rasmussen,"The Bible's Role in Christian Ethics," *Cross Talk*, part 4: 6.

With Larry L. Rasmussen, "Character Formation, Decision-making, and the Bible," *The Circuit Rider* (April): 1, 3-5.

1978 "Energy Ethics Reaches the Church's Agenda," *The Christian Century* 95 (November 1), 1034-1038.

"Global Hunger: New Images for the Powerful," *The Hunger Notebook*, 4th edition. New York: Hunger Program, United Presbyterian Church in the U.S.A.

1979 "Global Hunger: New Images for the Powerful," *Today's Word for Adults*. Christian Education: Shared Approaches, vol. 2, course 2.

1980 "Shalom: Toward a Vision of Human Wholeness," *Response* 12 (February): 4-5, 42-43.

"Tradition, Canon, and Biblical Theology," *Horizons in Biblical Theology* 2: 113-126.

1981 "The Psalter as Preaching Text," *Quarterly Review* 1 (Winter): 61-93.

1982 "Discipleship and Patriarchy: A Response to Elisabeth Schussler Fiorenza," *The Annual of the Society of Christian Ethics*, 173-180.

"National Power and Responsibility," *Engage/Social Action* 10 (January): 22-23.

1983 "Biblical Faith and the Loss of Children," *The Christian Century* 100 (October 26): 965-967.

"The Role of the Bible in Social Witness," *Engage/Social Action* 11 (July): 14-17.

1984 "Biblical Hermeneutics in Recent Discussion: Old Testament," *Religious Studies Review* 10: 1-7.

"By the Waters of Babylon. What Does the Lord Require? Part 5," *Sojourners* 13 (October): 26-29.

"From Promise to Deliverance. What Does the Lord Require? Part 2," *Sojourners* 13 (March): 28-31.

"In the Image of God. What Does the Lord Require? Part 1," *Sojourners* 13, (January): 10-15.

"Like the Other Nations. What Does the Lord Require? Part 4," *Sojourners* 13 (August): 29-32.

"Old Testament Theology: Its Task and Future," *Horizons in Biblical Theology*, 6 (June): iii-viii.

"The Role of Scripture in Public Theology," *Word and World* 4 (Summer): 260-268.

"Sages, Visionaries, and Poets. What Does the Lord Require? Part 6," *Sojourners* 13 (December): 24-28.

"You Shall Be My People. What Does the Lord Require? Part 3," *Sojourners*, 13 (May): 31-33.

1985	"Economics and Faith in Biblical Perspective," *Journal of Stewardship* 38 (December): 1-14. "Old Testament Foundations for Peacemaking in the Nuclear Era," *The Christian Century* 102 (December 4): 115-119. "To Safeguard the Common Heritage of the Earth's Resources," *Engage/Social Action* 13 (May): 31-32. "The Shalom of Creation," *Engage/Social Action* 13 (December): 8, 41. With Larry L. Rasmussen, "These All Look to Thee: A Relational Theology of Nature,", *Engage/Social Action* 13 (May): 33-39.
1988	"Biblical Theology: Issues in Authority and Hermeneutics," *The A.M.E. Zion Quarterly Review* 99 (October): 10-19.
1989	"Memory in Congregational Life," *Weavings* 4 (January-February): 7-17.
1990	"Stewards of Our Leadership: Biblical Images," *Journal of Stewardship* 42 (NCC Commission on Stewardship): 2-15.
1991	"Exegeses: Deuteronomy. 6:1-9; 1 Kings 17:8-16; Hebrews 10:11-18; John 18:33-37," *Lectionary Homiletics* 2 (November): 3-4, 11-12, 15, 27-28.
1992	"Biblical Preaching as Moral Reflection," *Journal for Preachers* 15:3 (March): 13-17. With Douglas Meeks, "Stewardship and Theological Education: A Dialogue," *Journal of Stewardship* 44 (Ecumenical Center for Stewardship Studies): 44-50.
1994	"Moral Agency, Community, and the Character of God in the Hebrew Bible," *Semeia* 66: 23-41.
1995	"Behold, I am Doing a New Thing," *Bread* 7 (May): 5.
2000	"Divine Character and the Formation of Moral Community in the Book of Exodus," *Journal of Korean Old Testament Society*, 8: 281-302.
2001	"Bread for the Journey," *Seminary Development News* 14:1 (January): 4-5. "Exegeses: 1 Corinthians 15:1-11; Jeremiah 17: 5-10; Luke 6:27-38; Exodus 34:29-35," *Lectionary Homiletics* 12:3 (February): 1-2, 9-10, 17-18, 25-26. With Larry L. Rasmussen, "The Prosperity of the Righteous," *Alive Now* (September/October): 10-11.
2002	"Biblical Stewardship" section in "Why We Apportion: A Theology of Giving," (Evanston, Ill.: General Council on Finance and Administration, The United Methodist Church), 2-3.

"Leadership as Stewardship," *Quarterly Review* 22, (Winter): 358-369.

2003 "Integrating Welcome into the Seminary Curriculum," *Journal of Religion, Disability, and Health*, 7: 23-31; published simultaneously in *Graduate Theological Education and the Human Experience of Disability*, Robert C. Anderson, editor. New York: The Haworth Pastoral Press: 23-31.

With Lewis Parks, "Leading from Providence," *Quarterly Review*, 23 (Fall): 274-285.

2005 "The Arts, Midrash, and Biblical Teaching," *Teaching Theology and Religion*, 8 (April): 114-122.

"Exegeses: Genesis 24:34-38, 42-49, 58-67; 25:19-34; Matthew 13:24-30, 36-43; 13:31-33, 44-52; Genesis 32:22-31," *Lectionary Homiletics* 16:4 (June/July): 41-42, 49-50, 57, 65-66, 73-74.

2006 "Reclaiming Prophetic Leadership," *Ex Auditu: An International Journal of the Theological Interpretation of Scripture*, 22: 10-25.

2007 "Response to Barbara Green, How Are the Mighty Fallen?" *Horizons in Biblical Theology*, 29: 9-16.

FILMS AND VIDEOTAPES

1984 Producer, "One Faith, Many Visions," a film for the Bicentennial of American Methodism, sponsored by Wesley Theological Seminary on a grant from the United Methodist Bicentennial Commission.

1991 Videotapes, "The Just Laws of God," and "Protector of the Powerless," *Disciple: Into the Word, Into the World*, sessions 13 and 14. Nashville: Graded Press, United Methodist Publishing House.

2008 DVD Kit, "Concluding Bible Study on Creation Care," with others. *Religion and Science: Pathways to Truth*, Lesson 9. Washington DC: Wesley Ministry Network.

ARTICLES ABOUT THE AUTHOR

1976 "Young Builders of America," *U.S. News and World Report*, 80 (February 9): 42-45.

2002 Cited in "Deacon Candidates and Diaconal Ministers Attend Candidacy Formation Retreat," *Connections* (Spring): 1-2.

Featured in article by Robin Lind, "Theological Education in a Time of Crisis," *In Trust* 13 (New Year): 3-4.

Quoted in article by Missy Daniel of *Religion & Ethics News Weekly*, "Bush liaison lends ear to mainline churches," in *The Christian Century* 119:8 (April 10-17): 9-10.

REVIEWS

1965   Max Warren, editor, *A Conversation About the Holy Communion* and Karl Barth, *Prayer and Preaching* in *Student World,* 58: 101-102.

1973   J. Blenkinsopp, *Gibeon and Israel* in *Journal of Biblical Literature*, 92 (Fall): 440-441.

1977   A. F. Campbell, *The Ark Narrative (1 Samuel 4-6; 2 Samuel 6)* in *Interpretation*, 31 (July): 316.

1978   David Robertson, *The Old Testament and the Literary Critic* in *The Virginia Seminary Journal*, 30: 46-47.

Letty M. Russell, editor, *The Liberating Word: A Guide to Nonsexist Interpretation of the Bible* in *Religious Studies Review*, 4: 75.

Norman Gottwald, editor, *The Bible and Liberation: Political and Social Hermeneutics* in *Religious Studies Review*, 4: 72.

Tomoo Ishida, *The Royal Dynasties in Ancient Israel* in *Catholic Biblical Quarterly*, 40 (July): 405-407.

Walter Brueggemann, *The Land* in *Interpretation*, 32 (July): 322-323.

1979   J. Robert Vannoy, *Covenant Renewal at Gilgal: A Study of 1 Samuel 11:14; 12:25* in *Catholic Biblical Quarterly*, 41 (October): 637-638.

Simon J. DeVries, *Prophet Against Prophet* in *Journal of Biblical Literature*, 98 (Winter): 594-595.

1980   David M. Gunn, *The Story of King David* in *Interpretation*, 34 (January): 93-94.

Victor P. Furnish, *The Moral Teachings of Paul*, reviewed with Larry L. Rasmussen in *Interpretation*, 34 (October): 417-420.

1981   P. Kyle McCarter, Jr., *1 Samuel. The Anchor Bible*, vol. 8. in *Catholic Biblical Quarterly*, 43 (October): 626-627.

1983   Walter Harrelson, *The Ten Commandments and Human Rights* in *Journal of Biblical Literature*, 102 (Spring): 123-124.

1987   Katherine Doob Sakenfeld, *Faithfulness in Action: Loyalty in Biblical Perspective* in *The Princeton Seminary Bulletin*, 8: 72-73.

1994   Richard Bauckman, *The Bible in Politics: How to Read the Bible Politically* in *Critical Review of Books in Religion*, 6: 121-122.

2003 S. Rodd, *Glimpses of a Strange Land: Studies in Old Testament Ethics*, and Gordon J. Wenham, *Story as Torah: Reading the Old Testament Ethically* in *Interpretation*, 57 (Summer): 199-202.

William P. Brown, editor. *Character and Scripture: Moral Formation, Community, and Biblical Interpretation*, in *Review of Biblical Literature*, (November 1) [http://www.bookreviews.org].

Name Index

A
Aeneas 38
Alexander, Robin 20, 27, 28
Allen, Ronald 85, 86, 87
Augustine 37

B
Barnard, Tom 49
Barth, Karl 134
Beal, Timothy 46, 47, 50
Beall, Myrtle 73
Beatrice 35–42
Benhabib, Seyla 24, 27, 28
Benigni, Roberto 94
Blickenstaff, Marianne 134
Boehmer, Julius 146-150
Boethius 37-PB 42
Boniface 30-PB 42
Boomershine, Tom 46-51
Borg, Marcus 23-28
Branham, William 60-73
Brueggemann, Walter 52-53, 57, 84, 89, 95
Brumback, Carl 70, 73

C
Cacciaguida 30, 32, 34, 39, 40, 41
Cangrande dela Scala 33
Carter, Warren 134
Cavalcanti, Guido 30, 42
Clinton,Hillary 15-18, 127-128
Cole, Jr., Allan Hugh 115-116, 119
Crawford, Sidney White 49-50
Cross, Peggy 91

D

da Vinci, Leonardo 140, 143, 144
Dante 3, 29–42
Danto 141, 142, 143, 144
Darrand, Tom Craig 72, 73
Daughtry, Leah 14
Dean, Howard 14
Dionne, E. J. 14
Dube, Musa 134
Dudley, Carl S. 127, 128

E

Elkins, James 138, 143, 144
Epstein, David 127, 128
Everding, Edward 85, 86, 87, 88

F

Feuerbach, Ludwig 152, 154, 155
Foucault, Michael 124, 127
Franklin, Franklin 61, 71, 106, 110, 111
Franzen, Barbara 71, 72
Fretheim, Terrence E. 52

G

Gaglardi, Maureen 72, 73
Garnet, Henry Highland 107, 109, 110, 111
Goleman, Daniel 95
Gonzalez, Justo 84
Grubb, Paul 63, 71, 72

H

Hall, Franklin 61, 71
Hawtin, Ernest 61, 62, 71
Hawtin, George 60, 61, 62, 65, 66, 67, 71, 72
Hellerman, Joseph H. 127, 128
Hemingway, Ernst 32
Hilkert, Mary Catherine 82, 87
Hoekstra, Raymond 62, 71, 72
Holdcroft, L. Thomas 70, 73
Hollenweger, Walter 70, 73
Holt, Herrick 60, 61
Hopkins, Denise Dombkowski 3, 43, 90, 95, 118
Hume, David 142, 143
Huntington, Samuel 26

I

Ignatius of Antioch 147
Iverson, Richard 73

J

Jaenen, Cornelius 62, 71
Jeter, Joseph 85, 86, 87
Jones, Serene 116, 117, 118

K

Karaban, Roslyn A 118
Kerry, John 13, 14, 15, 16, 17, 18
Kirkpatrick, Milford 60, 65, 71, 72
Koppel, Michael 3, 89, 95
Kriewald, Diedra 46, 50

L

Laffey, Alice 49, 50
Lamott, Anne 127, 128
Law, Eric 79, 83, 86, 87
Layzell, Reg 65, 68, 69, 72, 73
Leighton, Frederick 33, 34
Levenson, Jon D. 49, 50
Levinas, Emmanuel 83, 84
Lischer, Richard 127, 128
Lozada, Francisco 134
Luther, Martin 61, 102, 137, 140, 141, 143, 144

M

McCain, John 15
McCann, J. Clinton 127, 128
McClure, John 83, 84, 86, 87, 88
McNeill, Noel 71

N

Neumark, Heidi B 127, 128
Nieman, James 85, 87, 88

O

O'Day, Gail R 135
Obama, Barack 13, 15, 16, 18

P

Park, Andrew Sung 95
Pelosi, Nancy 14, 15
Pennington, James 107, 109, 110, 111
Petersen, David L. 52

R

Raboteau, Albert 110, 111
Ramsay, Nancy J. 118, 119

Rasmussen, A. W. 62, 64, 71, 72
Reid, Harry 14
Reinhartz, Adele 135
Ringe, Sharon H 4, 129, 134, 135
Riss, Richard 70, 71, 73
Roberts, Edith 92
Rogers, Thomas 85, 86, 87, 88

S
Said, Edward 32
Sapp, Eric 14
Saussy, Carroll 95
Scholtes, Peter 83
Schreiter, Robert J 20, 27, 28
Schwartz, Regina 153, 154, 155
Shupe, Anson 72, 73
Smith, Christine 84
Smith, Daniel 49
Staley, Jeffrey 134
Stewart, Paul 71, 72
Stiles, J. E. 62, 71
Strider, Burns 14
Sugirtharajah, R. S. 49, 50
Sullivan, Amy 14
Sunderland, Ronald. H 118, 119
Synan, Vinson 70, 73

T
Tetzel, Johann 140
Thatcher, Tom 134
Tillich, Paul 23, 26, 28
Troeger, Thomas 85, 86, 87, 88

U
Ulanov, Ann Belford 94, 95
Urgren, Morris R. 71, 72

V
Vanderslice, Mara 14
Villani, Giovanni 30
Virgil 38, 39, 42
Von Rad, Gerhard 152, 153, 155
Vrudny, Kimberly 49, 50

W
Waldman, J. T. 49, 50
Walker, David 108, 109, 110, 111
Wallis, Jim 14

Ward, Samuel Ringgold 25, 107, 109, 110, 111
Warnock, George 65, 66, 68, 72
Watt, James 62, 68, 72
Webber, Robert E. 127, 128
Wesley, John 61
White, Michael 127
Williams, Raymond 27, 28
Wogaman, Philip 84
Wright, N. T. 78
Wyatt, Thomas 65, 70

Subject Index

A
Abolitionist movement 107, 109
Abortion 16, 17
Abraham 81, 107
Acceptance 84, 90, 100, 117
Advocate 56, 104, 133
Aesthetics 141, 143–44
Africa 66, 106, 130
African American 21, 98–103, 108, 110, 111
African Diaspora 98–99
African Methodist Episcopal Church 102
African Methodist Episcopal Zion Church 102
Ahasuerus 44, 47–49
Alexandria 130
Aliens 77–78, 81, 84, 152–53
America 2, 7–8, 17, 43, 71–72, 99, 105–111, 121, 127, 130
Anōthen 131
Apocalyptic 76
Appeal (David Walker's *Appeal*) 108, 110–11
Ascension Gift Ministries 64–65, 72–73
Asylum seekers 130
Atlantic slave trade 106
Awareness 80, 86, 94–95, 108, 126–27, 141–42

B
Babylon 13, 41, 45, 53–54, 76–79, 81, 122–23, 126
Babylonia 153
Babylonian Captivity 105, 109
Baptist 39, 41, 101, 104
Basileia 129
Beauty 35, 44–45, 47, 116, 141–44
Bethany 129–30
Bi-cultural 132
Biblical storytelling 43, 46, 50, 56
Black abolitionists 4, 105, 107–09
Black Religion 98

Body of Christ 9, 21, 55, 64–71, 73, 82, 84, 87
Boston University 100, 103

C
Calendar 130
Canaan 69, 152, 154
Canaanite woman 81
Canonicity 44
Care 3, 16, 17, 19, 81, 84, 91, 96, 114–19
Catholic 13, 15–18, 30, 49–50, 66
Catholics in Alliance for the Common Good 15
Centripetal exegesis 85
Charismatic 60, 71, 74
China 66, 134
Choice 16, 21, 47, 81, 90, 95, 100, 109, 153
Christ 9, 15, 20–21, 23, 36, 40, 49, 55, 57, 62, 64–73, 76–79, 82–84, 87, 94, 107–108, 115, 123, 127, 140, 146, 148–49
Christian formation 3, 52, 55–56
Christian Gospel 19, 23, 25–26, 107
Christology 133, 135–135
Church 3, 5–8, 10, 17, 30, 38–40, 42, 45, 49–50, 52, 56–57, 60–80, 82, 87, 90, 91, 92, 95, 101–104, 108, 107–109, 115, 117, 121, 123–28, 131, 138,–42, 147
CIVA (Christians in the Visual Arts) 138, 143–44
Civil War, the (American) 55, 102, 109
Cognitive dissonance 54, 56
Comforter 133
Communal dining 21
Compassion 15, 90, 94, 101
Compassion Forum 15
Congregational exile 92
Congress 2, 14
Contra-diction 84–85
Conversion 107, 109
Convivio 36–37, 39
Corporate worship 21, 92
Corso Donati 30–31
Covenantal Relationship 13, 52
Creative play 91–92, 95
Creativity 3, 21–23, 32, 43–46, 57, 90, 95, 125
Creator 22, 154
Cult of the Virgin 36
Culture 3, 17, 19, 20–28, 45–46, 78, 80, 86, 90, 110–11, 130–31, 133
Culture is ideational 20

D
Daniel 49, 50, 58, 68, 77–78, 96
Dante in Exile 33
Darfur 134
Deacons 65, 70, 71
Death 15, 30–37, 40, 42, 57–58, 67, 95, 99, 102, 110–11, 114–17, 131, 133–34, 146, 148

Deliverance 10, 43, 47, 53, 57, 105, 115
Democratic 13-14, 16-18, 65
Democrats 3, 13-18
Despair 17, 52-55, 87, 94, 108, 114
Deuteronomistic history 153-54
Dharma 26
Diaspora/Dispersion 44-45, 47, 53, 77, 79, 98-99, 130, 132
Dignity 48, 99, 105, 108, 110, 111
Disease 17, 106
Disequilibrium 54, 56
Disorientation 52, 56

E
Earthquake 134
Egypt 39-40, 53, 69, 81, 109, 152
Election 13-14, 15-16, 18
Eleison Group 15
Elohim 154
Empire 43, 47-48, 130, 135
Ephesus 130
Equipping 53, 56-57
Equipping lay ministry 57
Esther 3, 43-50
Evangelical 13, 15, 17, 72, 74, 107-108
Evangelicalism 109, 110-11
Evangelization 65-66, 73, 107
Exile 3, 4, 9-13, 18, 29, 30-60, 76-79, 84, 90-95, 98, 99, 101, 105-109, 117, 122, 124, 134, 138, 140-42, 153
Exodus 4, 10, 18, 40, 53, 58, 69, 80, 98, 101, 106, 115, 117-18, 147-48, 152-54
Ezekiel 39, 41, 53, 64, 147

F
Faith in Public Life 15
Family tree 129
Fasting 48, 61-63, 69, 72
Feast of Pentecost 61, 69, 82
Feminist interpretations 46
Florence 29-34, 39-41, 140
Followers of the Nazarene 131
Four Square Gospel 61
Fourth Gospel 4, 129-35
Fragmentation 52, 54, 71, 106
Fugitive slaves 108

G
Genre 14, 44
Gentiles 132
Gifts of the Spirit 61-63, 66
Good news 5, 20, 23, 87, 107, 129, 131-32, 134
Gospel 4, 5, 19, 23-27, 61, 66, 74, 80, 82, 86-88, 106-109, 129-135, 148-49, 154

Graphic novel 43, 49–50
Great Awakenings 107
Grief 13, 52, 91, 108, 114–19, 122–23, 126
Guelphs 30
Gustav 134

H
Haman 44, 46–49
Healing 20, 27, 61–63, 67, 72, 96, 114–15, 117–18, 127, 131
Hebrew 9, 40–41, 43, 46–49, 84, 95–96, 98, 101, 105, 115–16, 132, 152–53, 154
Helper 133
Heretics 131
Hiding 46, 48, 50, 124
Hoi Ioudaioi 131
Holy Other 85
Holy Spirit 63, 69–74, 82–84, 133
Hope 3–4, 11, 17, 31, 33, 39, 42, 45, 52–57, 67, 76–79, 87, 90–91, 95, 101, 105–106, 108, 110–118, 124, 147,–48
Hopelessness 52, 55, 91
Hypocrisy 107

I
Identity 3, 10–11, 21, 33, 38, 43–50, 52–57, 85, 91–92, 100, 105, 108, 130, 132, 149, 153
Identity-negation 52
Idolatry 77–78, 140, 141
Illness 90
Imagination 42, 44, 50, 54, 88, 95–96, 117
Incarnation 23, 83, 140
India 24, 26, 66, 134
Indian 24
Inferno 30–34, 39–41
Inter-testamental Judaism 76
Internal refugees 130
Isaiah 5, 39, 41, 53, 77, 110–11, 148
    Second Isaiah 53
Israel 13, 40–41, 45, 53–56, 69, 76–78, 81, 95, 147, 152–55
Israelites 40, 105, 108–09, 152–53

J
Jehoiachin 53
Jeremiah 5, 41, 45, 53, 76–79, 147, 153
Jerusalem 38–40, 45, 49, 52–53, 67, 69, 76, 79, 82–84, 123–124, 126, 130, 132, 153
Jesus Christ 20, 57, 77–78, 83, 107, 148
Jesus-tradition 129
Johannine community 130–33
John of Zebedee 129
John the Baptist 39, 41
Josiah, King 4, 153
Jubilee Year 30
Judah 41, 45, 47, 53–54, 122–23, 153

Judeans 153
Justification 23, 62, 67

K
Katrina 134
Koine 132

L
Lament 53–56, 91, 93, 114, 117, 122
Lamentations 43, 53
Latter Rain 60, 62, 66, 68–74
Laughter 94, 123
Laying on of Hands 61, 63, 65, 68–72
Lazarus 130
Leadership 5–6, 11, 14, 17, 31, 50, 56–60, 63–64, 66, 69–70, 88, 90, 95–96, 105, 109, 121, 124, 125
Leviticus 152–53
Little Brown Church in the Vale 124
Logos 132
Love 5, 17, 20, 29, 32, 35–37, 42, 52, 54–57, 86, 93, 101–102, 116–17, 133, 152, 154
Lucia, Saint 38
Luke 76, 82–83, 147

M
Maccabean Revolt 78
Magnolia Missions 100
Manifested Sons of God 67–68
Martha 130–31
Mary 38, 67, 107, 130, 154
Material aspect of culture 21
Megillot 43
Memory 3, 36, 46, 52–58, 69, 93, 98, 121–24, 126–28, 154
Mesopotamia 53
Messiah College 15
Methodism 60
Methodists 101–102
Middle Passage 98, 106
Midrash 46, 49–50
Miscarriage 116–17
Mission-shaped seminary 27
Mordecai 44–48
Moses 39–40, 57, 64, 69, 79, 81, 84, 95, 101, 116, 152, 155
Mourning 42, 115, 118
Multiple intelligences 86

N
Narrative collapse 4, 121–22, 124
Nebuchadnezzar 45, 53
Negro 102, 108–111
Negro spirituals 109
"Negro-hate" 108

178 Subject Index

Neighbor 52, 56, 86, 133
New Covenant 76
New culture zones 20
New order 60, 70–71, 74
New Orleans 102, 134
New Testament (NT) 64, 72, 76–77, 115–16, 129, 132, 146–47
New World, the 105–106
New York 50, 73, 74, 88, 96, 102–103, 110–111, 127–28, 131, 138, 143–44, 155
NOBS 46, 50
Non-elect 155

O
Old culture components 20
Other-wise Preaching 84–85, 88, 89
Overcomers 67–68

P
Pain 34, 36, 90–91, 100, 107, 114–16, 122, 124, 131, 154
Palimpsest 47
Paraclete 133
Paraklētos 133
Paul 38, 64, 67, 76, 95
Pentateuch 153–54
Pentecost 61, 68–69, 72, 82–84, 87
Pentecostalism 60, 71, 74
Pepperdine 13, 15, 18
Pepperdine University 13, 15
Performative culture 21
Peter 39, 41, 68, 76–78, 82–84, 87, 140–44
Pharaoh 101, 154–55
Philadelphia 49, 50, 58–59, 102, 110, 143–44
Pilgrims 30, 40, 77, 81
Play 30, 36, 54, 56, 67, 91–96, 124, 131, 139
Playful teaching 93
Poverty 16, 17, 99, 130, 141
Practical Theology 53, 58–59
Praise 40, 68–70, 103, 114–15
Prayer 42, 61–62, 69,–70, 72, 90, 95, 101–102, 104, 115–116, 126, 131, 146–47
Preaching 3, 10, 21, 80,–89, 100
Presidential campaign 14–15, 18
Pride, deadly sin of 30
Promised Land 10, 40, 69, 101, 106, 108–109
Prophecy 61, 63–68, 73
Prophetic witness 41, 53–57, 64, 68, 72–73, 78–79, 85, 101, 105, 108–109
Psalms 52–53, 96, 114, 118, 127–28
Psychic numbing 127
Purgatory 30–31, 33, 35, 37, 39–40
Purim 43, 46–47, 50
Purimshpiel 46
Purpose 21, 25, 37–38, 42, 52, 66, 78, 93–94, 99, 141, 143

R
Reconstruction 54, 110
Red Sea 101, 154
Refugees 49, 131, 134
Renewal 3, 57, 60, 68, 71, 74, 90, 95
Republican Party 13
Restoration 54, 62–64, 68, 73–74, 77–78, 108
Restoration of all things 68
Resurrection 40, 77, 101, 115, 117, 133, 146
Revival 60–74, 108, 126
Roe V. Wade 16
Roman Catholic 13, 30, 66
Roman Empire 129, 134
Rome 30, 31, 38, 76, 77, 140, 143

S
Sacred space 68, 117
Sanctification 62, 67
Second Temple period 132, 149
Sectarianism 78
Self-deprecation 123
Semeion 130
Semitic 130, 132
Sermon 68, 82, 85–86
Sheep Gate Pool 132
Shema 52
Shtetls 131
Sing the Lord's Song 4, 9–10, 54, 91, 106, 109, 121–22
Slavery 102, 105–110, 152
Slaves 99, 106–111, 152
Social location 55–56, 82
Society for the Propagation of the Gospel in Foreign Parts, The 107
Sofia 133
Sojourner 81
Spanish 98
Story 10, 17, 34, 37, 43–44, 46–47, 53, 56–57, 92, 114, 116–17, 121–26, 129–30, 154
Stranger 3, 9, 77, 80–81, 84–87
Suffering 32, 35, 36, 44, 54, 56, 68, 95, 100–101, 106 108, 114–18, 129
Suffering Servant 108
Synagogue 43, 49, 130–33
Synoptic Gospels 129

T
Teacher training 56, 57
Tenth Plague 154
Testimony 50, 85, 133
Theodicy 105
Theologia crucis 108
Theologia gloriae 108
Theological education 3, 10, 19, 20–27, 57

Theology of Art 138, 141–44
Tithēmi 133
Transition 90, 92–93, 95, 99

U
Ulysses 32
Uprooted people 129–130, 134

V
Vacation Bible School 93
Vatican II 15
Vietnam War 15
Visual art 44, 143
Vita Nuova 32, 35, 36–37, 41–42

W
Wesleyan Revival 60
Wesleyans 101
White supremacy 105, 108
Wilderness 10, 11, 15, 32, 41, 67, 69, 81, 98, 153
Wisdom 14, 22, 36, 37, 44, 49–50, 63–64, 70, 114, 132, 134–35
Witness 11, 24, 31, 55–57, 95, 105–110, 115, 133, 146–47
Word of knowledge 63–64
world, world-wide 62–63
Worship 21, 46, 68–71, 93, 99–102, 119, 122, 124

Y
YHWH 147, 149, 152, 154

Z
Zion 98, 101–102, 104, 122, 124

About the Authors

Casey, Shaun A.
Shaun A. Casey is Associate Professor of Christian Ethics at Wesley Theological Seminary. He attended Abilene Christian University where he earned a B.A. He graduated from Harvard Divinity School with a M.Div. He earned a M. P. A. from the Kennedy School of Government and was awarded the Th.D. from Harvard Divinity School. In addition to teaching at Wesley since 2000, he was a visiting professor at Pepperdine University. He has served congregations in Massachusetts, Rhode Island, and Mississippi in the Churches of Christ. His most recent publication is *The Making of a Catholic President: Kennedy vs. Nixon 1960* (2009).

Clarke, Sathianathan
Sathianathan Clarke joined the Wesley faculty in 2005. He serves in the Bishop Sundo Kim Chair of World Christianity and as Professor of Theology, Culture and Mission. He holds degrees from the University of Madras (B.A., M.A.); United Theological College (B.D.); Yale Divinity School (S.T.M.); and Harvard Divinity School (Th.D.). His publications include: *Dalits and Christianity: Subaltern Religion and Liberation Theology in India* (1999); *Religion Conversion in India: Modes, Motivations and Meanings* (2003); and "Global Cultural Traffic, Christian Mission, and Biblical Interpretation: Rereading Luke 10:1-12 Through the Eyes of an Indian Mission Recipient," *Ex auditu* (2007).

Davis, Deryl A.
Deryl A. Davis is Associate Faculty in Drama and Religion at Wesley Theological Seminary. He also supervises The Sunday Forum and Disciples of Christ in Community programs at Washington National Cathedral. Deryl has advanced degrees in literature and theology from the University of Edinburgh (Scotland) and in journalism from Columbia University. He is the author of short plays and a number of print and magazine articles. *From Darkness to Light: A Spiritual Journey Through 'The Divine Comedy'* (2009) is his first book.

Dombkowski Hopkins, Denise
Denise Dombkowski Hopkins is Professor of Hebrew Bible at Wesley Theological Seminary, where she has taught since 1986. She received her undergraduate degree from Syracuse University and her M.A. and Ph.D. degrees in Biblical Studies from Vanderbilt University. She also studied twice at

the Ecumenical Institute (Tantur) on the West Bank. Dr. Hopkins is the author of *Journey Through the Psalms* (2002), the introduction and annotations for Judith and 1,2,3, and 4 Maccabees in *The Discipleship Study Bible* (2008), and the forthcoming *Grounded in the Living Word: The Hebrew Bible and Pastoral Care Practices*, co-authored with Michael Koppel (2009).

Duncan, Howertine Farrell

Howertine Farrell Duncan , head of Public Services at the Wesley Library, joined the staff in 1991. She received her B. S. in Education from the University of Omaha (now, University of Nebraska at Omaha) in 1967; her MLS from the University of Oklahoma in 1968; and her M.Div. from Wesley Theological Seminary in 2005. Her publications include: "Selected Reference Aids for Small Medical Libraries." *Bulletin of the Medical Library Association* (1970); and "Genealogy Sources," *Summary of Proceedings of the Fifty-sixth Annual Conference of the American Theological Library Association* (2002)—A report as facilitator of the Roundtable discussion.

Duckworth, Jessicah Krey

Jessicah Krey Duckworth joined the Wesley Theological Seminary faculty in 2007. She is an instructor of Christian Formation and Teaching. She is a graduate of The Lutheran Theological Seminary at Philadelphia and is a doctoral candidate in Practical Theology with an emphasis on Christian Education at Princeton Theological Seminary.

Faupel, D. William

D. William Faupel joined the Wesley Theological Seminary faculty in 2004 as Director of the Library and Professor of the History of Christianity. He received his Ph.D. from the University of Birmingham, England in 1989 in the field of historical theology. He earned an M.Div degree from Asbury Theological Seminary in 1972 and an M.S. degree in Library Science from the University of Kentucky in 1971. He also took the B.A. degree from Evangel College in 1967 and an A.B. degree from Central Bible College in 1966. He is the author of *The Everlasting Gospel: The Significance of Eschatology in the Development of Pentecostal Thought* (1994).

Gease, Eleanor Marshall

Eleanor Marshall Gease has been executive assistant to the Dean of Wesley Theological Seminary since 2006. She holds a B.A. from The Ohio State University, an M.T.S. from Wesley Theological Seminary, and is currently pursuing doctoral studies in history at The American University in Washington, D. C.

Hill, Craig C.

Craig C. Hill is Professor of New Testament and Director of the Wesley

Ministry Network. He joined the Wesley Faculty in 1995. Dr. Hill received his B.A. from Illinois Wesleyan University; his M.Div. from Garrett-Evangelical Theological Seminary; and his D.Phil. from University of Oxford. He is the author of : *Hellenists and Hebrews: Reappraising Division within the Earliest Church* (1992); *In God's Time: The Bible and the Future* (2002); and Romans Commentary in *The Oxford Bible Commentary* (2001).

Hogan, Lucy Lind

Lucy Lind Hogan is Hugh Latimer Elderdice Professor of Preaching and Worship. Joining the faculty as an adjunct professor in 1987, she became a full-time faculty member in 1994 and was promoted to full professor in 2000. She holds a B.A. from Macalester College; an M.Div. from Virginia Theological Seminary; a D.Min. from Wesley Theological Seminary; and a Ph.D. from the University of Maryland. She is the author of *Connecting with the Congregation: Rhetoric and the Art of Preaching* with Robert Reid (1999); *Graceful Speech: An Invitation to Preaching* (2006); and her most recent book, *Lenten Services* (2009).

Koppel, Michael S.

Michael S. Koppel is Associate Professor of Pastoral Theology and Congregational Care. He came to Wesley Theological Seminary in 2002. He is an ordained minister of the National Capital Presbytery of the Presbyterian Church. He received the BA from the University of California, Davis; a M.Div. from Yale Divinity School and the Ph.D. from Claremont School of Theology. He is the author of *Open-Hearted Ministry: Play as Key to Pastoral Leadership* (2008), and co-author with Denise Dombkowski Hopkins, *Grounded in the Living Word: Hebrew Bible and Pastoral Care Practices* (2009).

McAllister-Wilson, David F.

David F. McAllister-Wilson assumed the office of President at Wesley Theological Seminary in July of 2002. He has served the institution for over 20 years. He came to Wesley from California, first as a student. He received his B.A. from California State University, Northridge, and both his M.Div. and D.Min. from Wesley. He is the co-author of *Christian Reflections on the Leadership Challenge* (2004).

McClain, William B.

William B. McClain is Mary Elizabeth McGehee Joyce Professor of Preaching. He joined the faculty in 1981. Dr. McClain holds an A. B. from Clarke College and an M.Div. and the D.Min. from Boston University. He is the author of *Traveling Light: Christian Perspectives on Pilgrimage and Pluralism* (1981); *Black People in the Methodist Church* (1984); and *Come Sunday: The Liturgy of Zion* (1990).

Moschella, Mary Clark

Mary Clark Moschella is Associate Professor of Pastoral Theology and Congregational Care. She came to Wesley in January 2001. She has been ordained in the United Church of Christ for 25 years. She holds an M.Div. from Harvard Divinity School and the Ph.D. from Claremont School of Theology. Her recent publications include *Ethnography as a Pastoral Practice: An Introduction* (2008); and *Living Devotions: Reflections on Immigration, Identity, and Religious Imagination* (2008).

Mitchell, Beverly Eileen

Beverly Eileen Mitchell is Professor of Historical Theology at Wesley Theological Seminary, in Washington, D.C., where she teaches courses in theology, church history, African American Religious History, and human rights. She has been a member of the faculty at Wesley Seminary since July 1998. She earned a B.A. from Temple University; an M.T.S. from Wesley Theological Seminary; and a Ph.D. in systematic theology from Boston College-Andover Newton Theological School. Among Dr. Mitchell's recent publications are two books, *Plantations and Death Camps: Religion, Ideology, and Human Dignity* (2009); and *Black Abolitionism: A Quest for Human Dignity* (2005).

Parks, Lewis A.

Lewis A. Parks is Professor of Theology, Ministry, and Congregational Development and directs the doctor of ministry program. He came to Wesley Theological Seminary in 1998. He received degrees from Lock Haven University (BS), Wesley (MDiv), and Saint Mary's Seminary and University, Baltimore (PhD). He is an ordained United Methodist pastor of the Central Pennsylvania Conference. He co-authored *Ducking Spears, Dancing Madly* (2004) with Bruce Birch and wrote *Preaching in the Small Membership Church* (2009).

Ringe, Sharon H.

Sharon H. Ringe, Professor of New Testament, joined the Wesley faculty in 1991. She holds a B. A. from the University of New Hampshire, and received both an M.Div. and Ph.D. from Union Theological Seminary in New York. Her recent publications include: *Jesus, Liberation, and the Biblical Jubilee: Images for Ethics and Christology* (1985); *Wisdom's Friends* (1999); and *Luke: A Commentary* (1999).

Sokolove, Deborah

Deborah Sokolove is the Director of the Henry Luce III Center for the Arts and Religion. Previously, she served as Curator for the Dadian Gallery since 1994, and as Associate Faculty since 2005. She received her B.A. and M.F.A.

from California State University at Los Angeles; a Master of Theological Studies degree from Wesley Theological Seminary; and the Ph.D. in Liturgical Studies from Drew University. Publications include "Is This Art Liturgical?" in *Image: Art, Faith, Mystery,*(2006); "Walking Towards the Cross with Jesus" in *Call to Worship: The Work of Our Hands* (2009); "Wholly Porcelain: Mimesis and Meaning in the Sculpture of Ginger Henry Geyer" in Robin M. Jensen and Kimberly Vrudny, eds, *Theology, Visual Art, and Contemporary Culture* (2009).

Soulen, R. Kendall

R. Kendall Soulen has been Professor of Systematic Theology at Wesley Theological Seminary since 1992. He holds a B.A., Yale University (1982), an M. Div. from Candler School of Theology (1986), and a PhD from Yale University (1992). He is the author of *The God of Israel and Christian Theology* (1996); *Handbook of Biblical Criticism* (2001); and *God and Human Dignity*, with Linda Woodhead (2006).

Willhauck, Susan B.

Susan B. Willhauck served as faculty at Wesley Theological Seminary in Christian Formation and as Director of Equipping Lay Ministry from 1998-2008. She is now Associate Professor of Pastoral Theology at Atlantic School of Theology in Halifax, Nova Scotia. She holds a Ph.D. in Religious Education and Catechetics from The Catholic University of America, a Master of Theological Studies from Wesley Theological Seminary and a B.A. from Emory and Henry College. Her publications include *The Web of Women's Leadership: Recasting Congregational Ministry* with Jacqulyn Thorpe, (2001); and *Backtalk! Women Leaders Changing the Church* (2005).

Young, Josiah Ulysses II

Josiah Ulysses Young, Professor of Systematic Theology, holds a bachelor's degree from Morehouse College. His M.Div., M.Phil. and Ph.D. degrees are from Union Theological Seminary in New York. He began his teaching career at Colgate University and joined the Wesley faculty in 1988 where he was promoted to full professor in 1992. Among his publications are: *Dogged Strength within the Veil: Africana Spirituality and the Mysterious Love of God* (2003), *No Difference in the Fare: Dietrich Bonhoeffer and the Problem of Racism* (1998), and *Black and African Theologies: Siblings or Distant Cousins?*(1986).

Printed in the United States
213670BV00002B/2/P